ONEIDA LAKE
"The only happiness"

Place Names and History

Jack Henke

North Country Books, Inc.
18 Irving Place
Utica, New York 13501-5618

ONEIDA LAKE
"The Only Happiness"

Place Names and History

Copyright © 1989
by Jack Henke

All Rights Reserved
No part of this book may be reproduced
in any manner without written
permission of the publisher.

ISBN 978-0-932052-77-3
First Paperback Edition 1993

Library of Congress Cataloging-in-Publication Data

Henke, Jack.
    Oneida Lake: the only happiness: place names
and history/by Jack Henke.
    p.   cm.
    Includes bibliographical references.
    ISBN 978-0-925168-19-1
    1. Oneida Lake Region (NY)—History.
Local. 2. Names, Geographical—New York (State)
—Oneida Lake Region. I. Title.
F127.052H46   1989
974.7'62—dc20   89-27237
                                                             CIP

North Country Books, Inc.
18 Irving Place
Utica, New York 13501-5618

For
Gramps and Brookfield's Children

TABLE OF CONTENTS

Preface	vii
Onondaga County	1
Madison County	38
Oswego County	92
Oneida County	148
Contemporary Oneida Lake Scenes	188
Isles and Shoals	208
Tangents	219
Afterthoughts	235
My Debts	238

The good life indeed - Oneida Lake tourists, 1907

PREFACE

Oneida Lake, the largest lake entirely within New York State's borders, is approximately twenty-two miles long and from one to five miles wide, its width varying with the numerous bays and points that contour its shoreline. For its dimensions, it is a shallow body of water, having fifty-five feet as a maximum depth and a mean depth of slightly more than twenty feet. Oneida is fertile water, naturally enriched by its tributaries. Canaseraga and Chittenango Creeks, south shore tributaries which drain Madison County's "Great Marsh," and Oneida Creek, which meanders through the agriculturally rich Stockbridge Valley, provide the bulk of the lake's nutrients. These minerals constitute sustenance for plankton, basis for the productive Oneida Lake food web. The lake's largest tributary is Fish Creek, which enters Oneida through the Barge Canal at Sylvan Beach. Other feeder streams include Big Bay Creek, Scriba Creek at Constantia, and Black Creek at Cleveland.

Four counties border Oneida Lake. The north shore includes Oswego and, to the east, Oneida County. On the south, Onondaga County oversees the lake's western basin, while Madison County borders the east end. Lakeshore townships within the counties encompass West Monroe, Hastings and Constantia in Oswego County, Vienna and Verona in Oneida, Sullivan and Lenox in Madison, and Cicero in Onondaga. The lakeside communities include Brewerton at the Oneida River outlet and Sylvan Beach at the Barge Canal inlet. Along the north shore are Constantia, Bernhard's Bay, Cleveland, Jewell and North Bay, while the south shore settlements are Lower South Bay, Bridgeport, Lakeport, Oneida Lake and Upper South Bay.

My first meaningful experience with Oneida Lake occurred in late September of 1971. Rob Ziegler, a Hamilton College classmate and friend, accompanied me on an impromptu self-guided tour of Sylvan Beach. It was a perfect Indian summer day—a hazy sun overlooking, the oranges and reds of the trees mixing with the season's vanishing warmth. Autumn was vintage; the omnipresent crunching of the Beach's fallen leaf carpeting constantly emphasized the time of year. Rob and I photographed the scene, conversed with the village's friendly population, and walked the beach, appreciating the lake's glimmerglass calm. On that fall day I decided to research Sylvan Beach's past. This labor culminated, four years later, in the publication of *Sylvan Beach - A History*. During this time, I acquired a deep affinity for Oneida Lake and its environs. As Beach people would say, I "got sand in my shoes." My research brought me in contact with innumerable source materials; interviews, diaries, news articles, journals, scrapbook entries and the like filled my files. I was astounded by the fact that, despite its size, relative importance, and the fact that millions of people have come in close contact with it, Oneida Lake was a very underdeveloped historical subject. Aside from a brief general history published in 1926 and some odd news coverage, college papers, or terse textbook citings, the lake's past had no formal recording.

Oneida Lake and its people possess a fine history, full of life and rich with tradition. The lake's story is a chronicle that merits documentation and appreciation. In this volume I discuss the origin of all lake-oriented place names and, in doing so, address the major themes in Oneida's history. By no means is this book to be considered a complete work on Oneida Lake's past. Such an undertaking would require far more pages than are herein included and could easily mire the reader amidst scads of trivia which, in local history writing, too often bury important details.

The book's organization proceeds as follows. I have divided the lake into five parts, each section dealing with place name origins of every point, bay, shoal, settlement, creek, township and county within it. Four chapters deal with the four counties and any place names in the waters near them. The fifth, "Isles and Shoals," discusses the mid-lake area. Many of the place name entries contain information relative to the total picture of Oneida Lake history, while a sixth chapter, "Tangents," covers some additional topics about the lake's history that I encountered in the research process.

My basic map for researching the project was the 1933 C.P. Grimes map, published by the Anglers' Association of Onondaga. This map's place names were expanded and edited as new information from historical sources reached me. No one authoritative Oneida Lake place name map has ever existed. The maps which introduce each chapter are syntheses of my research and the names on them are a consensus of my sources.

Although the "My Debts" section lists the people who helped me with this book, it is only fair that certain persons be noted further. Chittenango historian, Clara Houck, and Bridgeport historian, Carol Greene, went "above and beyond" in assisting me with the Madison County chapter. Constantia historian, Leonard Cooper, lectured me on the north shore's past and Millard Rogers, of Brewerton, always found time in his busy schedule to answer my questions about the lake's western basin. Bruce and Erma Stallknecht, of Big Bay, gave me hours of knowledge and introduced me to the fine, informative people of the Brewerton Historical Society. Glenn Chesebrough, of Sylvan Beach, was the guide on my first historic tour around the lake and exposed me to the informative wealth of the Brewerton Library's Milton Papers. And finally, I wish to thank David Ellis and David Millar of Hamilton College, my teachers.

Oneida Lake history is a saga of princes and poachers, of land barons and humble homespun farmers, of revolutionary patriots, obscure Indians, Civil War veterans, boatmen, hermits and above all, the average American. The labor of these people and their contemporaries has developed the lake we know today. Their story is a tapestry of delightful, informative tales which aptly show that the lake, as an early journalist once wrote of Sylvan Beach, is a most "picturesque spot . . . and, in addition to what nature has done for it, has a history that makes comment about it always interesting."

ONEIDA LAKE
THE VISUAL HISTORY

The steamer Manhattan, *Lower South Bay, 1885*

The written word of Oneida Lake history is perfectly supplemented by the magnificent photographs and prints that visually capture life during the lake's past. These primary sources, gleaned from scrapbooks, mustied files, display cases, shoe boxes and historical society collections are essential components of historical expression for they capture facts and feelings that elude the historian's pen's grasp.

This book contains five photo sections. The first embraces images of Brewerton, Frenchman's Island and Lower South Bay. The second takes in Bridgeport, Lakeport, Upper South Bay and points between, and the third portrays Constantia, Bernhard's Bay and Cleveland. Sylvan and Verona Beaches are illustrated in the fourth section and the final grouping illustrates the contemporary lake environs.

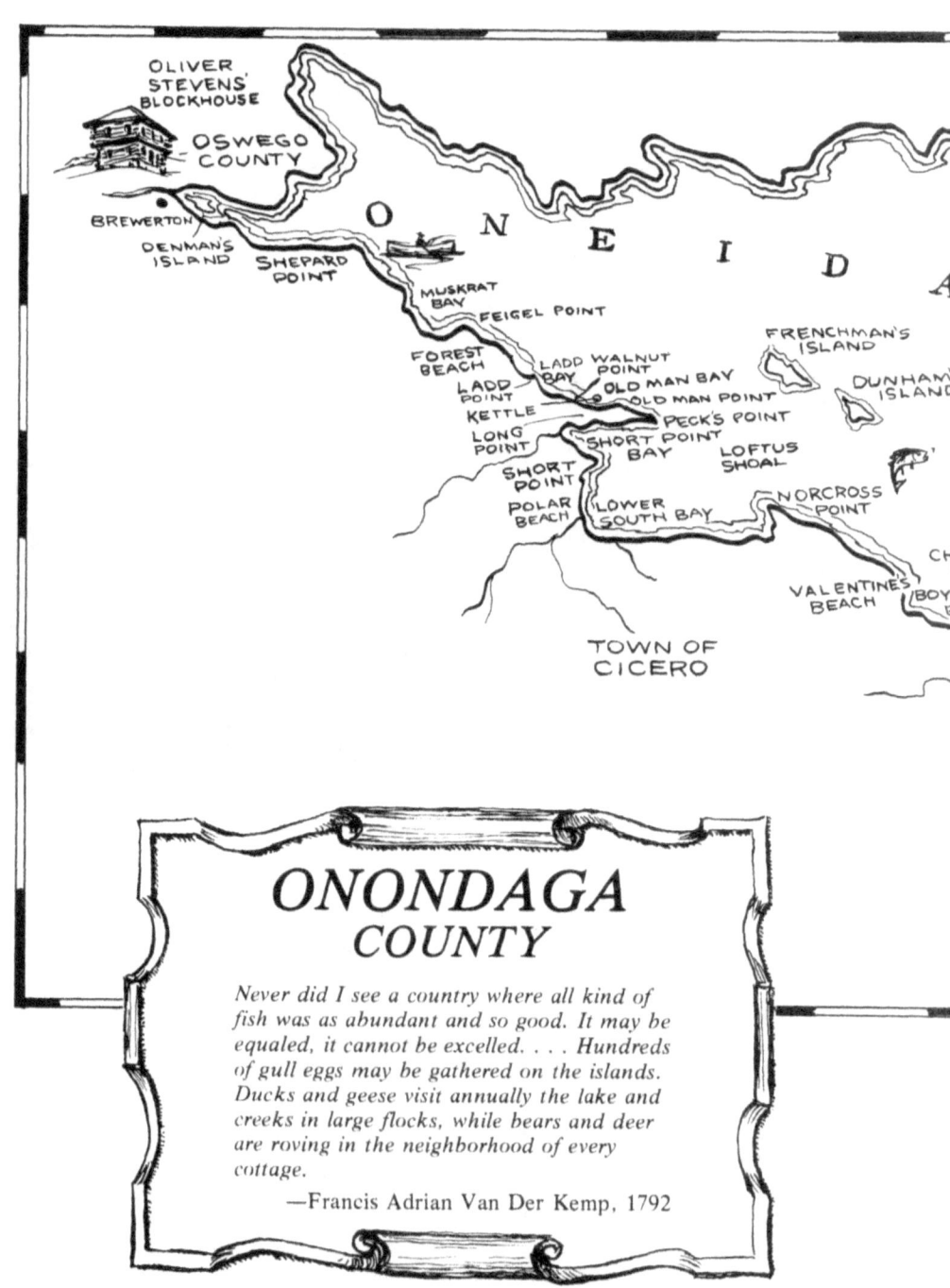

ONONDAGA COUNTY

Never did I see a country where all kind of fish was as abundant and so good. It may be equaled, it cannot be excelled. . . . Hundreds of gull eggs may be gathered on the islands. Ducks and geese visit annually the lake and creeks in large flocks, while bears and deer are roving in the neighborhood of every cottage.

—Francis Adrian Van Der Kemp, 1792

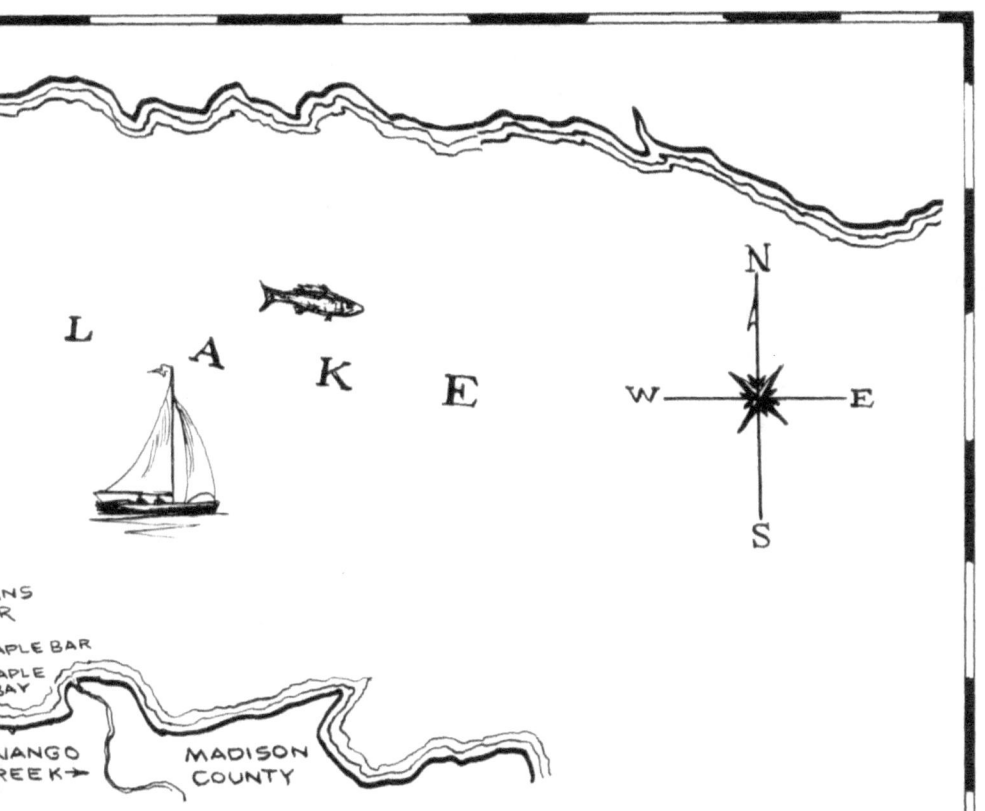

This county takes its name from the Iroquois tribe that lived there and kept the famed Iroquois Confederacy's council fire. The word "Onondaga," according to the *Illustrated Dictionary of Place Names, United States and Canada*, means "hill people." Beauchamp's *Indian Names in New York* closely agrees, defining Onondaga as "people of the mountain." Cicero is the county's only township bordering Oneida Lake. It was named by Simeon DeWitt, surveyor of the town, for the Roman statesman/orator, Marcus Tullius Cicero (106-43 B.C.). The title was consistent with an early nineteenth century upstate "classicism fad" for community naming. The town was officially formed on February 20, 1807; it lost territory in April 1817, when the town of Clay was created. Cicero's boundaries have remained constant since the latter date.

Brewerton begins this chapter's place names and Maple Bay, on the county's far eastern lakeshore, concludes. Technically, the bays, shoals, and bars included in this chapter are in Oswego

County. They are placed in this section because their proximity to the Onondaga County shoreline makes such an adjustment logical. The same grouping occurs in the Madison County chapter, where off-shore places are actually in Oneida County. In addition, for every county, place names are ordered from west to east, except for a slight variation in Oneida County, where names are sequenced from Cleveland east to North Bay and then south to Oneida Creek.

Summary histories of Brewerton and Lower South Bay are included within this chapter. This section's place names' order reads as follows:

Brewerton	Short Point and Bay
Denman's Island	Polar Beach
Shepard Point	Lower South Bay
Muskrat Bay	Loftus Shoal
Feigel Point	Norcross Point
Forest Beach	Valentine's Beach
Ladd's Point and Bay	Boysen's Bay
Walnut Point and the "Kettle"	Chimney Bar
Old Man Point and Bay	Crans Bar
Long Point and Peck's Point	Maple Bay and Bar

BREWERTON

Historical information concerning this village has been gleaned from two major sources: the Milton Papers, filed in the Brewerton Free Library, and the book *Brewerton, New York, U.S.A.*, copyrighted in 1973 as a joint effort of the Brewerton Library and several local historians. Both have provided the data for my re-creation of Brewerton's past. The latter book, based largely on Elet Milton's exhaustive Brewerton research, is a fine local history text, containing a well-organized topical survey of this community's heritage.

The first recorded white man's sighting of Oneida Lake occurred at Brewerton when Samuel de Champlain, on October 8, 1615, observed the lake from a spot near there. Brewerton's location at the Oneida River's junction with the lake made it a strategic place in colonial times. The British recognized this fact and, during late summer and early fall of 1759, built Fort Brewerton, overlooking a slightly raised bank on the river's north side. This small fortification (100 feet by 100 feet), along with the Royal Blockhouse, erected the previous year near Fish Creek's mouth on Oneida Lake's eastern shore, was intended to guard the frontier against attacks from marauding French and from the Indians. The fort was named for Major George Brewerton Jr., reputed to be a supervisor of its construction. It was an isolated outpost and witnessed no major military activity during the French and Indian Wars. Upon the close of that conflict the Iroquois, feeling threatened by British military bases, agitated for these forts' elimination. The Crown, having previously guaranteed that the forts were temporary, complied with Iroquois wishes and Fort Brewerton was abandoned around 1767. Soon after, Indians burned the fort's stockade and blockhouse.

The first settlement in Brewerton and Oswego County occurred in 1789 when Oliver Stevens brought his family from Canaan, Connecticut, to a site on the Oneida River outlet's north side. Stevens, an enterprising Yankee, engaged in the Indian fur trade and built a small tavern catering to boatmen. In 1794, fearing unruly Indians, Stevens constructed a protective blockhouse subsidized by state funding. His family, at times, inhabited the fortification, and it also served as a convenient location for his tavern business. The Stevens blockhouse continued to function as a tavern under several proprietors well into the 1800's. Eventually it proved cumbersome and was razed, a part of its site later being occupied by the Fort Brewerton House, erected by Benjamin and Orson Emmons in 1851. A replica of Stevens' blockhouse, built by William Ennis and the Brewerton Historical Society in 1977, now serves as that organization's headquarters and houses a fine museum of local Indian and Oneida Lake artifacts.

Brewerton's economy has, throughout its history, been strongly influenced by the Oneida Lake and River. Hotels, such as the above cited Fort Brewerton House, took advantage of the itinerant boating trade as well as business engendered by early sportsmen and tourists. Other Brewerton public houses and their founders included the Fort Brewerton Hotel (Henry Emmons, 1867), the Oneida River House (Frank Dickson, 1906), the River Side House (B.N. Wood, 1884) and the Washburn House (Charles E. Washburn, 1870's). The latter hotel, Brewerton's largest and grandest, was constructed on the site of several earlier inns, the first of which was Patrick MaGee's log tavern, opened in 1791. MaGee's enterprise, near the Oneida River's south bank, lasted until 1795 and was later purchased by Jonathan Emmons, who initiated ferry service across the Oneida River.

Like their counterparts at other Oneida Lake resorts, Brewerton hotels advertised in city newspapers to attract summer clientele. An ad for the Washburn House, from the Syracuse *Journal* of August 27, 1872, described the establishment as follows:

> This is a new, large and commodius brick edifice, situated at the outlet of Oneida Lake, and offers excellent accommodations for summer boarders, pleasure parties, picnics, etc., on reasonable terms. Row boats and fishing tackle in abundance.
>
> This beautiful Summer Resort is easily accessible by Syracuse Northern Railroad, four trains of which arrive and depart daily.

A look into other Brewerton businesses and industry reveals more of the lake and river's impact on this community. In the nineteenth century, the village boasted two steam-powered sawmills, one established by Samuel Gilson and the other by the Hulburt Brothers. These mills, essential businesses in a growing community, received timber via the lake and river. Logs cut from Oneida Lake's surrounding forests were assembled into rafts at locations like Oneida Creek, Chittenango Creek, Black Creek, Scriba Creek and Toad Harbor. In early years, these rafts were poled or sailed through lake shallows by rugged lumbermen. Eventually, steamboats such as the Oneida Lake and River Steamboat Company's *Oswego* provided power for log transportation, but even with steamboats, log moving was a slow process. The log rafting trade flourished on Oneida until the 1890's, by which time the lake's forest garland had been so depleted as to render the business unprofitable.

Brewerton's small industrial "complex" in the late 1800's included a cider mill, ashery, cheese factory, apple evaporator and numerous craftmen's shops. The Thomas M. Milton Boat Building Company was for years a village landmark. Canal, steam and pleasure vessels took form at the Milton boat works. Brewerton was a center for the Oneida Lake fishing industry throughout its recorded history. Iroquois Indians sought sustenance spearing fish at Brewerton's Oneida River rifts, eels exported in the 1800's brought supplementary income to many

Brewerton families, and the village was a haven for the Oneida Lake fish "pirate" in the early part of this century.

Contemporary Brewerton exhibits scenes reminiscent of its history. On the whole the village, connected to Syracuse via Interstate 81, has a suburban character reflected in its housing projects, "quick-stop" gas-grocery combos, and Route 11 business "strip." Beneath this neon surface, however, lies a different Brewerton. Along the Oneida River, state canal scows, commercial barges and pleasure boats still moor at the ramshackle concrete pier. The site of Fort Brewerton and the restored Stevens' blockhouse, both symbolic of their eras, overlook the river scene. On a side street, a fish company still purchases panfish and bullheads caught by local anglers. The Brewerton Free Library, built on land donated by Elet Milton, serves scores of local reading enthusiasts and the occasional historian who delights in the library's Oneida Lake oriented Milton papers. The Brewerton Sports' Shop, with its cornucopia of taxidermy masterworks and seemingly endless selections, is a mecca for regional sportsmen.

One can, indeed, experience Oneida Lake history at Brewerton today. Talk with Millard or Chuck Rogers at Brewerton Sports and get to know the sagas of the ancient fish pirate and of the history of conservation on Oneida. View the exhibits or attend a lecture at the Brewerton Historical Society and become a bit more appreciative of our Indian and colonial legacies. Examine the voluminous files of Elet Milton's research and marvel at the details of Oneida Lake life during the 1800's and early 1900's. The historical experience is typified by one of my ice-fishing ventures on Big Bay, ten years ago. A pre-dawn morning was clear and quiet, the air a crisp ten degrees as I walked across the bay's icecap. The sun rose with brilliance, silhouetting Frenchman's Island to the east, reflecting in duplicate on the snowless ice. A timeless scene unfolded, a spectacle in which the Indian, the pioneer, the pirate, logger, innkeeper, and cottager were all once a part.

DENMAN'S ISLAND

This tiny isle has, like so many Oneida Lake sites, claimed several titles throughout history. It was once named "Indian Isle" and "Iroquois Isle," both appellations referring to the extensive native American activity that occurred there. Prehistoric Indians and the Onondaga Iroquois used the island as a fishing camp from which they could spear the formerly plentiful eel. Archaeologists have uncovered scores of significant artifacts on the isle that give vivid documentation to its Indian occupation. In July of 1806, James Geddes surveyed the isle, discovered it to have 1.24 acres and assessed its value at six dollars. Geddes alluded to the island's history and potential in his writing:

> It is a noal (sic) of a pretty good natural soil, but has been in such severe use so long, that it is pretty much worn out. It might be fancied by a gentleman owning the South Shore for a piece to ornament as pleasure ground.

In the middle 1800's Indian Isle became "Baldwin's Isle." Harvey Baldwin, son of Jonas Baldwin, founder of Baldwinsville, was the isle's owner when Brewerton was surveyed in 1836. Harvey, perhaps the "gentleman" of Geddes' musing, became mayor of Syracuse in 1848. The island remained in the Baldwin family hands until this century, when it was sold to Hubert W. Smith of Smith-Corona typewriter fame. In latter years, people have called it "Denman's Isle," for Charles A. Denman and family who purchased the spot from Smith in 1952. Charles Denman's son, Raymond, succeeded his father in island ownership.

SHEPARD POINT

New York State rewarded its veterans of the American Revolution with free land, consisting of lots drawn from a large area known as the "Military Tract." This holding was situated in central New York and touched the southwest shore of Oneida Lake. One person to take advantage of this early veterans' benefit was the Reverend John Shepard. Shepard, originally from the lower Hudson Valley, joined the Continental Army in 1777 and eventually rose to the rank of captain. Among the engagements he participated in was General "Mad" Anthony Wayne's fierce struggle for Stoney Point. In 1781, Shepard's health forced him to resign his commission. He studied for the ministry and was ordained at the Stamford Congregational Church in 1787; this career lasted until 1794. At the drawing for Military Tract acreage, Shepard selected Lot 11 in the Town of Cicero, including Shepard Point lakeshore property. Around 1802 he erected a home on this land, cleared adjacent acreage and operated a small farm. By the time of his death, in 1822, he had sold all of his land grant. He died virtually penniless, with an estate valued at $66.96, no land, and debts totaling $16.00.

When John Shepard came to Oneida Lake, the area was very much a primeval wilderness. Vast forests and impenetrable swamps made life difficult for even the hardiest pioneer. Bears and panthers prowled these habitats, adding danger. Undoubtedly, Shepard's life was spartan and an incident in 1811 illustrates this. In that year, two of Shepard's daughters became lost in the woods surrounding Lower South Bay and despite the proximity to the family home, it took searchers three days to locate the girls. It was said that, during their ordeal, the Shepards subsisted on "nuts and greens." Doubtless, their wilderness upbringing prepared them for such a crisis.

MUSKRAT BAY

Wetlands once formed a nearly impassable barrier to travelers in the Oneida Lake region. The "Great Marsh" south of the lake, the Big Bay Swamp, and the bogs east of Verona Beach were significant obstructions to early wayfarers. Another such morass was the "Great Muskrat Swamp," stretching from near Brewerton to Lower South Bay. Named for the animal whose dwellings once formed the marsh's only "houses," this swamp was of concern to local residents as early as 1858. In that year a commission was appointed to investigate swamp drainage. Parts of the marsh were drained, but technological limitations prevented a large-scale effort. Over the years the marsh has diminished in size, but it still retains much of its primeval qualities and dangers. Several years ago, for instance, cases of Eastern equine encephalitis were traced to mosquitoes which flourish in the swamp.

Today, the Great Muskrat Swamp is often referred to as the Cicero Swamp. Muskrat Bay has been named for the imposing wetland it borders.

FEIGEL POINT

Richard Feigel purchased a sixty acre farm on the point on June 20, 1901. Feigel and his wife, Elizabeth, ran the farm until 1929, when it was conveyed to his son, Richard William Feigel of Syracuse. For the younger Feigel, the farm was primarily an investment and it proved a useful one. Feigel ran a men's clothing store in Syracuse and, during the Great Depression, was able to keep his business afloat by selling lots in the lakeshore property. The Feigel family is still in possession of much of the original tract. Laurence Fournier, great-grandson of Richard Feigel, owns the old farmhouse, an adjoining woodlot and Feigel Point. The farm's barn, west of the Fournier property on Muskrat Bay Road, is also in family ownership.

FOREST BEACH

This lakefront stretch, east of Feigel Point along Muskrat Bay Road, was originally called "Lake Forest Beach," taking its name from the thick woods surrounding.

LADD POINT AND BAY

In 1872, Douglas and Jane Cook Ladd packed their belongings in an ox-drawn wagon and traveled from Constantia Center to Oneida's south shore. The couple chose winter for their move, perceiving the ice to be of sufficient thickness. Ice depths exceeding two feet are not uncommon on Oneida. The ice mass often shifts, however, causing formation of dangerous cracks and air pockets. One of Ladd's oxen stepped into a hidden crack and was unable to extract itself. Undaunted, Douglas walked to Frenchman's Island, borrowed a horse from the proprietor of the Frenchman's Island Hotel, and towed the beast from its potential demise. The Ladds settled near Ladd Point, farmed the land, and raised a family of ten chldren. Such large families provided a needed labor supply for early unmechanized farms.

Evidence of tragedy was discovered at the Ladd farm site in the

1950's. Hikers, wandering about the area, found a plain tombstone, hidden in tall grass six feet from a large maple. The stone bore only the name "EDGAR." Research, conducted by Elet Milton, revealed it to be the grave of an infant son of Douglas and Jane Ladd. The stone was placed in the Ladd family plot in the Pine Plains Cemetery, but the child's remains were left undisturbed.

WALNUT POINT AND THE "KETTLE"

Like Willow Point and Maple Bay, the first place name originates from notable vegetation at the site. A fine grove of walnut trees once graced this little point. Walnut trees were so common around Oneida Lake that Christopher Martin, an early settler of Constantia Township, described the lake's shore as being "lined" with them, and with chestnut trees.

The "Kettle" is an area in the lake directly east of Walnut Point. The term is of fish pirate origin and refers to a sudden kettle-shaped dip in the lake bottom. Pirates were very attuned to such spots because the depth change required a net adjustment which, if not properly done, would result in a decline in their harvest.

OLD MAN POINT AND BAY

These place names were among the most mystifying of all. Neither county histories, maps, nor deeds gave me clues as to who the "old man" was. Fortunately, lady luck sometimes smiles on historians. In the summer of 1985 I went to the Syracuse Public Library to examine maps of Onondaga County. After studying these sources, I asked the reference librarian if he had anything else concerning the county's lakeshore area. He retreated to the reference room "off-limits" stacks and returned, ten minutes later, with two very dusty manila folders. Leafing through the contents, I was struck by a Syracuse newspaper article from September of 1905 entitled "The Hermit of Lewis Point." A. S. Hall was a hermit. Deduction and one confirming interview revealed Hall to be the "old man."

Hall's early life was beset with hardship. He was born in Amboy, Oswego County, in 1830. In his teens, he migrated to America's undeveloped west where he worked as a lumberjack and even dabbled in mining during the famous California gold rush. Returning to Syracuse, he worked as a teamster, coach driver and milk deliverer. He married twice, but both unions failed. Frustration led him to fighting and an assault charge. Fleeing justice, he went to Canada, where he lived for some time.

When Hall returned from Canada, he came to the Lower South Bay area. There he built a crude houseboat and "lived night and day on the water, an exile from his fellow men." He was a recluse. At sixty years of age but looking much older, he acquired the nickname "Old Man Hall - the Hermit of Oneida Lake."

Around 1890 Hall drifted east, from Lower South Bay to Lewis Point. There he fashioned a crude tarpaper shack. He supported himself by fishing until his shack was destroyed by high water and outgoing ice in February of 1903. After this date, his fate is unknown. His hermit years had made him a colorful Oneida Lake character. The paper said he "has seen the lake in every mood and knows no fear." He was dubbed a "modern Thoreau" whose "pipe and whiskey bottle provided solace." He was "tanned and weatherbeaten . . . a striking picture of rugged health." He had not shaved in thirty years. Rip Van Winkle had serious competition in A.S. Hall.

Why do I say Hall was the "old man?" First, the "old man" title was a part of his nickname. Secondly, in the Lower South Bay area, Hall tried to be totally isolated from others. He lived on a makeshift barge. Old Man's Bay would have been the best spot for Hall. Walnut Point and Old Man Point shelter both sides of this small bay. More importantly, however, there was absolutely no settlement on the bay when Hall arrived. The swamps on the bay's land side guarded his privacy. Lower South Bay itself had camps and small resorts; Hall avoided all company. Old Man Bay would have given him sanctuary.

Fred Scriba of Constantia is a veteran Oneida Lake fisherman. He traces his ancestry back to the 1790's, to George Scriba (re: Constantia, Oswego County chapter), an original lake area developer. Fred and I were talking once, about place names, when I asked him if he knew anything about the Lower South Bay area. I unfolded a map and Fred pointed to Peck's Point, saying that Duncan Peck had done some business with his father. Fred then mentioned the name "Hall's Point." Anticipating his answer, I asked Fred where it was. "Why right up from Peck's," said Fred pointing to Old Man Point. "We used to fish a lot there." The "old man's" identity, once an enigma, was now confirmed.

LONG POINT AND PECK'S POINT

From a geographer's viewpoint, this is an archetypal point; long and thin, it juts out from land to form a perfect breakwater, shielding Lower South Bay from the north wind's rage. Nineteenth century maps and deeds consistently name it "Long Point." In 1890, however, Duncan W. Peck of Syracuse purchased the eastern tip of the point from Douglas Ladd. Peck was a prominent Syracuse businessman and public figure. In the year he acquired the point, he was manager of the John White and Company Salt Manufacturers. Later, he owned a large lumber business on Syracuse's Clinton Block, selling pilings, posts, railroad ties and other bulky wood products. Peck purchased much of his timber from dealers along Oneida's north shore. During his public service tenure, Peck was Syracuse's Commissioner of Public Safety, a position he held at the turn of the century. He was also an avid waterfowl hunter and purchased Long Point's tip for building duck blinds. Waterfowl flocked to Oneida in such numbers during the 19th century that local folk often talked of the sky being "blackened" by fall's great migrating flocks. Peck's hunting prowess was such that, on October 25, 1880, he was cited by a Syracuse newspaper as returning from an Oneida Lake "marsh a day or two ago with as fine a lot of game as one could wish to feast his eyes upon." After Peck's acquisition of Long Point's extremity, that spot became known as "Peck's Point."

SHORT POINT AND BAY

Short Point, directly south of Long Point in Lower South Bay, derives its name from its size and a comparison to the other point. Less than half the length of Long Point, Short Point has also given its name to the bay which separates it from its lengthier cousin.

THE WEST END — BREWERTON, FRENCHMAN'S ISLAND AND LOWER SOUTH BAY

Constructed in the 1870's, Brewerton's Washburn House was that community's largest inn. The hotel maintained a fleet of rental fishing boats and catered to sportsmen.

The muddied morass of Brewerton's State Street, looking south, in the "horse and buggy" era is contrasted with the icy paved quality of that thoroughfare, viewed north, in the early auto years. The Brewerton Bait Shop, an anglers' mecca, was formerly housed in the structure between the Washburn House and the gas station. The store is now located by Route 81.

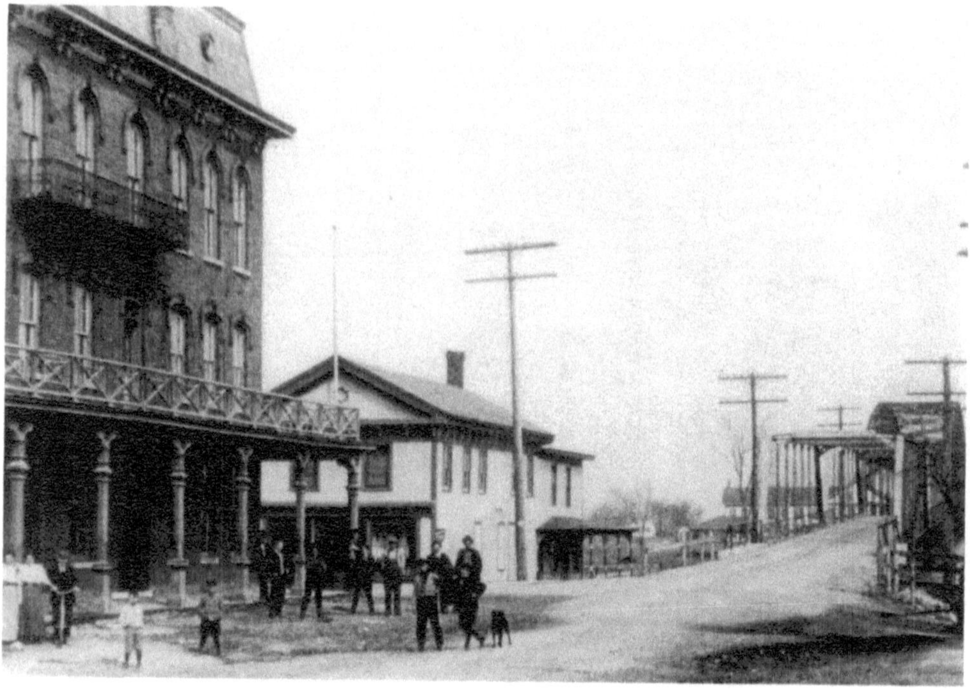

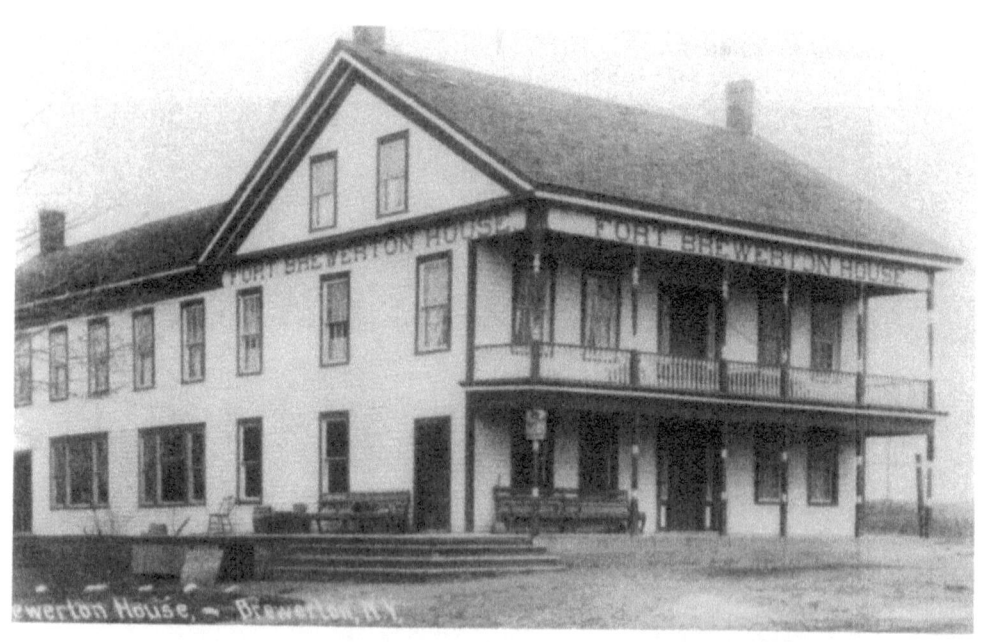

A view of Brewerton, looking north from the Washburn House. This highway bridge, the community's second, was built in 1883.

Henry Emmons established the Fort Brewerton Hotel in 1867 on a site on the Oneida River's north bank, where the contemporary Brewerton Historical Society Blockhouse Museum is located.

Brewerton Historical Society

The Lake View House, erected around the turn of the century, complimented Brewerton's already productive tourist industry. The inn's breeze-catching verandas were a common feature of Oneida Lake resorts.

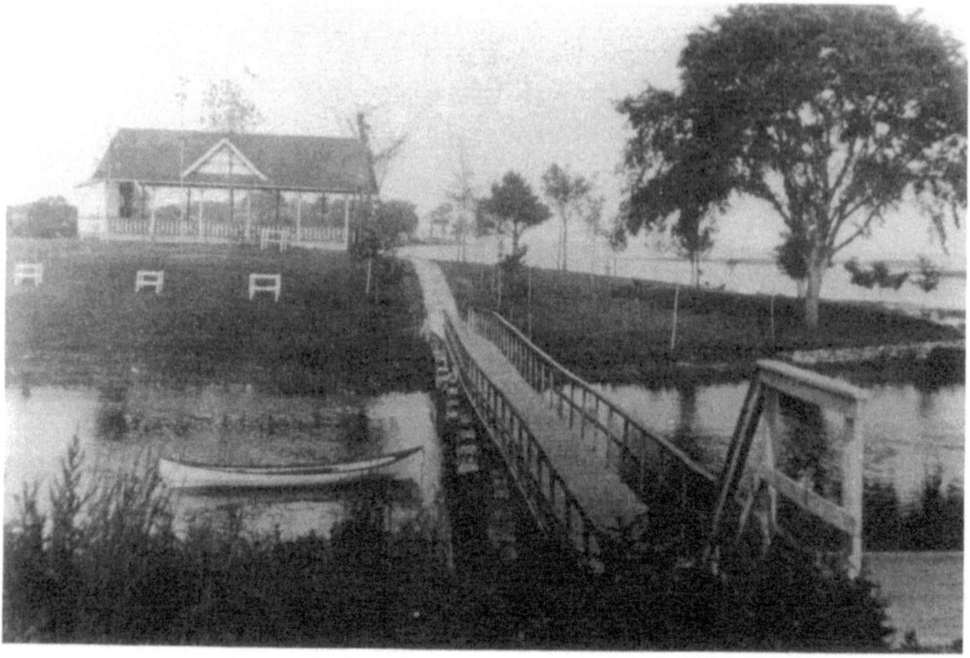

Brewerton Historical Society

Denman's Island, pictured here when it was called Baldwin's Island, is a tiny isle at Brewerton that was heavily used by pre-historic and Iroquois Indians as a fishing camp. Oneida River's rifts on the isle's north were prime angling territory.

Brewerton Historical Society

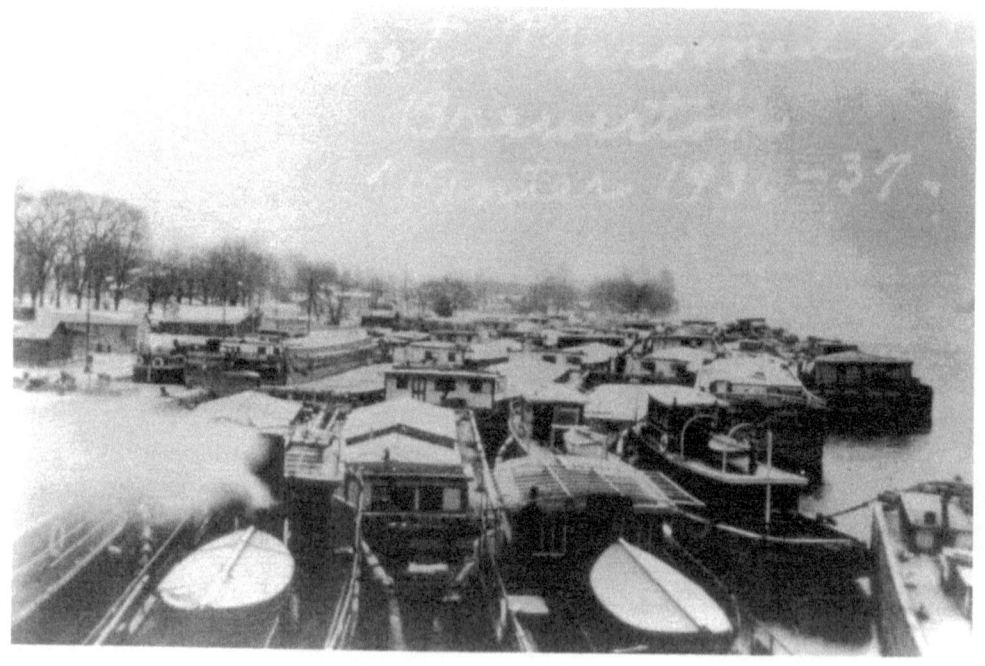

Brewerton's Barge Canal harbor was never busier than during the winter of 1936-37, when a sudden freeze marooned dozens of canal vessels. Sylvan Beach's harbor was also jammed with canal craft.

The Oneida River outlet at Brewerton, circa 1900. Wood Point juts out on the left, while Shepard Point forms the right-hand border. Several grass islands punctuate the water's expanse and, in the distance, Frenchman's Island peeks through the summer's mist.

Another outlet vista, looking north from the grass islands to the Oswego County shore. Sailing craft like these were commonly used by early fishing guides as they greatly increased the guides' rowboat-oriented angling range.

The first Oneida River bridge in Brewerton was erected in 1824. Winter evening light accented the span's wavy, and dangerously weathered, character. This photo was taken in the 1870's.

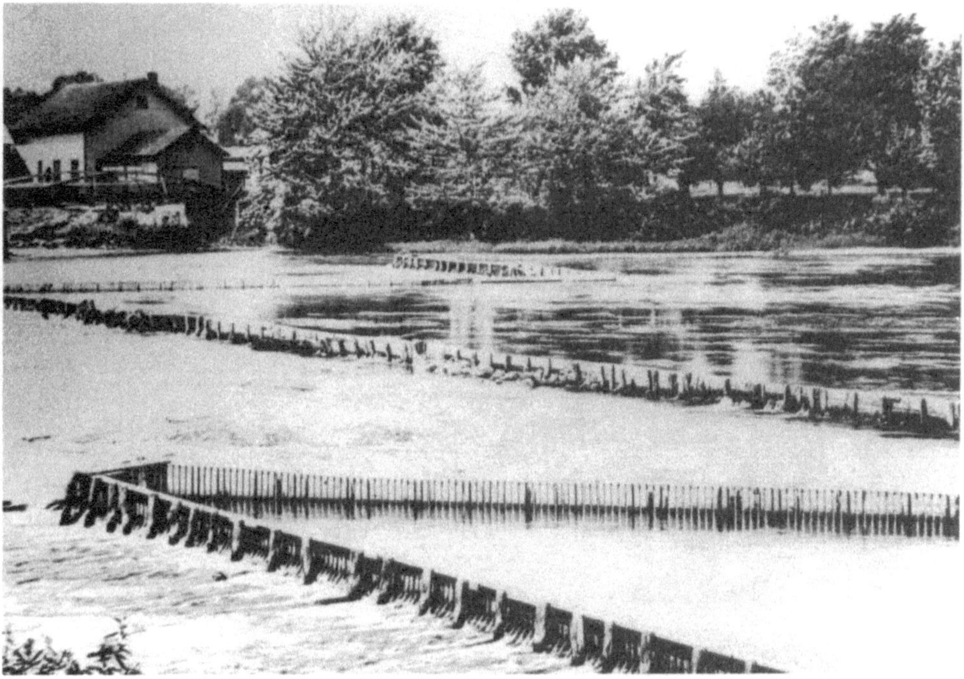

Brewerton Historical Society

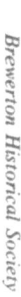

Caughdenoy, west of Brewerton, was the capital of Oneida's eel fishing industry. Pictured here are the eel weirs, funnel-shaped traps that ensnared eels on their migration from the lake. Tons of raw and smoked eels were exported from Caughdenoy and Brewerton during the business's best years.

Brewerton Historical Society

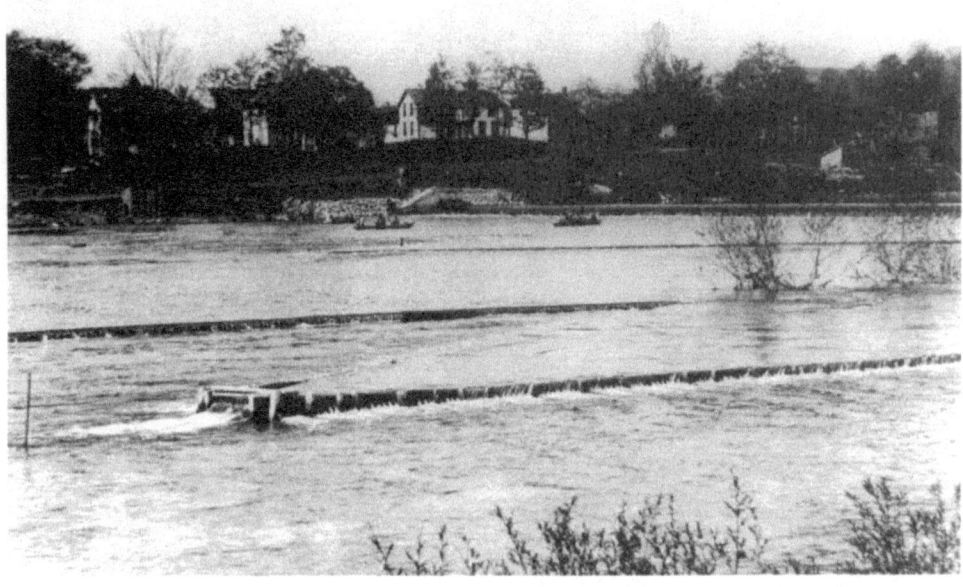

Smokehouses imparted succulent flavor to Oneida Lake eels and brought additional income to the fishermen.

Other eel products included dried skins and eel oil. The skins were used for livestock whips while the oil had a supposed medicinal value.

Onondaga Historical Association

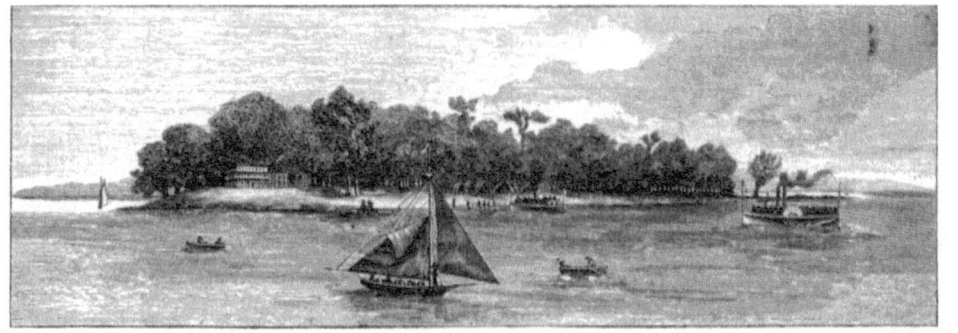

Built in 1858 by Leonard Hoadley and Larmon Dunham, the Sylvan House was Frenchman's Island's sole tourist facility. A modest hotel, the Sylvan House's duration lasted until its razing in 1901. The above print is from an 1860's advertisement while the photo below dates to the 1870's.

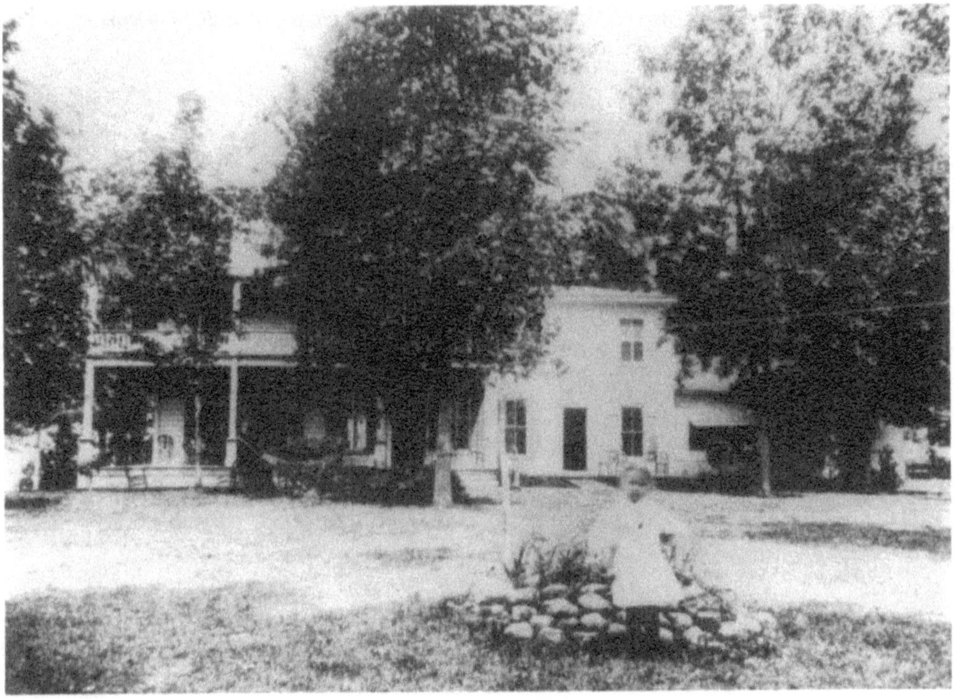

Brewerton Historical Society

Clifford Beebe maintained a large wharf at Frenchman's to accommodate steamboats. The above print shows the Sagamore *while in the lower photo the vessel* North Shore, *which traveled from Brewerton to South Bay, is moored dockside.*

Dunham's Island, viewed from a "cobble beach" on Frenchman's, circa 1910. Unlike its western twin, which was acquired by New York State, Dunham's has remained in private ownership.

Tourists picnic in a Frenchman's Island grove. At this time the island was owned by South Bay's Beebe syndicate.

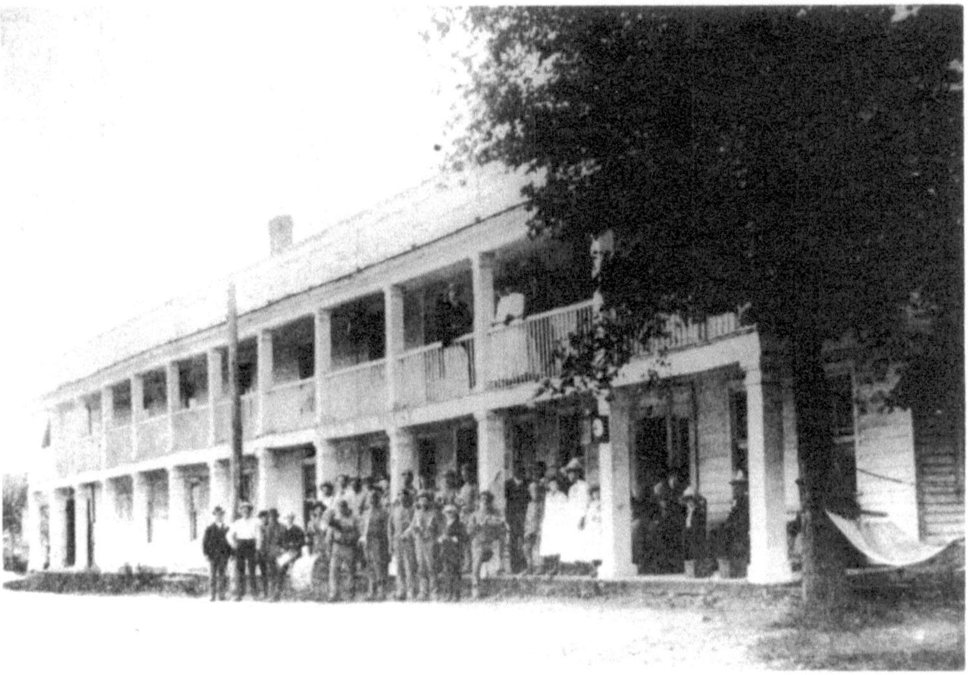

Brewerton Historical Society

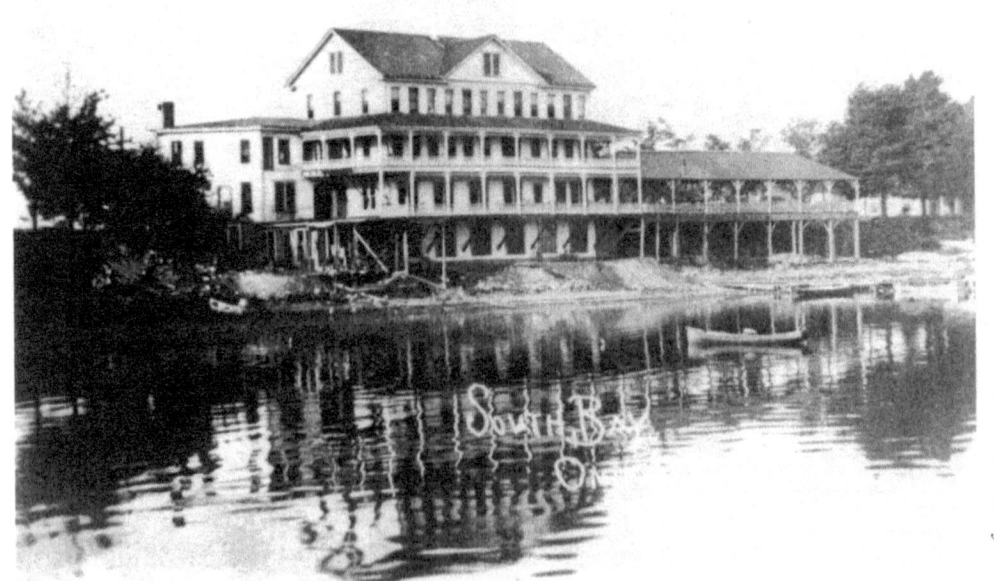

The South Bay House, erected by David Terpenny in 1804, was that area's first tourist spa. The hotel catered to Bay patrons until its fiery destruction in 1898.

Brewerton Historical Society

George Crownhart built the second South Bay Hotel in 1897. Crownhart was an active entrepreneur, having been involved with the Ocean House in the 1880's and having owned the South Bay House at the time of its demise.

The Beebe company installed this railroad pier at Lower South Bay, enabling trains from the Syracuse-to-South Bay trolley line to deliver passengers to the awaiting Sagamore.

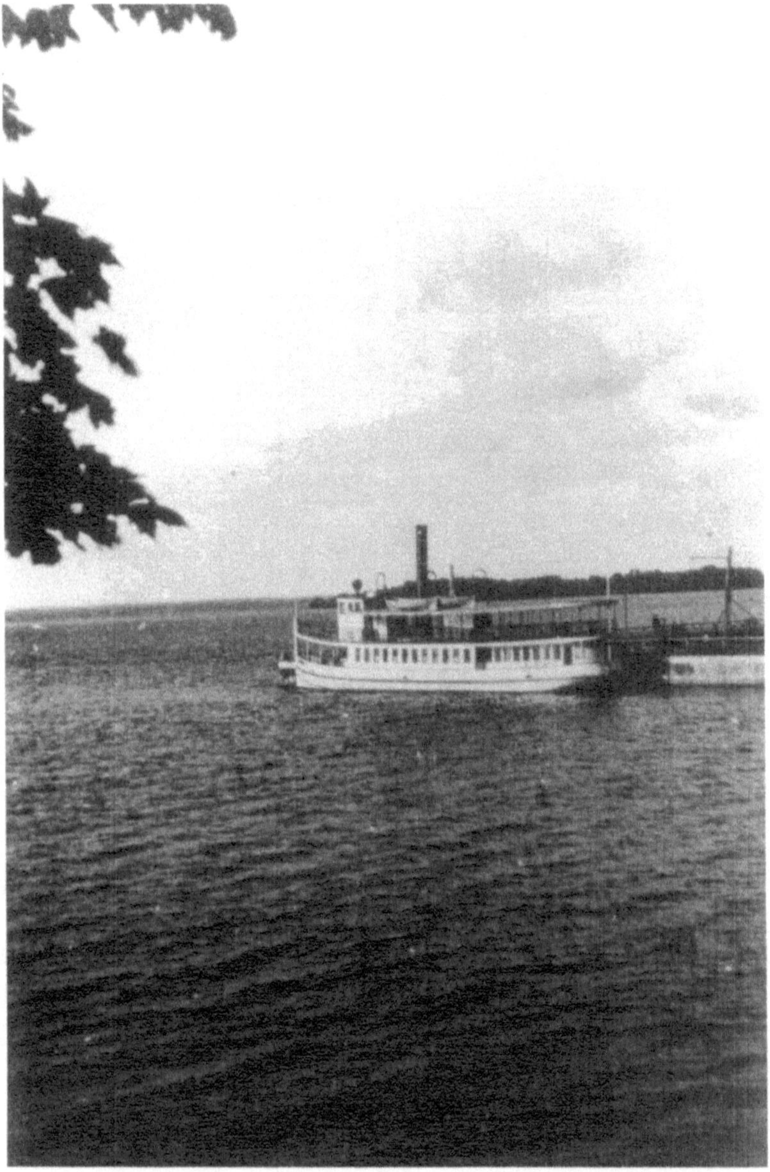

Brewerton Historical Society

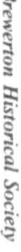

Oneida Lake has never seen a steamboat as grand as the Sagamore. *Owned by the Beebe company, the 122-foot boat could carry several hundred people. Its Oneida Lake service lasted from 1909 to 1915.*

Charles Losky, pictured here in 1911, was the Beebe Company's ticket agent at the South Bay wharf.

Formerly the Oneida Lake and River Steamboat Company's Oswego, *the* Manhattan *was a barge-towing steamer and, as is evident in this "over-loaded" print, had a busy tourist function.*

Not all Oneida Lake steamers were large. Frances *was a family yacht, owned by Thomas Milton, a Brewerton boat builder. Pictured here at Frenchman's in 1890 is the little steamer, with Milton sitting to the right and his youngest child, J. Elet Milton to the left. Elet Milton later became a fine Oneida Lake historian.*

Duck hunters at Lower South Bay, 1898. Note the drums in the boat to the left. This percussion unit was used to call ducks, a bizarre but effective sporting technique.

Joseph Norcross, a noted South Bay steamboat builder, constructed a boat called Twins, *named for his children. In 1861 the vessel was rechristened* Teaser.

The Sagamore Inn, Lower South Bay's fanciest resort was established by William Dunham in 1901. The Beebe organization bought the hotel in 1907 but sold it to the South Bay Angler's Clubhouse Association. Fire claimed the inn on November 30, 1908. The South Bay Yacht and Country Club currently occupies the site.

Ice-boating has thrilled Oneida Lake's daredevils throughout the twentieth century. These ice-boat aficionados are from the South Bay Yacht Club during the 1940's.

POLAR BEACH

This beach borders the western end of Lower South Bay, stretching south from Short Point. The Polar Beach area was originally surveyed and mapped in December of 1910. At that time the area's three owners, Frank Hoyt, Hiram Carter, and H.J. Horner had their holdings divided into the customary "cottage lots." Lots sold extremely well in the following fifteen years and a "beach road" was built in 1917. At that time, Polar Beach was known as "Park Row," a name given to it by the developers. It has also been called "Sandy Bay Beach," as per its physical qualities. The "Polar Beach" title emerged in the 1930's. Marvin Ladd and George Scriba recalled that "Polar Beach" was a nickname given to the area by local residents during that decade.

LOWER SOUTH BAY

This large and beautiful bay is called "Lower" by virtue of its location. "Upper" South Bay, on Oneida's eastern end is on the "head" or higher part of the lake, while Lower South Bay is near the Oneida River, the lake's outlet near its "foot," or lower section, at Brewerton. Lower South Bay has a significant history in Oneida Lake's resort saga.

The first resort facility on Lower South Bay was the South Bay House, built by David Terpenny in 1804. The hotel, with a capacity of seventy-five, was a long building of two stories, adorned by a double veranda on the lake side, supported by thirteen square pillars. Adjoining the property were five acres of land, an orchard and an ice house. Captain Valentine Dunham, of Valentine's Beach fame, served the hotel's sportsmen with his fleet of fishing boats. In its ninety-four-year history, the South Bay House had twenty-five proprietors, the last being George Crownhart who witnessed the hotel's demise by fire on March 15, 1898. A local paper, when notified of the fire, wrote of the hotel, "Since its first days it had been a headquarters for sportsmen, it not being an infrequent thing for a company from Philadelphia, New York or Boston to visit the hotel to hunt and fish. Its steep low roofs and wide veranda made it a picturesque place."

The owners of the South Bay House took pride in their hotel.

Although not a luxurious spa, the place was an adequate, neat accommodation for anglers, its primary customers. Evidence of ownership pride emanates from advertisements which appeared in the Syracuse newspapers in the mid-1800's. One paper correspondent, titled "Ivanhoe," wrote, "I feel confident in expressing the opinion that this house is kept in a style second to no country hotel in Western New York." J. Pettibone, hotel proprietor in the 1850's, described his business in the Syracuse *Standard* of June 9, 1858.

> The well known and popular South Bay House, having been recently refitted from cellar to garret, is now in order for the reception of guests and visitors. . . . The rooms are large, comfortable and airy, and the Hotel furnishes the greatest inducements for those who wish to spend a few days or weeks in the country.
>
> P.S. - There is also connected with the above Hotel a splendid fleet of sail and row boats, owned under the command of Captain V. Dunham. . . . The boats are safe and will be managed by experienced and skillful sailors. Fish are now being taken in the lake in great abundance.

The South Bay House was one of several hotels that catered to sportsmen in the bay's golden resort years. In the early 1880's, Henry and George Crownhart operated the Ocean House. Built on former Norcross family lands on Norcross Point, this hotel was also a fisherman's haven, boasting of its fine boats and access to prime angling territory. The hotel maintained a private steam yacht, the *Bessie Waldron*, to meet patrons embarking from trains at Brewerton; this same steamer towed fishing boats to spots such as the islands off Constantia.

By far the most glamourous hotel of South Bay was the Sagamore Inn. It was called a "splendid hotel," built in 1901 by Valentine Dunham's son, William, on land purchased from Henry Loftus (re: Loftus Shoal). William Dunham invested $4,000 in the property and spent approximately $65,000 on the inn. The hotel was a three story structure with spacious verandas and decorative ornamentation surrounding its entry and rooftop pediments. It very much resembled the luxury inns of the Thousand Islands region. Ironically, Dunham's investment bankrupted him; he could not afford to manage such a commodious hotel. During the year of the Sagamore Inn's construction, Dunham sold it to Arthur Jenkins of Syracuse.

Jenkins operated the inn until 1904, when the Bay Road Construction Company purchased it and invested an additional $25,000 in the structure. The Clifford Beebe interests acquired the South Bay Railroad in 1907 and, with it, the Sagamore. Beebe operated the inn as an exclusive hotel, employing George Crownhart and Smith Soule as managers. When the railroad needed capital, the inn was sold to the South Bay Angler's Clubhouse Association. This group, numbering over 2,500 members, rented rooms to club members as well as to the general public. On November 30, 1908, fire brought tragic destruction to this beautiful lake landmark. The Anglers' Association rebuilt on the site; their clubhouse is now the South Bay Yacht and Country Club.

What vitality Lower South Bay possessed as a resort came from its natural blessings and from the transportation facilities that brought people there. In 1895, the Syracuse and Oneida Lake Electric Railway Company was chartered; its attempts to connect the bay with Syracuse failed, primarily due to national financial woes. In 1904 the Syracuse and South Bay Electric Railroad Corporation acquired control of the Syracuse and Oneida Lake Company. This second corporation fared better, building the railroad line to the bay, terminating with a large loop that took the tracks to steamboat/pleasure boat connections at the water's edge. However, the Syracuse and South Bay Corporation could not maintain sufficient capital and, on February 21, 1907, Clifford Beebe purchased the line at a receiver's sale. Beebe renamed the railroad the Syracuse and South Bay Electric Railway Company, issued stock, and finally got the cars rolling in the summer of 1908.

Clifford Beebe and associates had a fine plan for South Bay resort development. Their ideal South Bay entailed the Sagamore Inn, the *Sagamore* steamboat, recreational facilities, picnic areas, fishing and pleasure boat rentals and, through the steamboat, connections to Frenchman's Island and other resorts of Oneida Lake. The South Bay Electric Railroad started operating on August 27, 1908. In the resort season, the railroad did well, and crowded cars filled with fishermen and vacationers were common. However, the off seasons were disastrous, causing the road to continually lose money. Other Beebe railroad ventures were equally burdensome, putting the company in financial trouble, culminating in a public auction of the South Bay line in 1916. A new company, the Syracuse Northern Electric Railway took over the road and operated it for several years. Eventually, as in the case of most New York State passenger railroads, the availability and convenience of the automobile killed the South Bay line.

Today, Lower South Bay is a delightful retreat on Oneida. By and large isolated from the major highways that encircle the lake, the Bay's shores are dotted with camps, marinas and restaurants. The water's broad expanse is fairly sheltered and usually calm, save for the effects of a nasty northeasterly blow. A perfect view of Frenchman's and Dunham's Islands frames the northern end of the Bay while Long Point guards the western portal and Norcross Point the eastern door. Many fishermen take advantage of the Bay's fine angling and scores of boaters ply its waters. The days of the Sagamore Inn, of the electric railway, of the steamers, of Valentine Dunham, Joseph Norcross and Clifford Beebe may be gone, but Lower South Bay maintains a vitality in which these once thrived.

LOFTUS SHOAL

Sometimes called "Loftie" Shoal, this reef was named for Henry Loftus, a dealer and manufacturer of wigs and hair goods in Syracuse. Around 1885 Loftus built a cottage on a Lower South Bay land tract that included two acres and five hundred feet of lakefront. He operated a small marina there. Loftus Shoal was one of the favorite fishing spots for the "rowboat-powered" anglers of that era.

NORCROSS POINT

Joseph W. Norcross, in 1854, built his house, barn, several outbuildings and a boatyard on the point named for him. In the boatyard he and his workers constructed steamboats, then the fastest conveyance on Oneida. Among the Norcross line of steamers were the *Queen of the Lake* and *Citizen's Corps*, both christened in 1857. In 1858 Norcross launched a steamer named for himself and also created the boat, *Twins*. Many smaller craft were built in the Norcross boatyard. Norcross and his family left the point in the 1860's. The Ocean House, a hotel operated by

Henry Crownhart, was built on the site of the Norcross home. Norcross was also one of the first to enjoy the sport of ice-boating on Oneida.

VALENTINE'S BEACH

Born in Hamilton, New York on May 15, 1816, Valentine Dunham left the state's heartland, "went to sea" and became a professional sailor. Upon returning, he settled on Dunham's Island with his father, Hazael (see that island's entry in "Isles and Shoals" chapter). Later he purchased the isle, but never developed it, choosing instead to enter the boating business. After acquiring real estate on Lower South Bay, Dunham constructed a marina, rented fishing and sail boats, and became a renowned Oneida Lake guide for both pleasure and angling parties. Dunham's business endured from 1853 until his death in 1898. Some of my sources stated that Valentine's Beach was named for the enterprising Valentine Dunham, but a more probable explanation of this place name's origin comes from Edward Boysen, son of George W. Boysen (Boysen's Bay). Mr. Boysen wrote me concerning the subject: "My father sold the beach property to William E. Valentine, a Syracuse coal dealer, in the 1930's. Mr. Valentine built a restaurant there and the area became known as Valentine's Beach." The Dunhams had an earlier connection to the area, but the recollections of a person who knew William Valentine (Ed Boysen even had a treehouse on the latter's land) bear greater historical validity.

BOYSEN'S BAY

This bay was named for George W. Boysen, who bought a 54-acre farm bordering the lake in 1909. At that time the bay was known as Grave's Bay. Boysen's name has stuck with the bay and is often associated, erroneously, with the small amusement park that made the spot famous. "Boysen's Bay Park" was a significant attraction in the 1920's and 1930's. The park contained a carousel and many child-pleasing "kiddy rides." A skating rink brought pleasure to dating couples who went there to swoon away romantic evenings. The picnic grove was a popular place for corporate outings. The Smith Corona Typewriter Company, formerly of Cortland, held their annual picnic there. A swimming area and a rowboat rental service attracted additional patrons. George Boysen sold land to the park's developers and while he never operated the small resort, his name was attached to the spa and enhancing bay.

CHIMNEY BAR

Long and narrow, this Boysen's Bay bar reminded old-time fishermen of a chimney.

CRANS BAR

This little bar crosses the northern part of Maple Bay. The bar was named for the Crans family, farmers who for years owned shore land opposite it. The family originally came from Ulster County in New York's lower Hudson Valley. An 1854 map of Cicero Township shows a Moses Cranse (sic) living on the property near the bar. Moses's son, Merrit, also became a farmer, cultivating over a hundred acres by 1890. Another son, Oliver, followed the family trade and settled in the Maple Bay homestead. In the late 1800's, the Crans family name was quite common in the Cicero area. By 1917, however, the only Crans listed as a Cicero "agriculturist" was Willis Crans. Richard Brown and Marvin Ladd, both life-long residents of the lake area, recall Willis's 100 acre dairy farm, on the bay near the first Crans settlement. This business operated until 1952. The farm, with its barn and outbuildings, was most likely an orientation point for anglers in the lake that were trying to locate the Crans Bar. Shore reference points are still extensively used by anglers, though today's electronic depth finders facilitate the locating task.

MAPLE BAY AND BAR

Like Walnut Point, this bay took its name from the trees that once grew there. Prior to its Maple Bay naming, the bay was called Deyo's Dock. During the middle and latter 1800's, Nathaniel, Jonathan and Abigail Deyo owned farms that bordered Maple Bay lakeshore. The family maintained a dock on the bay that was used by steamboats, sportsmen and pleasure craft. This dock was, without a doubt, highly convenient for larger boats that could not navigate some of the bay's shallow shoals or ascend Chittenango Creek to Bridgeport.

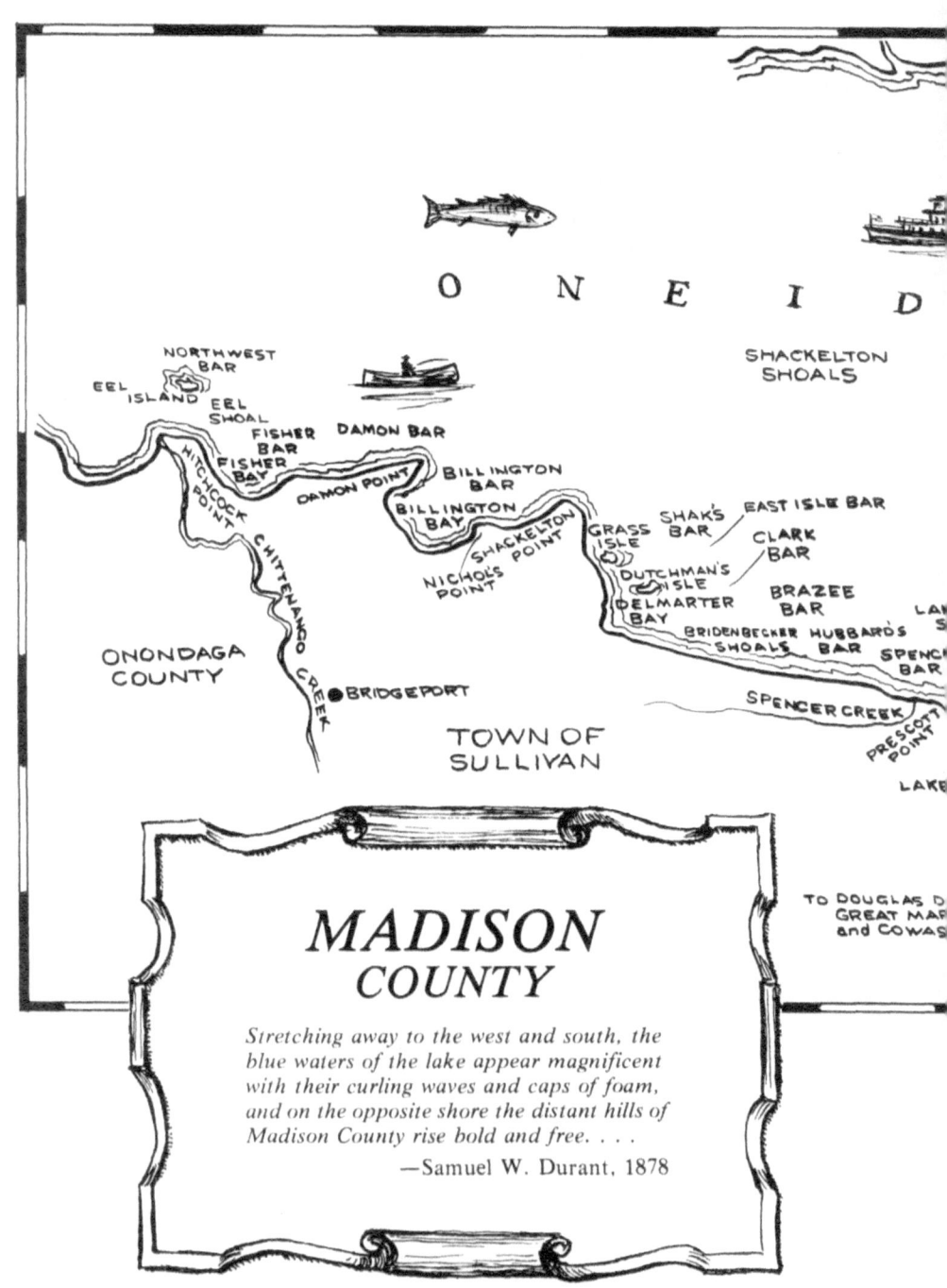

MADISON COUNTY

Stretching away to the west and south, the blue waters of the lake appear magnificent with their curling waves and caps of foam, and on the opposite shore the distant hills of Madison County rise bold and free....

—Samuel W. Durant, 1878

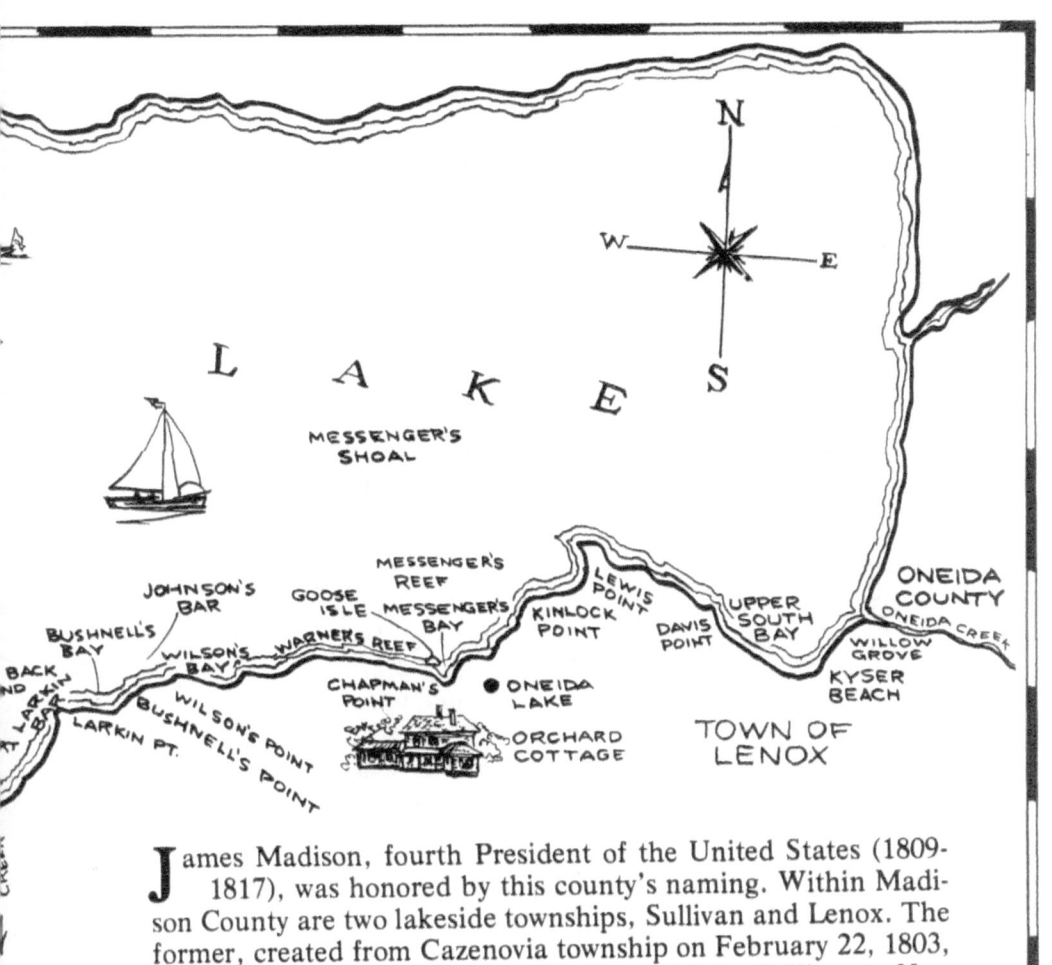

James Madison, fourth President of the United States (1809-1817), was honored by this county's naming. Within Madison County are two lakeside townships, Sullivan and Lenox. The former, created from Cazenovia township on February 22, 1803, was named for Revolutionary War General John Sullivan, a New Hampshire native, who led the patriots' successful campaign that destroyed countless villages and essential crop fields in the Iroquois Indians' western New York heartland. Lenox was separated from Sullivan township on March 3, 1809. The origin of its title is subject for conjecture. An *Oneida Dispatch* writer wrote, on February 13, 1964, that "legend has it that there was an old fort near Wampsville and a family named Lenox lived at (the fort) or nearby." The name originates in the British Isles and crossed the Atlantic with colonists destined for New England. More than likely, Yankee settlers to Madison County gave Lenox its title.

Bridgeport constitutes the western lead-in to this chapter; Willow Grove, on Oneida Creek, ends the section. Brief histories of Lakeport, Bridgeport, Messenger's Bay and Upper South Bay are included within.

Place names, in order of appearance, are:

- Bridgeport
- Chittenango Creek
- Hitchcock Point
- Northwest Bar
- Eel Island and Shoal
- Fisher's Bay and Bar
- Damon Point and Bar
- Goose Island
- Billington Bay and Bar
- Nichols Point
- Shackelton Point and Shoals and Shak's Bar
- Delmarter Bay
- Grass Isle
- Dutchman's Isle
- East Isle Bar
- Clark Bar
- Brazee Bar
- Bridenbecker Shoals
- Hubbard's Bar
- Spencer Creek and Bar
- Prescott's Point
- Blind Isle
- Lakeport, Lakeport Shoals and Bar
- Canaseraga Creek, Douglas Ditch, Great Marsh and Cowaselon Creek
- Hog's Back Mound
- Larkin Point and Bar
- Johnson's Bar
- Bushnell's Point and Bay
- Wilson's Point and Bay
- Warner's Reef
- Chapman Point
- Messenger's Bay, Shoal and Reef, Oneida Lake hamlet
- Kinlock Point
- Lewis Point
- Davis Point
- Upper South Bay
- Kyser Beach
- Willow Grove

BRIDGEPORT

Captain Rosel Barnes was the Bridgeport area's first settler and, for a brief time, the infant community was called Barnesville. Barnes constructed the village's first frame house, a dwelling that replaced his pioneer log cabin-tavern building. Evidently Bridgeport's promise proved insufficient for Barnes and the innkeeper soon moved to Illinois. Hammond's Madison County history cites Clark's *Onondaga* in explaining two other early names for Bridgeport:

> Messrs. Isaac and John Delamarter made a settlement at the Chittenango Rifts, or Rapids, as the place (Bridgeport) was then called, in 1802. . . . There is a sudden fall in the Chittenango Creek here of about ten feet, which yields an

immense water power, which is very little employed. It is a famous place for taking suckers and other fish, early in the spring, and from this circumstance has been denominated the sucker bank. It was once a great place for taking salmon. It was not uncommon to take them from the nets weighing from twelve to twenty-five pounds.

Despite Hammond's statement that the rapids were little used, the Chittenango Creek rifts provided power for several early Bridgeport factories, among which were a sawmill, woolen mill and gristmill. Such small industries stimulated community growth and Bridgeport soon outgrew Lakeport in the 1800's primarily because of the creek's power source. Lakeport's stream, Canaseraga Creek, is a lethargic water, incapable of generating enough energy for even small, primitive industries.

A commonly accepted idea concerning the origin of the name "Bridgeport" was that it came about during construction of the first bridge over Chittenango Creek. Although located a mile inland from Oneida Lake, the settlement became a "port" through this creek's navigability. One of the first settlers, a Captain John Rector, built 100-ton boats at Bridgeport and sailed them down the creek for use in the lake trade. An obituary for a Mrs. Moses Jennings, however, published in the *Madison County Times* on March 18, 1898, casts doubt on the bridge-naming theory. The obituary read:

> Mrs. Jennings was born in Hartland, Hartford County (Connecticut), December 16, 1806. Her father, Captain John Rector, came to this country in the spring of 1808. There were no mail or milling privileges at that time short of Manlius village. Among the pioneers that soon followed was Levi Jennings from Fairfield County, Bridgeport, Connecticut, with his patriarchal family of twelve children, attracted hither by the water power, also surrounding heavy timber lands. Soon, with energy and capital, he established mills and named the little hamlet Bridgeport, which had hitherto been called The Rapids or Rifts.

David Burr's 1829 Madison County map has Bridgeport labeled as such. This date occurred before construction of the community's first bridge. The naming of upstate communities for New England towns was common in the early 1800's. This was the period of the "Yankee invasion" of New York, when thousands of New Englanders left home to settle upstate's fertile, undeveloped lands. Places like New Hartford, Springfield and Norwich were of Yankee origin, hence the Bridgeport naming was consistent with a common practice.

Oneida Lake place names near Bridgeport reflect some of the area's early families. The Damons of Damon Point, the Billingtons of Billington Bay and the Briggs and Delamarter families of Briggs (Delmarter) Bay were all pioneers of the area. Bridgeport, by the latter nineteenth century, had matured into a prosperous small town. A county history of that era described the settlement's commercial aspects:

> Bridgeport . . . contains two hotels (one kept by Joseph Lewis, built in 1873, on the site of one burned in 1867; and the other by Udell Mayo, who commenced the spring of 1880, succeeded by John Nichols); three blacksmith shops; four stores, kept by Dunham and Sharpe, Orson Terpenny, Charles Billington and Brother (general stores), and Horace Draper (hardware store and tinshop), and a gristmill. The postmaster is A. P. Briggs, who has held the office since the spring of 1879, and succeeded George Rector.
>
> There are two physicians in the place, Dr. David Dunham and David Dunham, Jr.
>
> The Bridgeport Mills are run by the Snyder Bros. (W. J. and C. D.), who bought the mills in 1879 of Oney Sayles, who had run them about four years. The mills contain two runs of stones which are propelled by water power, and do only custom work.
>
> Near Bridgeport are located two cheese factories.

The account continued, stating that the cheese factories processed the milk of 375 cows. This point is a key to understanding the vitality of early Bridgeport. Like many upstate country towns, Bridgeport served as a trading and social center for its numerous surrounding farms. Farmers hauled their milk to the cheese factories, brought their grain to the gristmill, purchased lumber at the sawmill, and shopped for necessities at the general stores. Some farm children attended school at Bridgeport and many farm families belonged to the local Methodist or Baptist church. Farmers were Bridgeport's raison d'etre. True, the community drew some benefit from Oneida Lake tourism, but in the nineteenth century this enterprise ran second to businesses catering to the farmer. Bridgeport was over a mile from the lake and thus, unlike Constantia, Lakeport, or Sylvan Beach, could not take full advantage of the vacation trade.

Some interesting details characterized life in early Bridgeport.

Barrels, manufactured there, were exported, via the lake and Oneida River, to Syracuse where they were exchanged for salt. The village's first school was situated near Chittenango Creek and, during spring floods, taller boys carried the younger children to class. Half way from Bridgeport to the lake was a spot on the creek called "Bloody Point," named for the tons of salmon butchered there. Bridgeport pioneers braved many hardships, not the least of which was the dangers of wild animals. A Madison County Directory of 1869 contained the following story:

> Mrs. Cuppernoll, an aged lady living at Bridgeport, and daughter of Mr. Carter, relates that when she was first married, her husband used to change works with a friend at a distance, leaving her alone sometimes for a week. On one occasion, before he left home she prepared for their supper a dish of thickened milk. It being late, she deferred washing the kettle, but filling it with water, set it outside of her cabin door and retired. This door was only a 'rag rug' hung up temporarily. During the night she heard what she supposed to be the fighting and scrambling of dogs over her kettle, and only wondering where they all came from, she gave herself no further trouble and went to sleep. Early in the morning she was awakened by the halooing of her nearest neighbor, who having heard the howling of a pack of wolves near the dwelling in the night, and knowing the frail character of her door, fully expected to find that she had been devoured by the ravenous beasts. Her kettle was licked clean but no damage was done. Afterwards, until her husband's return, she slept in the loft.

Bears, too, were common in the vicinity. An account from the same county directory told of Bridgeport citizen Robert Carter's being treed for five hours by an enraged bear.

Today, Bridgeport is three types of communities merged into one. Along the lakefront and Chittenango Creek is resort Bridgeport, with large marinas and summer houses, most of which have been converted to year-round homes, dominating the scene. West of the creek, along Route 31, stretches suburban Bridgeport, a Syracuse commuter development characterized by modern housing projects and a shopping plaza. On Route 31, east of the creek bridge, lies an older Bridgeport, its buildings a mix of nineteenth century relics and newer structures. Here, one finds establishments such as the venerable Bottings Hotel, formerly the Union Hotel owned by "Mine Host" J.W. Nichols, contrasted with neighboring new businesses like Bridgeport Pizza, a marvelous bakery-Italian restaurant combination, particularly attractive to this writer's taste buds. While not an historic area in the sense of Cazenovia's Route 20 strip, old Bridgeport's buildings bear physical witness to the village's formative days.

CHITTENANGO CREEK

Place names of Indian origin often inspire differing historical interpretation and this major south shore tributary is a fine example. In *Body, Boots and Britches*, Harold Thompson wrote of the Chittenango quandary:

> Chu-de-nang, 'Where the sun shines out,' according to Morgan. Chittenango Creek. Others, however, have defined it as 'Where waters divide and run north,' which is really without any true meaning. On a map of 1825 it is called Chit-e-ning, and in land treaties Chit-i-lin-go creek. A Cusick thinks this means 'Marshy place,' the stream passing for many miles through low lands before it reaches the lake. After the Tuscaroras came into Madison County it was sometimes called Tuscarora Creek, from them. In 1767 Sir William Johnson said, 'I met the Indians at the Tuscarora creek, in Oneida Lake.' The Indians now know it as O-wah-ge-nah, or 'Perch Creek.''

George Stewart's *American Place Names*, echoing Thompson's analysis, states that the creek's name is of meaning "uncertain." Early settlers liked this Indian word, however, and used it.

The creek has always been important in Oneida Lake history. The Iroquois and their predecessors, of course, fished it heavily. The shoals formed by its alluvial deposits in Maple Bay were, and are, fine angling grounds. Water power provided by the creek was a primary reason for the settlement of Bridgeport, once allegedly called "Chittenango Rifts." Today, the creek's lower reaches are lined with summer camps and fishermen remain attracted by its spring walleye migrations.

SOUTH SHORE PAST PICTORIALS — BRIDGEPORT, LAKEPORT, UPPER SOUTH BAY AND POINTS BETWEEN

Bridgeport's Stamberg Hotel was a landmark in the village's "downtown." The building, now greatly altered, currently houses Botting's Hotel.

Chittenango Creek powered Bridgeport's nineteenth century factories. This establishment, the first water-run gristmill, was situated on the creek's east bank, by the Main Street bridge.

Reflections along Chittenango Creek, near its mouth, beg for the romantic writer's words while the lower view of that stream and its rich flood plain, south of Bridgeport, illustrate what attracted many of the lake area's pioneer agrarians.

Bridgeport was named for Bridgeport, Connecticut, but many folk have erroneously thought that its bridges inspired the title. The first "advanced" structure, pictured above, was raised in 1871 while the lower, contemporary bridge initially spanned Chittenango Creek in 1910.

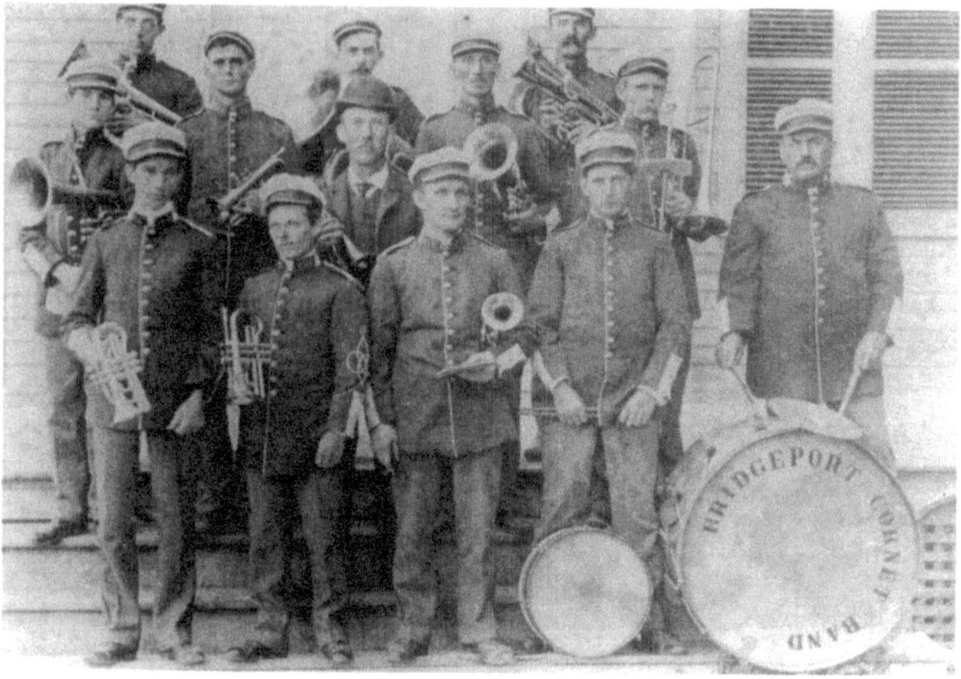

Sullivan Library

A village is its people and Bridgeport was no exception, from the somber Cornet Band to a child postcard "cutie."

Sullivan Library

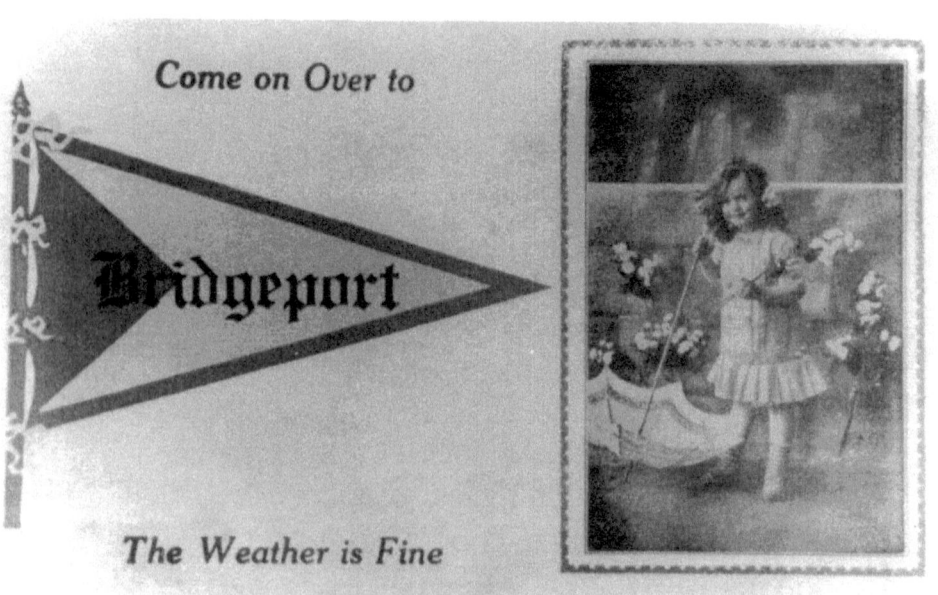

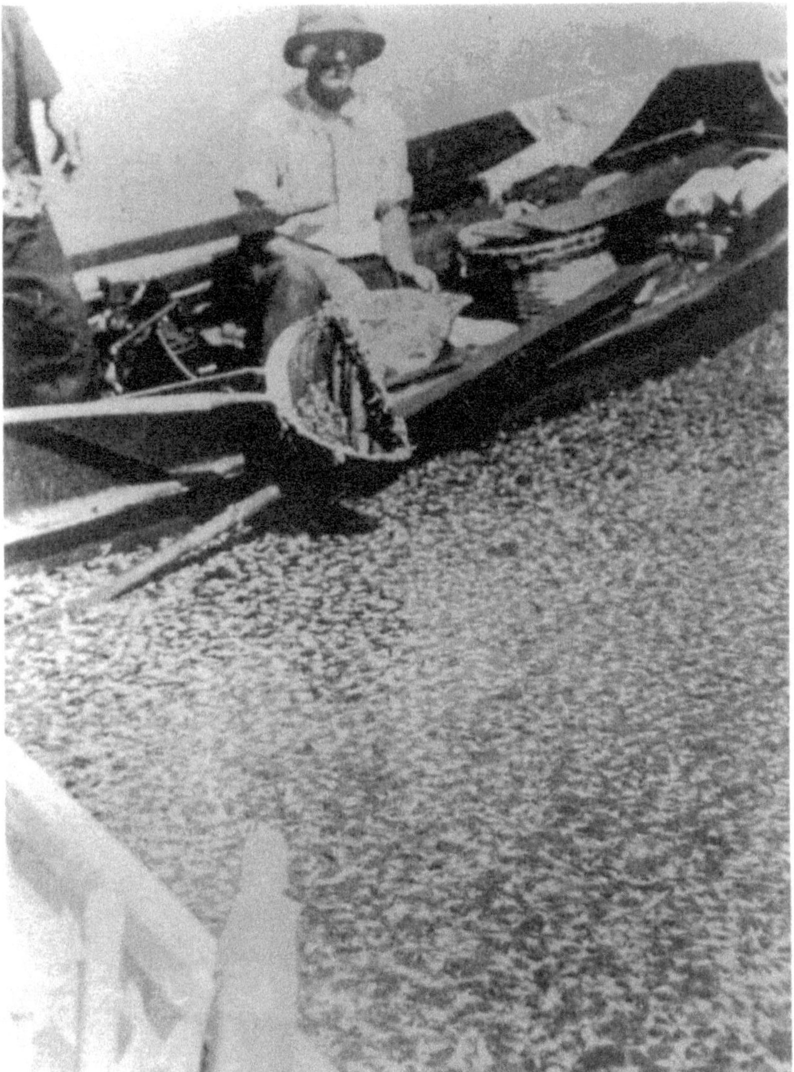

Cornell University

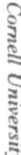

Mayflies, commonly known around Oneida as "eel flies," were once an annoying part of lake area life. After reproduction, the flies would die and their carcasses washed ashore in such numbers that clean-up proved to be a herculean labor.

Sullivan Library

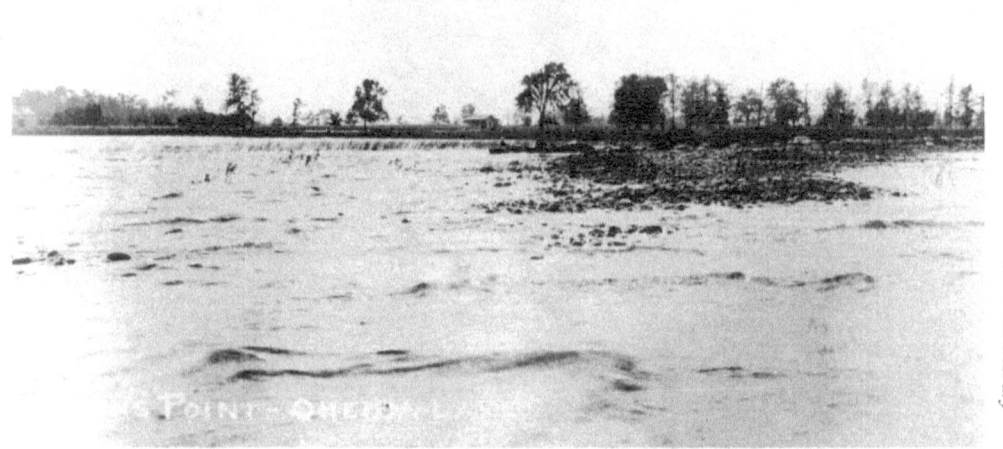

The "cottaging" movement in the early 20th century transformed Damon's Point from largely undeveloped farmland to a crowded summer community. Much of the lake's shore was altered in a similar manner during this era.

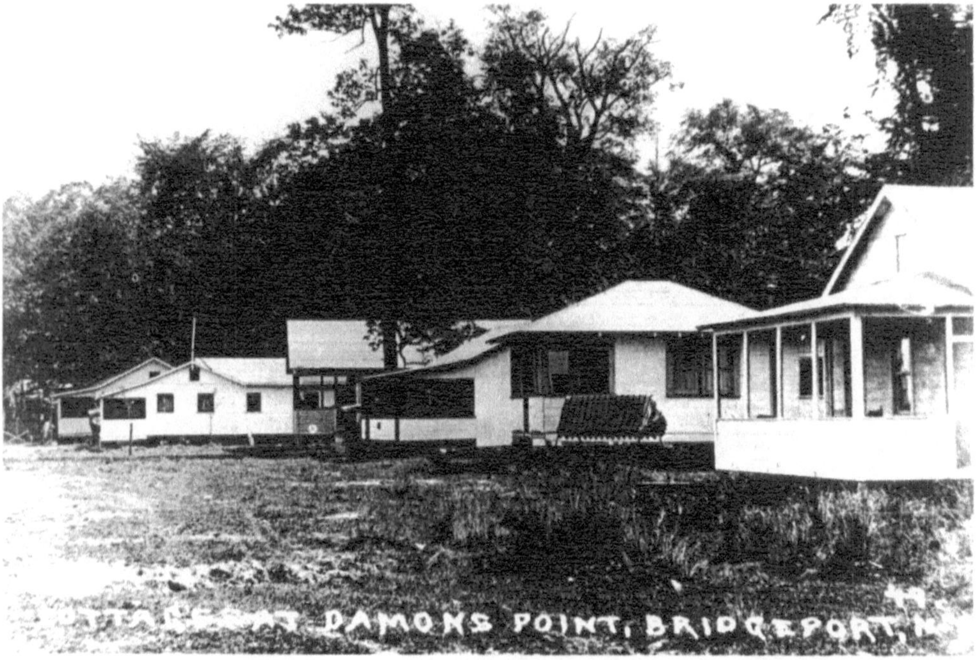

Sullivan Library

Billington's Bay during the agricultural days of the late 1800's. Livestock graze by the shore while anglers unload their catch. Many lakeside farmers supplemented their income by commercial fishing.

This shot of the Billington's Bay marsh clearly shows the emergent vegetation that was once common along Oneida's periphery. Development filled in most of this lush border, eliminating breeding grounds for northern pike and pickerel, thus contributing to the walleye's ascension as Oneida's premier game fish.

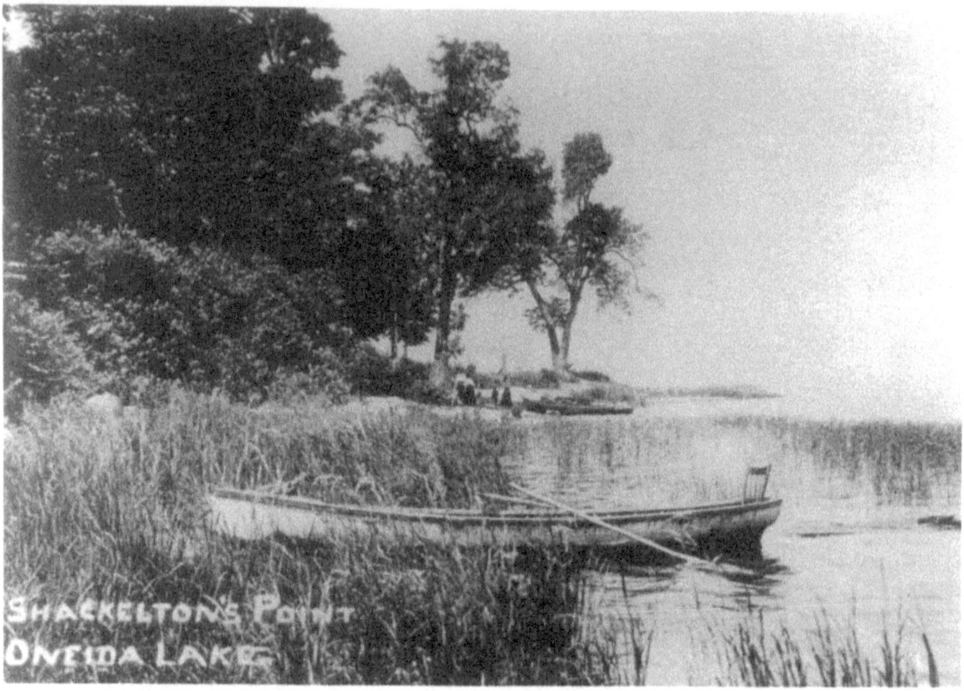

Sullivan Library

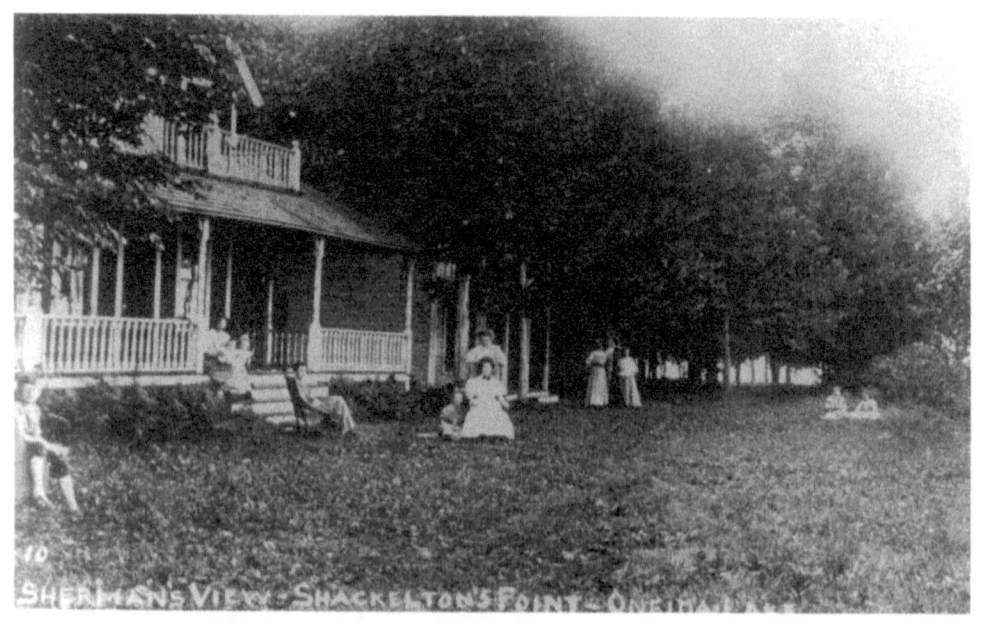

Shackelton's Point, in the days before Brown's Xandria estate, was a family resort, offering boat and cottage rentals, a picnic grove, and plenty of old-fashioned "R and R."

Sullivan Library

Two of the Cornell Shackelton Point Research Station's tests are collecting perch fry samples and electroshocking adult fish. These research tools, depicted here in two photos from the early 1960's, are among the techniques that enable the station to monitor Oneida's fluctuating fish populations. At the left of each print is John Forney, the biologist who has guided the station throughout its three-decade history.

Canaseraga Creek enters Oneida at Lakeport. A sluggish, meandering stream, it was once called Douglas Creek, for Colonel Zebulon Douglas, a state legislator whose efforts were largely responsible for constructing Douglas Ditch, a drainage canal which lowered water levels in Madison County's Great Marsh.

Cooper's Place, a precursor to today's fast food outlets, catered to motorists traversing Lakeport's Main Street, now Route 31. Small, family-operated restaurants were common around Oneida in the early twentieth century.

David Larkin's Hotel and Grove was Lakeport's commercial hub. Abram Larkin, David's father, was one of the community's pioneers, emigrating there from Rhode Island in 1813.

If You Have that Tired Feeling and Need Rest, Pack Up a Few Duds and Light Out for the

Larkin Grove Farm

LAKE PORT, N. Y.

No Better Fishing Grounds in Oneida Lake

MEALS AND BOATS

A quaint card highlights some of the Larkin Grove attractions while, below, the Progressive Era's reform legislation is evidenced in a pastoral advertisement.

Warm Meals at The Larkin Grove Farm, Lakeport, N. Y., under the Pure Food Law.

Lakeport Bay and "beach," around 1900. The cobble beach characterizes most lakeshore locales, except for the sandy, shelving beaches along the eastern end. Larkin Point provides the bay's backdrop.

The Lakeport School was typical of the one-room country schools in which many early Oneida Lakers received their education.

View of Rustic Tavern, Portion of Lawn and Old Well House, Lewis Point, N. Y., Oneida Lake

Started as the "Rural Retreat" by Osbert Messenger in the 1890's, the Rustic Tavern was the first tourist spa on Lewis Point. The photo of its airy veranda, below, illustrates the rough wood, wickered delight that its patrons savored.

View of Portion of Veranda of Rustic Tavern at Lewis Point, N. Y., Oneida Lake

Byron Scoville's Lottie *emerges from the lakeside lock of the second Oneida Lake Canal at Upper South Bay, 1900. The lock and a neighboring sister structure are now a part of the Oneida Lake Marina.*

The Bard of Avon would doubtless cringe upon reading this bit of Oneida Lake poetry, but the verse's lines give specific reference to reasons why people patronized the lake's resorts.

> Just a word of consolation,
>   To those seeking recreation,
> If you want to spend a mighty pleasant day,
>   Take the Lehigh train on Sunday,
>   For it's cheaper than on Monday,
> And tell them to unload you at South Bay,
>   The round trip's but a dollar,
>   On the price you can not holler,
> It's only just three miles from Sylvan Beach,
>   Back and forth the boats are running
>   And the scenery is stunning,
> Oneida Lake is certainly a peach,
>   We will feed you fish and chicken
>   And frog's legs, all good picken,
> Our meals you'll find are strictly up to date,
>   The wet goods they are splendid,
>   We have whiskies straight and blended,
> And we'll keator to your wants while you wait.
>
>   Yours truly,
>   J. S. SULLIVAN, Proprietor.

STEPHENS HOUSE

SOUTH BAY (Madison Co.) N.Y.

ORDERS RECEIVED BY PHONE OR MAIL

South Bay's Main Street as it appeared in the early motoring days. Jake Kyser's Hotel, pictured below, was the community's primary inn. Kyser, an accomplished Oneida Lake pirate, gained fame by rescuing many victims of the lake's storms. As might be expected, "pike dinners" were a specialty of Jake's hotel.

HITCHCOCK POINT

This point, which extends into the eastern half of Maple Bay, was named for Charles Hitchcock, a prominent Madison County resident around the turn of the century. Hitchcock was born in Seneca Falls in 1859. He moved to Madison County and, at age twenty-five, began his legal studies. In 1888 he passed the bar exam; for years, he practiced his profession in Syracuse while residing in Chittenango. Hitchcock was an attorney with a solid reputation. Governor Al Smith recognized this and, in 1923, appointed him to fill a vacancy in the State's Supreme Court. Hitchcock served for seven months on the court, losing the election following his appointment. He had a great interest in history, serving as president of the Madison County Historical Society and publishing, in 1905, a brief history of Chittenango.

Another of Hitchcock's interests was real estate; Madison County records show numerous transactions involving him. His first land dealing on Oneida occurred in 1886, when he purchased three-quarters of an acre on the Lakeport shore. In September of 1897, Hitchcock bought the Snyder and Shetler farms comprising most of Hitchcock Point. The late 1800's and early 1900's were years of great economic expansion around Oneida. A person with Hitchcock's background was bound to realize lakeshore property's potential. His purchase was speculative in nature, and he eventually sold the land. Like most larger Oneida Lake tracts, it was surveyed and divided into cottage lots.

Hitchcock Point has had one other name in its history. Early maps refer to is as Long Point, an appropriate name considering its length.

NORTHWEST BAR

This shoal is northwest of Fisher's Bay and was named by anglers and fish pirates who used that bay as a port for their vessels.

EEL ISLAND AND SHOALS

Eel Island and its adjoining shoals were, obviously, named for the long, slender, slimy fish that once constituted a considerable economic plus for Oneida Lake anglers. The island, now submerged due to a rise in the lake's level that accompanied Barge Canal construction, was formerly called "Long Point Island." French's map of 1860 shows it as such, directly north of Hitchcock Point, then called Long Point.

FISHER'S BAY AND BAR

This bay's earliest recorded name was "Froher Bay," a title probably referring to a squatter or seasonal fisherman as no Froher is listed in any Madison County census or property records. Until around 1900 the bay was called Keller's Bay. Peter Keller, a farmer, purchased lakeshore land east of the bay in 1821 from Stephen Delamarter and sold the same property to John Delamarter a decade later. Keller moved two miles south to Bridgeport, near John and Alvin Keller, and cultivated a large acreage for many years. Directly across Chittenango Creek from the Keller holdings was a settlement called Matthews Mills (now North Manlius). Samuel Matthews's sawmill used logs brought from Oneida Lake's north shore to Keller's Bay. It is altogether possible that the Kellers assisted Matthews and towed logs, with their horse teams, overland to the sawmill. John Keller had a more than passing interest in the lumber business, boarding two English carpenters at his home. The Keller's Bay naming could easily have emanated from this lumber business association.

The Fisher family's history at this bay goes back to the turn of the century, when Conrad and Louise Fisher, from Minoa, purchased shore property at the terminus of Bridgeport's North Road. This transaction included a farm which the Fishers allowed their son-in-law and daughter, John and Florence Barrett, to manage. In 1958, the Barrett's son Conrad, and grandsons Bill and Jack Barrett, along with Burdette McAdam, constructed Fisher Bay Marina. Since then, Bill and Jack have acquired complete ownership and still operate the marina today, the former being involved in the harbor itself and the latter in its adjoining restaurant.

DAMON POINT AND BAR

One of the Bridgeport area's first settlers was Jason Damon, a Yankee immigrant and Revolutionary War veteran from Western Massachusetts. Arriving in Bridgeport around 1800, Damon settled near Shackelton Point, building a modest farm at the site. He and his wife, Lucy, had a large family of seven children. Jason's son, Norton, eventually established his own farm, the first building at Damon Point. An 1897 census shows that Norton's farm produced potatoes, apples, milk, eggs, beef, butter, pork and wool. This sustenance was supplemented by fish from the lake and a small income netted from Norton's wife's, Mary's, knitting business.

Norton Damon's son, Loren, took over the family farm upon his father's death and continued much the same operation. Around 1905, however, Loren moved to Bridgeport and established a boat building company. The "Damon Rowboat," framed with New York State oak, was an extremely sturdy craft, enjoyed by Oneida Lake fishermen for years. A common boast still recalled by Bridgeport old-timers was that no person ever drowned because of a Damon boat malfunction. Loren managed the boat building company until his death in 1938. During his nautical years, he supplemented his income by gradually parcelling off land at Damon Point for cottage lots.

Loren's sons, Leon, Ceylon and Raymond worked the farm and boat-building businesses. Leon once operated a grocery store at the point and continues to reside there today. Upon Loren's death in 1938, Leon and Ceylon took over the boat business. They streamlined their model, altering the vessel to accommodate outboard motors, then becoming popular on the lake. The Damon boat business continued for another two decades.

Damon Point takes its name from this long-time Bridgeport family. Damon Bar is often called Loren Bar, in honor of Loren Damon. Like Hitchcock Point, Damon Point is referred to in nineteenth century maps as Long Point, a term befitting its dimensions.

GOOSE ISLE

Two tiny shoals exist along the Madison County shore, one north of Damon Point and the other in the southeast corner of Messenger's Bay. When the Barge Canal raised the lake's level, both isles became submerged. Prior to the canal construction, exposed lake isles such as these gave migrating Canadian geese a wide, unobstructed view, a favored landing area for these security-conscious waterfowl.

BILLINGTON BAY AND BAR

Patriarch of the Billington family was Samuel Billington, a Revolutionary War veteran who served in the Essex Militia in New Jersey. In the early 1800's, Samuel migrated to Montgomery County, New York, but subsequently moved to the Billington Bay area, east of Bridgeport. He and his wife, Catherine, had a son, Charles. The latter and his spouse, Armenia, raised eleven sons and four daughters. Charles Billington was a farmer and several of his children followed in this vocation. Five of his sons, however, entered professional fields, two becoming doctors, two attorneys and one a dentist.

One of Charles Billington's grandsons, Pharon Billington, administered, with his brother Rutherford, two dairy farms on the bay. These were profitable affairs for their era and endured well into the 1930's. Pharon's daughter, Isabelle Billington Saunders, recalled details of her childhood on these farms in an interview for the *Chittenango-Bridgeport Times* in 1977. Saunders remembered such details as farmers driving pigs before oxen when plowing fields, the purpose of which was to frighten the then numerous snakes. Her father and uncle, in winter, would lead a horse and wagon team across the ice to Constantia to pick up lumber and, at times, livestock. During one particularly dangerous adventure, the Billington brothers were forced to whip their horse team across a gaping crack in the ice. Isabelle received her education at the Bridgeport school and, in this case, she was much more fortunate than most neighboring children. She had a horse which she rode to town each day and hitched in the school yard.

Pharon Billington also dabbled in Oneida's resort business. His farmhouse was used as a boarding house and he had cottages and boats for rent to the tourists. Tragedy struck his boarding house in 1910, as told in the following saga from the *Madison County Times*.

> The large farm dwelling on the Pharon Billington place between Shackelton's Point and Bridgeport, along the shore of Oneida Lake, burned to the ground about 11 o'clock Monday night. Everything was lost but some furniture was taken out of the front rooms. The origin of the fire is unknown. It started in the woodshed and before it was discovered the flames had eaten their way into the body of the house, and in no time the entire house was a roaring furnace. The Billington place was known far and wide as a summer boarding house, and nearly all summer long it had housed summer parties, fishing parties, and the like and been the center of many a lively time. It was especially adapted for the comfort of roomers and boarders, and occupied a prominent spot on the shore of the lake.

The era from 1850 to 1920 was a significant time in Oneida Lake history. The first major influx of tourists and the construction of facilities to accommodate them occurred then. Pharon Billington, a modestly prosperous farmer, undoubtedly realized the value of resort dollars and took advantage of the lake's newfound popularity. In the 1920's Billington divided much of his land into camp lots.

NICHOLS POINT

Pharon Billington's wife was Maude Nichols Billington. Her brother, Fred Nichols, was a multi-faceted businessman who, during his life, was a car salesman, operated a gas station, sold real estate and rented Florida apartments. When Billington began selling camp lots around his bay, Nichols purchased the first lot on what is now called Nichols' Point. Pharon Billington named the point for his brother-in-law, who was quite honored at the naming.

SHACKELTON POINT, SHOALS AND SHAK'S BAR

This prominent south shore point was once called Phillips' Point after Martin Phillips, son of Jacob Phillips (re: Oswego County, Phillips Point entry), who operated a small farm there. Later, the point was named Owen's Point; the Gideon Owen family, early Bridgeport area settlers, farmed the point after Phillips vacated it. The point had some archaeological significance, as related in this quote from a Madison County history:

> At Owen's Point are several Indian mounds, supposed to contain the remains of Oneida chiefs. Near them stands a large beech tree, hollow and open at one side, from which it is said the skeleton of an Indian was once taken.

Legend has it that the Oneida Indians used the point as a site for smoking salmon, a fish once plentiful in the lake. The "Bridgeport United Methodist Church History" tells of Theresa Deyo Halsey's finding, in her youth, scores of Indian beads and arrowheads at Shackelton Point.

The point was named for Charles Shackelton, a farmer, resort operator and game warden who occupied the point from the 1870's to around 1895. Shackelton's resort was known as "Shackelton's Grove," consisting of a hotel, a picnic area and related facilities. On June 22, 1888, the *Madison County Times* gave this description of his spa:

> A Bridgeport correspondent to the Union says, 'Shackelton's Point bids to be the place of resort on Oneida Lake. Three different parties from Syracuse have purchased lots and are now drawing lumber for the purpose of building fine cottages. . . . 'Shack' also has the best steamboat landing on the lake.'

The bulk of Charles Shackelton's business centered around the picnic trade, with large group clambakes and ox roasts being popular. Shackelton operated his grove until early 1895. Ill health forced him to lease the resort and, eventually, to auction off most of his holdings. He died on October 18, 1895, at age fifty-eight. His wife, Jane, died shortly thereafter. Shackelton's property was purchased by Orimel G. Jones, a family friend. Jones expanded the farm, building several barns, an ice house, and a "sugarshack" for boiling maple syrup. He later sold the land to Alexander T. Brown, a prominent Syracuse citizen.

Brown had humble origins, starting as a blacksmith in the village of Homer, Cortland County. His was an inventive mind, however, and he developed firearms and typewriter innovations that netted him a fortune. Brown used his point holdings as a retreat. Shackelton Point, in the early 1900's continued as an Oneida Lake resort. The large picnic grove attracted many community organizations, a building called the "Long House" was used for dances, and the Shackelton Point Hotel catered to fishermen and their families. It is said that Brown enjoyed coming to the point, mixing with local people, and savoring the relaxed air that this summer retreat afforded.

Alexander Brown died in 1929 and his son, Charles S. Brown, inherited the property. Charles enlarged his father's land holdings to over four hundred acres, purchasing several adjoining farms and cottages. In addition, he obtained a New York State lease on Leete (Dutchman's) and Grass Islands, just off shore from Shackelton Point. Thus, Brown established the "Xandria" estate, named for his father, on Shackelton Point. This was a unique property on Oneida Lake. Containing, at one time, forty-seven structures, Xandria included a main house, several guest cottages, servants' quarters, a six-car garage and a kennel for Great Dane dogs, a love of Brown's wife, Iola.

Brown had plans to further expand, but these were curtailed by his sudden death by a heart attack in 1953. He bequeathed the estate to his beloved Cornell University, of which he was an alumnus. In 1955, the Cornell University Biological Field Station was formally opened at Shackelton's. This teaching-research institution has become an invaluable asset in the conservation and enrichment of the Oneida Lake environment. The station annually monitors fish populations and water quality of the lake and makes recommendations to the state conservation department with regard to walleye fry stocking and catch size and number limitations. Numerous biological papers have emanated from the station. Many are intended for the scientific community; among these, for example, are Michael Clady's "Change in Abundance of Inshore Fishes in Oneida Lake, 1916 to 1970" and John Chevalier's "Cannibalism as a Factor in First Year Survival of Walleye in Oneida Lake." Other publications, such as Edward Mills' and John Gannon's "Oneida Lake Profile," explain the lake's ecology in layman's terms and have received a wide public distribution. For over twenty years, Dr. John Forney has been the leader of the Cornell Field Station. Through his research, writtings and public appearances, Dr. Forney has become synonymous with the concept of sound ecological management of Oneida Lake. His efforts at unlocking Oneida's biological secrets and insuring that the lake retains its amazing productivity have been tireless labors for environmental quality. The lake and its afficionados owe this biologist a sincere word of thanks.

DELMARTER BAY

The correct spelling of this bay should read Delamarter, as it was named for that pioneer Bridgeport family. In 1802, Isaac and John Delamarter came to the Bridgeport area and settled on the bay, approximately two miles east of town. Like most of their contemporaries they were farmers, tilling an existence out of the upstate wilderness. Isaac's son, Isaac, farmed the family homestead well into the latter nineteenth century. The Delamarter farm was eventually purchased by Charles Brown and incorporated into his Xandria estate.

Delmarter Bay was originally called Briggs Bay, after the Reverend Austin Briggs, a Methodist clergyman who came to Bridgeport in 1812. A veteran of the Revolution, Briggs tried to claim Military Tract land in Manlius, but had difficulty securing a title. He migrated to the lake, constructed a cabin on the shore and finally built a farm on the bay that once bore his name. The first clergyman in the Bridgeport area, Briggs was a "circuit rider," making long rounds to contact the faithful. An early county history said of Briggs, "He traversed the new country on horseback, and often on foot, on account of bad roads, and sometimes in canoes on the lake and rivers." One can imagine the arduous nature of Briggs' ministerial task. Austin Briggs' son, Austin, became a prominent Bridgeport citizen. He worked the family farm, practiced law, served as town postmaster, and owned a stage line. His wife was an accomplished milliner. The Briggs family, through their prosperity, were able to maintain a housekeeper, a rarity among lake families of this era.

GRASS ISLE

Madison County's Grass Isle is directly west of Dutchman's Island and derives its name from the aquatic grasses which cover it. There are many such isles in the lake, particularly in the west end, where shoals are most common.

DUTCHMAN'S ISLE

This isle, in the western end of Delmarter Bay, has had several names. Elet Milton, in his notes, stated that it was once called "Sly Island." Milton reasoned "perhaps when passing by it out in the lake, its low-lying surface and forest trees so blend into the adjacent shore as to cause it to be practically unobservable." Possibly, shallow reefs surrounding the island proved difficult or "sly" for old-time boatmen to navigate. In 1856 New York State granted the island to Professor Peletia Leete, a locally prominent person. Leete, a surveyor by profession, divided much of the land surrounding the lake, including numerous parcels at Sylvan Beach during that village's genesis. His professional and religious sides gained a unique characterization in one local paper's columns as he was termed a "distinguished surveyor and agnostic." Leete was an "old-time laker" and this reputation brought part-time employment as a historical local color guide for Sylvan Beach businessmen's steamboat tours. During his ownership, the island was referred to as Leete Island, sometimes misspelled "Loet Island."

"Dutchmen," in the upstate vernacular of the 1800's, were persons of German descent. Immigrant Germans called themselves, in their language, Deutschelanders, a term upstaters promptly reduced to Dutchmen. Our island derives its title from two such Germans.

In his fine series of articles entitled "Cleveland - Past and Present," written for the *North Shore Times* in the 1960's, Frederick G. Griesmyer narrated the saga of our first Dutchman:

> ... About 1861, a Prussian named Carl Hargood came, with his family, to Oneida Lake. He had some means and desired to purchase or rent the island, but was unable to do so. Mr. Leete, however, gave the Prussian leave to live on

the island until he wanted it himself. Hargood's wife and children did not like the location and went to the northern part of the state, purchased a farm and settled down. Hargood remained on the island - which consists of five acres - fishing and hunting. Net fishing was at that time legal. One day, in the summer of 1862, Hargood's dead body was found in shallow water near the shore of the island, face down. His head bore marks of violence, but nothing definite was ever ascertained.

Griesmyer's source for the story was the oral record, a common data gathering spot for local historians. Elet Milton's notes make reference to Hargood, citing the same source, emphasizing that "tradition has it" that the Dutchman was Hargood. Considering that Milton was born prior to 1900 and grew up with people exposed first-hand to the Dutchman story, his "tradition" account carries weight.

Evalena Hubbard's "Recollections of Northern Sullivan" gives an account of yet another Dutchman of the island, a distinctly different person than Hargood. A descendant of early lake settlers, Evalena, like Milton, had good access to the oral record. Listen to her words:

No local history would be complete without the mention of Joseph Sterling and the 'Old Dutchman' as he was familiarly called. Mr. Sterling came from New Hartford and bought the farm on the north side of the road, now owned by Mr. Wallace Billington. Farming, however, was not to his taste so he sold his land and his life hereafter was one long 'visit.' People who were used to his visits were not surprised to see him come downstairs to breakfast even though they had not seen him for weeks! Neither were they alarmed if he went out without a hat and did not return. He delighted in telling stories or repeating sermons. Occasionally he could be persuaded to do some farm work, but he was always in haste to visit some distant point. People were glad to entertain him as he could tell all the news which, as he used to say, was better than a letter from friends. The 'Old Dutchman' lived alone on the island for many years, though his wife and son visited him one summer and the son remained several months. It was supposed that he was a political exile, as it was not family trouble which caused his isolation. People who knew him well never believed he could have been guilty of any crime. He could speak little English and was a very quiet, inoffensive man. With his little dog he would come along the road two or three times a week with fish that he would exchange for money or provisions. He also made splint baskets of a peculiar shape unlike any made by the Indians. He was found in the lake by some fisherman who took the body and the little dog to shore. At the inquest it was decided that this was not a case of drowning, but of murder. The theory was that someone had placed him in the lake, after killing and robbing him. No money was found among his remaining possessions.

These accounts of the Dutchman lead me to conclude that there were two separate island occupants. Hargood inhabited the island for merely a year, Sterling for "many." Hargood appeared on the scene and asked Leete to sell him the island. Sterling was a neighborhood fixture before "squatting" on Dutchman's. Hargood had children; only one son of Sterling was mentioned. Hargood's death remains a mystery; Sterling's demise received an investigation with a conclusion. Our isle's Dutch*man* was actually plural, not singular.

A final mystery remains. As a student at Hamilton College in the early 1970's, I encountered an article in a treasure hunters' magazine that dealt with this Dutchman. The article said that the Dutchman possessed a collection of rare European gold and silver buttons. When the man died, no one knew the treasure's location. Was it buried on the island? In the lake? Or was the saga, perhaps, the wonderful creation of rural upstate imagination? If only the ghosts of Carl Hargood and Joseph Sterling could answer.

EAST ISLE BAR

This bar is situated to the east of Dutchman's Isle.

CLARK BAR

Clark Bar was named for Leonard Clark, a farmer who occupied land opposite the bar in the later 1800's. Leonard Clark came to the lake from Cortland County. The farm, owned by him and his wife, Harriet, was a modest establishment, typical for the lake area then. The 1875 census of Madison County reveals that Clark farmed forty-seven acres of land, nine of which he plowed, eighteen left to pasture and twenty used as meadow. In that year, his gross farm sales totaled $465. This was gleaned from twenty-seven bushels of winter wheat, two hundred five of oats (Clark's plowing "fuel"), ten of buckwheat, thirty of Indian corn, twenty-five of potatoes and ten of apples. Clark's enterprise produced two hundred fifty pounds of butter and twenty-two dollars worth of eggs. His stock included nine pigs, seven cows, two horses, one colt and one heifer. Total value of his farm was estimated at $3,800.

These statistics reveal much about farm lifestyle during this period. The farmer had to be a utilitarian individual, frugal and watchful. Leonard Clark produced most of his own food. His farm's celler certainly contained crocks for salted pork and pickled vegetables. Potatoes and apples were kept cool and fresh in the cellar's confines as well. Milk and eggs provided daily sustenance, with enough of a surplus of each to net Clark a small income. Clark most likely fished the lake, adding diversity to his family's diet. His land was adequate to produce feed for his stock. What profit Clark did take in was used for new tools, clothing and needed dry goods that were available in nearby stores. Despite its hardscrabble nature, this agrarian life was practiced by thousands in nineteenth century New York.

BRAZEE BAR

On April 13, 1883, Augustus Brazee purchased the old Carter farm, west of Lakeport on Delmarter Bay. Brazee Bar, north of Augustus' land holdings, was named for him. Brazee was a hardworking individual. He and his sons ran the farm and, in addition, he owned a boot and shoe factory. A far cry from such contemporary industries as Endicott-Johnson, Brazee's shoe establishment was a typical 19th century family factory, employing under ten people. Such factories were numerous in that era and provided needed employment and service for upstate's rural communities. Besides his farming and industrial ventures, Brazee profited from tourism, renting property to John Haley a Lakeport hotel owner, in 1885. He was active in community affairs and held office in the local American Legion, an organization for which he was qualified through his Civil War service.

BRIDENBECKER SHOALS

George Bridenbecker and his wife, Gertrude Wilson Bridenbecker (re: Wilson's Point), managed a family farm on lakeshore land opposite these shoals. Originally a large acreage, the farm was condensed around 1923 when Bridenbecker began selling cottage lots. George was an old-time lake fisherman, using long, multi-hooked set lines. His son, Roy Bridenbecker, kept up family tradition and, prior to retirement, operated a 102-acre, thirty-five milker dairy farm. Roy's farm income was also supplemented by commercial fishing.

HUBBARD'S BAR

Martin Hubbard was the vanguard of the Hubbard family migration to Oneida Lake, emigrating there in 1826. A Massachusetts native, Hubbard first came to the Town of Bridgewater in southern Oneida County. His father was of a patriotic background, being a Revolutionary War veteran and, at one time, having entertained George Washington and staff in his hotel in Hatfield, Massachusetts. Tragedy struck the Hubbard family soon after they arrived at the lake. Martin's wife died and, in 1829, Hubbard took his two youngest children, Hiram and Laura, and relocated on the lake shore, west of Lakeport and south of Hubbard's Bar.

The 1875 census for Madison County reveals that Hiram Hubbard, then sixty, was still operating the family farm on Delmarter Bay. Assisting him was his wife, Mercy Spencer Hubbard, and a son, Edwin. Another son, Lebbeus, operated a farm nearby. An interesting piece of trivia surrounds Mercy Hubbard. She and Hiram visited Saybrook, Connecticut in 1849, and brought back a rose bush cutting taken from a plant which her forefathers carried here from England in 1635. Mercy Hubbard planted the cutting and gave the resulting rose bush to Lebbeus and his wife as a wedding present. As of 1940, after three hundred years in America, it was still flowering.

SPENCER CREEK AND BAR

Evalena Hubbard, a direct descendant of Mercy Hubbard, wrote in her history of the Lakeport area of the man for whom these places were named:

> In 1814, because of the wonderful stories of the fertility of the soil often repeated in his family as told by his great-grandfather, Reuben Spencer sold his line of freight vessels which he sailed between the Connecticut River and the West Indies and with his wife and four children came to Northern Sullivan bringing his oxen, rafts (to be used to cross streams), rude lumber wagon, mud boat, all necessary tools, house furnishings, chickens and two splendid red Durham cows.

Spencer, one of Lakeport's first settlers, exhibited the pioneering spirit that developed our country in the early national era. He owned a profitable business in New England, had a comfortable family life but yet was willing to risk all to settle the vast New York wilderness. His venturesome spirit was evident during the War of 1812, when he converted several of his ships to military use and patrolled the Connecticut coast, guarding against British raiders. This same elan ran throughout his family tree - his father served in the Continental army and his grandfather fought in the French and Indian War. At Spencer's Lakeport bailiwyk, Reuben, assisted by friends, built the first sawmill in the region and later installed a turning lathe with which he manufactured salt vat covers. He was a respected and extremely sociable member of the Lakeport community, as is shown in this account from Hammond's *History of Madison County*:

> Mr. Spencer, who lived to be an old man, and to see all of his numerous family of children married and settled in life, with children of their own, departed this life some ten years ago (around 1862). Those who knew him best have always spoken of him as an excellent man. His wife was greatly respected and was in all respects a 'strong woman.' She had considerable knowledge of medicines and nursing; hence she was a useful woman withal, in those early times. . . . Mr. Spencer was a great story teller, and during the last few years of his life, lived almost entirely in the past, paying little attention to passing events around him. He could tell a story to the last, and tell it well, and no one delighted more

than he, when the apple harvest was over, and his cellar well supplied with the rich juice and the delicious fruit, to treat with good stories and good cheer, all who called upon him.

I only regret that he didn't write, and publish, for his knowledge of early lake history would have provided an invaluable chronicle of the time.

PRESCOTT'S POINT

Hammond's Madison County history cited this point's past:

> Sometime during the year 1811, a man by the name of Fogger came and built a cabin on what is now familiarly known as 'Randall's Point,' about a half mile northwest of Lakeport. At that time there was no regularly laid out road along the lake shore. Fogger stayed about three or four years, and then disappeared from the scene, leaving no other memento to those who should come after him, than his name associated with the point. . . . Tradition, however, if nothing more, will keep alive the name of Fogger.

Time, however, has worked to bury the Fogger name and no longer is this mystery man's title associated with Prescott's Point. The Randall referred to in Hammond's account was E.H. Randall, a Lakeport hotel proprietor. The June 3, 1861 edition of the Syracuse *Journal* contained the following note on Mr. Randall:

> A favorite fishing ground on Oneida Lake is Lakeport and the favorite stopping place is Union Grove House, kept by E.H. Randall. He has boats, fishing tackle, and all the conveniences for sporting, kept in prime order. His hotel accommodations are ample. Fishing and pleasure parties will do well to remember Lakeport and Mr. Randall. The best of pike and bass are caught there in abundance, as we have reason to know, having on Saturday received a box of fish from Mr. Randall.

Prescott's Point was named for Samuel J. Prescott, a dairy farmer in the early 1900's. Samuel's son, Glen, continued the family agrarian tradition until 1946, when he sold the farm. The barn of the old Prescott farm can still be seen on Route 31, west of Lakeport, being currently used as office-storage space for Fremac Marine.

BLIND ISLE

Oneida Lake's "blind isles" are shoals which, if the lake receded, would break the water's surface. Messenger's Shoal at Buoy 113 is often called "Blind Isle." These reefs can prove extremely dangerous if not marked by warning buoys. To the novice boatman they can appear to be navigable water, far from shore and seemingly safe. Many a boat excursion has met an untimely sheered pin or broken propeller when a vessel struck a blind isle.

LAKEPORT, LAKEPORT SHOAL AND BAR

Smith's 1880 *History of Madison County* described Lakeport as being "a small post (office) village situated five miles east of Bridgeport, and containing a sawmill, two hotels, one store, one blacksmith shop, and a shoe shop." Additional employment was furnished by the Spencer Brook (Creek) Cheese Factory, built west of the hamlet by John Gifford in 1868. Lakeport had its own school and about thirty homes at the time Smith's account was written. It was named for being a port on Oneida Lake. Located where Canaseraga Creek empties into Oneida, the hamlet's harbor, guarded by Prescott's Point on the west and Larkin Point on the east, gave shelter to early lake boatmen.

Lakeport's settlement dates back to 1811. Among its pioneers are several for whom lake places are named. Zina and Reuben Bushnell, and descendants, gave their name to Bushnell's Point and Bay. Abram and David Larkin lived on Larkin Point. Reuben Spencer settled near Spencer Creek. For these and most early Lakeport folk, farming was their initial sustenance, though some, such as the Larkins, took advantage of the mid-nineteenth century growth of Oneida Lake tourism. This latter industry, in Lakeport, centered around the Larkin House (see Larkin Point, this chapter), the Avon House, built by John Dempsey in 1877, and the Union Grove House, operated by E. H. Randall in the 1860's and later called the "Lower Hotel." Lakeport never rivaled Lower South Bay or Sylvan Beach as an Oneida tourist mecca, but its hotels added greatly to its economy. Today, the settlement remains a small community, with businesses centered along

Route 31 and many summer cottages lining the shore.

GREAT MARSH, DOUGLAS DITCH, CANASERAGA CREEK AND COWASELON CREEK

Between Oneida Lake and the Erie Canal, south of Bridgeport and Lakeport, was located the Great Marsh, parts of which are still in existence. This large swamp once covered an estimated 15,000 acres and had water depths up to four feet. Austin Briggs, Jr. of Bridgeport often told how he once could skate for miles across the marsh. The Great Marsh was formed as Chittenango and Canaseraga Creeks, and their tributaries, flowed north toward the lake. There, these streams encountered a rise in elevation that backed their waters into the Oneida Lake plain. Throughout history, this morass has had several names. Among these are the "Great Swamp" and the "Cowaselon Swamp." Many people referred to it as the "Vly" or "Fly," variations on a Dutch term meaning valley. The Vly was actually a large meadow, covered with muck, that bordered the Great Marsh on the south and extended through both Sullivan and Lenox townships.

The marsh presented early travelers and farmers with a significant dilemma. Journeys through it were virtually impossible and the land, although extremely fertile, was too wet for proper cultivation. For years there was talk of building a "Vly Road" connecting Bridgeport with Chittenango. One Bridgeport merchant, thinking that such construction would raise taxes exorbitantly, declared that he "did not want to live longer than the time that should see the first wagon cross the Vly." The following summer, a party from Chittenango, using wagons, blazed a trail through the marsh. Upon arriving at Bridgeport, they celebrated their achievement and, while visiting the above merchant, "advised him to prepare the ceremonials for his own funeral, as the time he had so often named as the desirable one at which to close his earthly existence had arrived." This story brought laughter to Bridgeport folk for years.

The Great Marsh was conquered in the first half of the nineteenth century. The trail broken by Chittenango explorers was widened to become the Cazenovia and Oneida Lake Stone Road. In 1848 the highway was planked and it became the DeRuyter, Cazenovia and Oneida Lake Plank Road. Two decades prior, much of the marsh got a needed draining. This reclamation process started in 1819, with the completion of Douglas Ditch, a drainage canal leading through the marsh to Canaseraga Creek. Initially funded through the New York State Drainage Act of 1816, the canal was enlarged in 1848, 1889 and 1936-37. Douglas Ditch was named for Colonel Zebulon Douglas, a pioneer Chittenango area settler. Originally from Columbia County, Douglas moved to this region in 1797, acquiring 350 acres. His talents were multi-faceted and, during his lifetime, he farmed, kept a tavern, served as a colonel in the militia during the War of 1812, worked as postmaster and was instrumental in organizing the first school in his neighborhood. In 1811 he was elected to the State Assembly and, through his influence in that lawmaking body, was able to secure funding for Douglas Ditch construction. This ditch converted thousands of useless swamp acres into top-flight farm land. Today, this land is among the most productive in Madison County. Zebulon Douglas certainly represented his Assembly district well.

The names Canaseraga and Cowaselon Creeks are Iroquoian in origin. Harold Thompson, in his book, *Body, Boots and Britches*, states that Canaseraga's approved meaning is "Several strings of beads, with one string lying across." Another interpretation, adds Thompson, is "Big Elkhorn." George Stewart, however, in his *American Place Names*, states that Canaseraga means "among milk weeds." Cowaselon Creek, according to Thompson, meant "bushes hanging over the water." This latter stream, Canaseraga's tributary, is often called "The Squash" in local vernacular. For years people mispronounced Cowaselon as "Squash-alone." DeWitt Clinton, upon hearing the creek's name, thought it to be "Squaw-alone" and repeated that title. From Clinton's version probably comes the erroneous Cowaselon translation of "Weeping Squaw."

HOG'S BACK MOUND

This shoal, sometimes referred to simply as "The Mound" is a hump-shaped reef just to the north of Lakeport Bay. The "Hog's Back" was an old-time expression used to describe geographic features that resembled the curved upper side of "old porky." Such reefs are excellent fishing areas as their shallowness allows for greater light penetration which, as it abets aquatic vegetation growth, attracts feed for gamefish.

LARKIN POINT AND BAR

Clara Houck is a fine local historian, specializing in Sullivan Township, and it is on her research that this acccount is based.

Abram Larkin came to Lakeport from Hopkinson, Rhode Island in 1813 and built a home on Larkin Point. David Larkin, Abram's son, was one of the most successful citizens in Lakeport's formative years. Born in 1815, David helped his father on the family farm and later served as local postmaster. Around 1850, the Larkins made their most significant contribution to Lakeport - establishing the "Lakeport House," a hotel on the northeast corner of what is now the intersection of Route 31 and North Chittenango Road. Later renamed the "Larkin House," the hotel had three stories and a spacious meeting hall. It was the center of Lakeport's commercial and social life. Among the events occurring at Larkin's were holiday parties for townsfolk, auctions, fox chases, picnics at the "grove," club meetings, fishermen's outings, plus the accommodation, over time, of thousands of boarders. A hotel register shows people from across the country, including groups such as the "Bavarian Band," "Heywood's Merrymakers," "Wilbur's Opera Company," circus performers and on January 18, 1883, the *Maid of Arran* acting troupe, the latter title being a play by L. Frank Baum, author of *The Wizard of Oz*. Intriguing political names appear on the register; among these are James G. Blaine, Grover Cleveland, Chester Arthur and Ulysses S. Grant. Commented historian Houck, "Some of these may have been written in by members of the Old Java Club who met upstairs quite frequently during the 1880's to discuss politics."

Later, David Larkin's sons helped with the business, once changing the hotel's name to "Commercial House." Larkin died in 1890 and the family lost interest in the hotel, renting it for several years before finally selling. When this Lakeport landmark burned in February, 1906, it was owned by Henry Weston of Syracuse. In 1921 Henry P. Larkin, David's son, authorized a surveying of Larkin Point land into cottage lots.

JOHNSON'S BAR

Elmer Johnson, a farmer, owned lakeshore property near the small bar named for him. Johnson's farm was a prosperous endeavor, valued in 1875 at $14,000, a high assessment for farms during that era. He, with his wife, Ellen, and their two children, lived in one of the most ornate homes on Oneida's south shore. Built in Etruscan villa style, the house was adorned with fancy scroll brackets and hooded moldings, and was topped by a widow's walk which afforded a sweeping panorama of the lake. The Johnson home still stands today on Route 31; in recent years it has been used as a tavern.

BUSHNELL POINT AND BAY

Like Reuben Spencer, the Bushnells were pioneers in the Lakeport region. Zina Bushnell, who was Spencer's cross-the-road neighbor in Saybrook, Connecticut, migrated to Lakeport at about the same time as Reuben. Bushnell, like his associate, possessed the qualities requisite for frontier survival. In addition to assisting Spencer in building the area's first sawmill, Bushnell constructed a large farmstead, eventually gaining ownership of over three hundred acres. Around 1818 Bushnell demonstrated masonry skill and built a brick home on his farm - the first structure of its type in the region. The brick house proved to be a blessing in disguise for Bushnell. It was sufficiently commodious for conversion to a tavern/inn that catered to workers then dredging the Douglas Ditch.

Prior to Zina Bushnell's coming to Lakeport, "Deacon" Reuben Bushnell settled in the area. Reuben, like Zina, was a farmer, but name and vocation provided these two pioneer's best similarities. An early county history cites Reuben and his friends saying that they "came, fully imbued with New England ideas, and when they became sufficiently numerous to form a religious society, they adopted the religious doctrines of Jonathan Edwards and lived in the full faith and simplicity of their day." No public house proprietorship for the "Deacon."

The Bushnell families flourished. Nineteenth century Madison County maps show numerous Bushnell farms dotting the bay and the immediate Lakeport environs. A mid-century county directory lists Almanza, Addison, Elias, Ezra, James, Luther, Reuben and Zina Bushnell, all farmers. In addition, the directory mentions Cady Bushnell, a cheesemaker, Franklin Bushnell, a cheesemaker and farmer, and William C. Bushnell, a carpenter and farmer. The combined landholdings of the Lakeport Bushnells totaled, at that time, over 1,500 acres. Most appropriately, the bay and point near the land they developed bear their name.

WILSON'S POINT AND BAY

Another of the Yankees who settled on Oneida's shores was Dr. Lyman H. Wilson, who came to the lake from Connecticut in 1841. Wilson, a physician, like the circuit-riding minister, Austin Briggs, employed horse and buggy to bring healing to the scattered lake area population. In addition, Wilson was a farmer managing, with his sons and hired man, a 265-acre spread. The 1875 Madison County census shows that Wilson's agrarian enterprise was valued at $12,000 and produced $1,200 in gross sales. The Wilson family operated their farm until around 1920. In 1921 their land was surveyed into cottage lots, a common fate of lakeshore farms.

WARNER'S REEF

Nathaniel Warner operated a farm on lakeshore property opposite this small reef. Warner purchased his farm in 1871 and kept it for four years, then moved to the environs of Oneida Creek. Warner was also a businessman, having managed a general store in Lakeport from 1859 to 1865.

CHAPMAN POINT

He came from Lincolnshire, England. He and his wife knew Charles Dickens and were written about by that famed author. He designed his home in the pattern of English country houses, with little expense being spared. He was an inventor and an author. He loved to fox hunt and would slaughter a beef cow to feed his prized hounds. He was John R. Chapman, a different sort of Oneida Lake pioneer.

Legend has it that Chapman was born into British aristocracy. His father was wealthy and talented; the elder Chapman worked on the steam locomotive invention and a model of such made by Chapman was once exhibited in the British Museum, London. By marrying a shopkeeper's daughter, Mary Pollett, Chapman displeased his family. While this bad feeling did not result in total ostracism, it persuaded Chapman and his bride to explore American opportunities. The couple left England on January 3, 1842. A co-voyageur, Charles Dickens, became acquainted with the Chapmans and described the couple in his book, *American Notes*:

> Fourthly, fifthly and lastly, another couple, newly married too, if one might judge from the endearments they frequently interchanged, of whom I know no more than that they were rather a mysterious, runaway sort of couple; that the lady had great personal attractions, also that the gentleman carried more guns than Robinson Crusoe, wore a shooting coat and had two great dogs on board. On further consideration, I remember that he tried roast pig and bottled ale as a cure for seasickness and that he took these remedies (usually in bed) with astonishing perseverence. I may add for the information of the curious that they failed decidedly.

The Chapmans traveled upstate and boarded with friends at Oneida Valley, a settlement one mile east of Upper South Bay. They liked the lakeshore countryside and determined to settle there. Around 1843, Chapman purchased several hundred acres east of Lakeport and erected the most unique home in the region. Styled after an English country house, it was a two-story brick structure with two one-story wings jutting out on opposite sides. Brick was imported from afar and, to accommodate the barges needed for hauling, Chapman built a seventy-five foot long lakefront pier, wide enough for a team of horses. Surrounding the house were ordered flower beds, a hawthorne hedge, balsam, tulip and whitewood trees, all arranged in a tasteful British style. The outbuildings included stables for Chapman's hunting horses, kennels that could accommodate fifty hounds, a boiling shed for preparing the dog's sustenance, a milking shed 125 feet long, several cow barns, and a cheese factory. Chapman financed his estate with a bequest from his parents, a sum rumored to total nearly ninety thousand dollars.

John and Mary Chapman lived in style, especially for their area. Theirs was not the arduous life of the average lakeshore farmer. Each afternoon had a tea hour set aside. Servants did much of the estate's labor. John delighted in the hunt and chased foxes with horses and hounds. During his years on the lake, Chapman made several accomplishments. He wrote a book, *Instructions to a Young Marksman*, which describes hunting principles and techniques. He was the inventor of the "spoon hook," an early lure that proved highly effective on Oneida. He also invented a four-barrel revolving rifle and a telescopic rifle attachment. Despite these achievements, his farm did not prosper. His lifestyle drained his inheritance and he was forced to sell most of his land, his elegant house, and live with his sons during his final years. There were nine Chapman sons and a "strapping" lot they were. The *Madison County Times* in 1888, published an article on the Chapman family. The piece noted that the Chapmans were loyal Democrats, cited that only one family member weighed under two hundred pounds and said, "Total weight of the family is 2,422 pounds, a little over a ton of democracy in one family."

Mary Chapman died on July 3, 1898. John R. Chapman passed away on February 3, 1899. He was mourned by the Lakeport community of which it was said that "older residents remember him with much pleasure and the visits of Mr. Chapman to this village and many pleasant incidents of his life in this town were told." The funeral occurred at the "white church," now the Oneida Lake Congregational Church, east of Lakeport. Today, other than Chapman Point, the primary reminder of John R. Chapman is his home, now known as "Orchard Cottage." The house is cited in Madison County's historic architecture volume, *Country Roads*.

MESSENGER'S BAY, SHOAL AND REEF, ONEIDA LAKE HAMLET

In 1814, George Messenger purchased 144 acres of lakeshore property on what is now called Messenger's Bay. Messenger, like most of his neighbors, was a farmer, but unlike his friends he diversified his business interests. In 1816 he built a hotel on Messenger's Bay; this inn has a long history in the Oneida Lake resort saga.

The Messenger House remained in family ownership throughout its duration. George's sons, George and E.O. Messenger, and his grandson, Osbert E. Messenger, managed the hotel through the nineteenth century. Several sources credit Osbert with being the Messenger for whom the bay was named, but probably it was the prolonged bay area occupation by the Messenger family that inspired this title.

Newspapers of the 1800's give clues to the activities at Messenger House during Osbert's proprietorship. Oyster suppers were common events, as were holiday parties, dances in the ballroom, picnics and the like. Most of the customers were Oneida Lake sportsmen. Osbert expanded the original business, adding a small Lewis Point resort in the 1870's. The *Madison County Times* of July 23, 1876, described Osbert's point endeavor:

> The present proprietor, O.E. Messenger, is a gentleman in every sense of the word, kind and accommodating, doing everything in his power to make it pleasant for his guests and, what is quite important in these times makes light charges. Mr. Messenger has built a convenient little cottage (Rural Retreat) on the point and, having fishing tackle and good boats, can supply the most fastidious with everything needful. Those wishing to spend a few days rusticating cannot do better than to go to a Rural Retreat at Lewis Point.

Osbert was, in addition, an avid fisherman and delighted in serving his friends elaborate meals that featured his prodigious catches.

Around 1910, the Messenger House was forced to close. Business had fallen off drastically and deterioration beset the old hotel. A Syracuse newspaper of that day contained the hotel's "obituary" in an article entitled, "The Passing of An Old Hotel." The author labeled the Messenger House an "ancient hostelry" and related hotel trivia regarding the grapevine, brought from Oneida Creek in 1814, and the poplars, imported from Massachusetts in 1822. The last proprietor was Sarah Huyck Messenger, Osbert's wife, who came to the hotel as a "June bride" in 1850. Warm nostalgia flowed in the author's words:

> The passing of the old Messenger House on Oneida Lake

calls to mind a long, quaint looking building with glass windows that open like doors on a porch supported by ivy-covered pillars, festooned with cobwebs spun by tiny spiders. One end of the roof has fallen in now and there will be no more whispered vows or gay badinage in its cool shelter. Maple trees border the avenue in front and evergreens shade the rear. . . .

The Messenger House was destroyed by fire soon after this article's publication.

Messenger's Bay was the old name given to a hamlet now known as Oneida Lake. While the present community consists of a road sign on Route 31 and a seemingly endless line of camps along the lake shore, the original hamlet was more of a concise settlement. Messenger's Bay revolved around the intersection of North Main Street, Canastota, and Route 31. The Messenger House was the community's central landmark, but across the street were a post office and general store. A one-room school and Methodist chapel served the community's educational and spiritual needs. The year-round population of Messenger's Bay, as recorded in the 1890 census, was forty but the summer population was considerably larger. Several hamlet residents were employed by the Messenger House to pick up tourists, using horse and buggy, at the Canastota railroad station. Most residents were small farmers.

Another landmark of the Messenger's Bay area is the Oneida Lake Congregational Church, located west of the bay on Route 31. This church began as the Union Congregational Society, a religious group organized in 1813. The society's members decided to build a meeting house in 1825, but, as a result of a membership dispute, two churches were begun, one in Whitelaw and the other at the lake. The "Church of the Lake" was not completed until around 1847, a situation emanating from congregational discord. New membership and spirit brought on the mid-century revitalization. Among the key people in this renaissance was Deacon Reuben Bushnell. The Messenger family was active in this church and Osbert, in 1892, became Sunday School Superintendent. The church building today retains its historical flair and is included in Madison County's *Country Roads* book.

KINLOCK POINT

Like many parcels of lakeshore property, Kinlock Point was purchased as a speculative investment. On July 23, 1913, Durand R. Kinlock, of Utica, bought the land and had it surveyed and subdivided into camp lots. Land on Kinlock Point sold well and, on May 8, 1922, a Kinlock Point Association of property owners was organized. The association is in existence to this day.

LEWIS POINT

At the eastern end of Oneida Lake, no landmark is more prominent than Lewis Point. Its vista greets the navigator as he enters the lake at Sylvan Beach. Coming from the west, a boatman can see the point for over twelve miles. The point forms an effective breakwater, sheltering Upper South Bay from vicious westerlies and Messenger's Bay from hard northeasters. It might easily have been named Long Point, for its tip is over a mile away from the junction of Lewis Point Road and Route 31.

Lewis Point provided one of the most frustrating episodes in my research for this book. I naturally assumed that a point of this size was named for a prominent landowner, but three days in the Madison County Clerk's office, days of dissecting countless deeds and abstracts, brought no landowning Lewis to light. Oral history sources offered no recollections of a Lewis on the point either. Frustrated, I shelved the point file. A week later, however, I was examining nineteenth century copies of the *Madison County Times* in the Sullivan Free Library and happened upon a listing of several articles that dealt with Lewis Point. One article, from the July 23, 1876 edition, contained the following:

> Of this romantic place, too much cannot be said in its favor. Lewis Point was named after a French Indian, Leweye, afterwards called Lewis.

So much for the "prominent landowner" theory. Leweye was most likely a squatter at the point, living like A. S. Hall, hunting, fishing, surviving mostly through native skills. An Alexander Brown or John R. Chapman he most certainly wasn't.

Lewis Point has a resort history dating back to the 1870's. The first recorded resort was Osbert Messenger's "Rural Retreat," a small facility. In 1885, Philander Nichols bought the point from Levi and Harriet Rogers, farmers who owned a large percentage of the promontory's acreage. Nichols made an unsuccessful attempt at resort development and ended up selling his holding in July of 1886 to Milton Delano, a prominent Canastota citizen. A hotel called "The Delano" was constructed and during his ownership, Delano leased the hotel to various proprietors. The hotel never showed a significant profit. This resort's era, however, witnessed considerable cottage construction at Lewis Point. The *Madison County Times* of May 3, 1885, stated, "Lewis Point will be known as Point Utica this summer and many Uticans are building handsome cottages at this place. The point is a favorite resort for ducks and many are bagged there daily."

In February of 1905, a local newspaper announced that the Lewis Point Land and Improvement Company of Syracuse had been started with the purpose of grandiose development. The company would operate the old point hotel and add "a bowling alley, shoot the chute, bath houses, Ferris wheel, automobile barn, dancing pavilion, yacht clubhouse, stables, etc." to the resort. J.F. Stewart's *Souvenir Booklet of Sylvan Beach*, 1907, contained architect's plans for the point facility and stated "wives and daughters will be as safe at this resort as they are in their own backyard." Like previous point development schemes, however, this plan fell short of its goals. Lewis Point was never destined to rival Sylvan Beach as the amusement mecca of Oneida Lake.

On February 10, 1937, the point was purchased by the Oneida Limited Corporation. From that time to the present, this company has owned Lewis Point. Oneida Limited operates an employee's clubhouse, provides picnic tables and dockage, and rents several camps to its workers at nominal fees. The company serves the general public by allowing ice fishermen parking rights to its spacious grounds and by giving bullheaders access to excellent spring fishing. Today, one physical reminder of the past is an old cannon which lies along the point's eastern shore. This artillery piece, one of Jewell's Justin cannons (see Jewell entry, Oneida County chapter), was mounted on a stone foundation in front of the Lewis Point Hotel in early June of 1909.

DAVIS POINT

This little point, jutting into the lake just to the east of Lewis Point was, like Kinlock Point, an example of lake real estate development. In November and December of 1920, Elmer and Elva Davis of Lake Geneva, Wisconsin, together with their partners, Fred and Georgena Dalrymple, purchased land surrounding the point. The "Davis and Dalrymple Lewis Point Addition" was surveyed and a cottage lot map was filed in the Madison County clerk's office on November 10, 1924. The tract included eighteen parcels by Davis Point and fifty-four sections along the Lewis Point Road.

UPPER SOUTH BAY

This south shore bay, named "upper" because of its location at the "head" or upper end of the lake, has served as a resort throughout its recorded history. The bay settlement's founder was DeWitt Clinton Stephens, who purchased 700 acres at eighty-three cents per acre at a public auction in Albany in the early 1800's. Stephens, named for New York's Erie Canal governor, possessed a deed that was signed by Clinton. When DeWitt and his wife, Sarah Conklin Stephens, came to South Bay, the community consisted of several houses and a mixed population of whites and Indians. Stephens had his land surveyed, advertised it, and sold tracts to permanent settlers, and built a brick-tile yard to facilitate home construction. A sawmill, located near the lake front, complimented Stephens' business.

Upper South Bay grew slowly in its early years. A Madison County atlas for 1875 shows the hamlet as containing a sawmill, the Stephens brickyard, a hop kiln, two blacksmith shops, a school, eighteen houses, and the "Upper South Bay House," a resort owned by J.W. Lewis. This hotel, recalled Charles Bushnell in his "Memories of the Town of Lenox" was a "public house, mostly occupied by fishermen." The hamlet grew somewhat in the next decade and boasted three hotels, the Stevens House, the Bruder or Lake View House, and the same Upper South Bay House. Railroad connections, established through the Lehigh Valley Railroad in 1887, brought scores of sportsmen and tourists to the bay and the resort experienced an era of genuine prosperity.

Summer was, of course, the hub of South Bay life, but winter was far from a resting season. Ice fishing on the bay was excellent, attracting a hardy angling crowd. Ice harvesting was important because the hotels needed to fill ice houses for summer refrigeration and, in connection with the harvest, a gala dance and oyster supper was held. Harness racing on the frozen lake drew many fans and horse-drawn wagons regularly crossed the ice, carrying hay from south shore farms to exchange for north shore logs (north shore Oneida Lake farms had far less fertile soil than their south side counterparts).

Bay residents envisioned added prosperity when the second Oneida Lake Canal, connecting the Erie at Durhamville with South Bay, was completed in 1877. This "feeder" canal, however, proved to be a financial disaster. Its locks were too small for larger barges and leaks developed in its lining banks. The state abandoned the ill-fated waterway soon after it opened. The only economic benefit the canal brought to the bay area was an influx of laborers during its construction. Today, remnants of the old canal can be viewed at the Oneida Lake Marina and along the east side of Route 13, south of that road's junction with Route 31.

Today's Upper South Bay is a far cry from the fishermen's retreat of the 1800's. It is an economically vital area, replete with large marinas, restaurants, stores and bait shops. Boating activity is intense. Breeze-filled spinakers, jibs and main sails of a sailing club's vessels make for one of the east end's most picturesque summer sights. Powerboats race across the bay's surface, carrying speed enthusiasts, water skiers, and those that just savor a summer's cruise. The bay's abundant weed areas attract vast schools of fish, and the piscatorial devotees who attempt to fool these sporting delights.

KYSER'S BEACH

This beach, stretching from South Bay's Marion Manor to Oneida Creek, was named in honor of Jake Kyser, one of the most renowned men in east shore history. Kyser was the sort from whom legends originated. He was a businessman, pirate, daredevil and, as Carl Moon once wrote for the *Oneida Dispatch*, a "fabulous character." The label "Oneida Laker" fit Jake perfectly.

Jake Kyser was an entrepreneur with diversified interests. In the early 1900's he captained a launch that carried passengers from South Bay to Sylvan Beach. Prior to prohibition he ran the South Bay Hotel, often known as Kyser's Hotel, quenching thirsts with nickel beers and satiating hearty appetites with fifty cent lake pike dinners. Kyser caught most of the walleyes he served, not always using legal means. Game constables consistently pursued Jake and the infamous pirate once boasted five concurrent poaching indictments. Seldom, however, was Jake convicted. Harassed by warden pursuit and possessing a keen sense of humor, Jake wrote to a local paper to protest his numerous arrests. The arrests were a waste of taxpayers' dollars, argued Jake, since so much state law enforcement time was spent for nil. History records no evidence of a Kyser-inspired taxpayer rebellion.

Jake had a habit of bicycling from his boat to the hotel or to other spots where walleyes were marketed. On the bike was attached a box in which illegal pike could be stored. Legend has it that a warden once stopped Jake en route to market. The constable inquired as to the box's contents. Quickly Jake responded, "Warden, you just wouldn't believe how full of pike that box is!" The game constable laughed - and left. Jake had the final chuckle.

Oneida Lake has claimed many lives; its storms can prove vicious, with five and six foot waves being common. Using his keen navigational skills and knowledge of the lake, Jake Kyser took his boat into many an Oneida tempest to rescue the capsized. He knew no fear of the lake. It was, after all, "his" Oneida Lake, a place where he was at home, in his element. Once he was awarded a medal commemorating his life-saving courage, but for Jake Kyser the real reward was the satisfaction of helping those in peril.

WILLOW GROVE

This is an old place name, seldom used today, that referred to the spot where Oneida Creek enters the lake. In the 1880's a

"Willow Grove Hotel" stood here and trains of the Lehigh Valley Railroad made regular stops. As with Oswego County's Willow Point, this place was named for its dominant flora. It has always been a commercially active place and today boasts a tavern, restaurant, bait shop and motel. Fishermen flock to Willow Grove in the spring and fall. Ice-out brings a large migration of bullheads and white perch to the Oneida Creek mouth. In autumn, usually during cold, blustery weather, large walleyes swim up the creek following schools of buckeye minnows. Until the late 1970's, the abandoned Lehigh Valley bridge served as a pier for anglers seeking these fine fish. The deteriorating bridge threatened to fall into the creek and was demolished. Several walleye anglers fly fish along the creek bank at night; working streamer patterns, they employ a technique seldom seen today on Oneida.

The Willow Grove vicinity was the site of one of Oneida Lake's first white settler's homestead. Pomroy Jones discussed this in his *Annals and Recollections of Oneida County*, 1851:

> George A. Smith, who was better known in his time by the Dutch sobriquet of Yearry Smith, was the first settler within the limits of the town (Verona). His location was near where the Oneida Creek empties into the lake. On Christmas eve, 1791, he and his family arrived at Jonathan Dean's tavern in Westmoreland, and the next day started for his destined place of residence. Such was their snail-like pace, occasioned by deep snow, and intervening swamps and thickets, that eight days were consumed in the journey (now hardly three hours' drive), and they reached their new home January 1st, 1792. Mr. Smith lived about eleven years after his arrival, and in his day he was somewhat prominent as a pioneer settler.

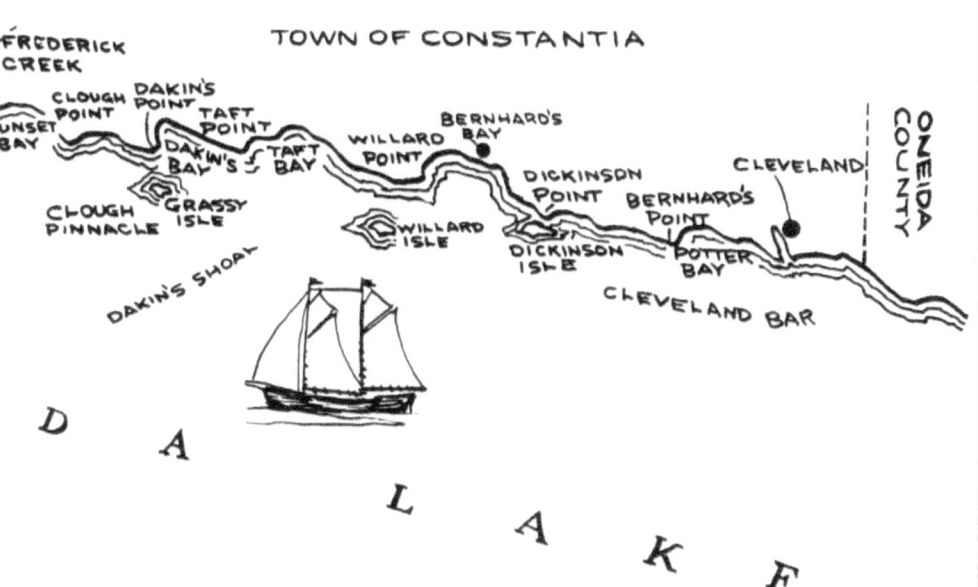

Harold Thompson attributes this county's title to the Iroquois word meaning "flowing out" or "small water flowing into that which is large." Anyone viewing the spot where the Oswego River empties into Lake Ontario will understand this name's logic. Along Oswego County's Oneida Lake shore are the towns of Constantia, West Monroe, and Hastings. Constantia, which originally engulfed the other two towns, was sectioned from Mexico Township and given official state sovereignty on April 8, 1808. George Scriba, Constantia's pioneer developer, named the town and based his choice on a variation of the Roman Emperor Constantine's name. West Monroe, which Scriba called "Delft" (a city near Rotterdam, the Netherlands), was separated from Constantia and incorporated by the state legislature on March 21, 1839. It is named to honor President James Monroe, who occupied that office from 1817 to 1825. Hastings, Scriba's "Breda," gained identity from Constantia in 1825. It was named for Hastings Curtis, who settled there in 1820, built the first brick hotel, the first post office, helped start the first stage line and was elected to the State Assembly in 1824.

The chapter begins with Fort Brewerton, on the north side of the lake's Oneida River outlet and proceeds eastward, ending in Cleveland. Brief histories of Constantia, Cleveland and Bernhard's Bay are included within.

The chapter's place names are sequenced as follows:

Fort Brewerton	Three Mile Bay
Wood Point	Sand Point
Milton Point	Baker Point
Big Bay & Big Bay Creek	Bullhead Bay
Big Bay Swamp and Dry Land Point	Constantia
	Scriba Creek and Frederick Creek
Deer Point	
Willow Point	Sunset Bay
Poddygut Point, Bay and Shoals	Clough Point and Pinnacle
	Dakin's Bay, Point and Shoal
Shaw Point and Bay	
Fairchild Point	Grassy Isle
Ed Nick Shoal	Taft Point and Bay
Wedgeworth Point	Bernhard's Bay and Point
Johnston Bay	Willard Isle and Point
Toad Harbor	Dickinson Isle and Point
Nannyberry Point	Potter Bay
Phillips Point and Bar	Cleveland and the Cleveland Bar
Mudturtle Point	

FORT BREWERTON

This term was formerly used to refer to that part of Brewerton village that lay north of the Oneida River. Fort Brewerton, a British outpost during the French and Indian War, overlooked the river here. Detailed information concerning this fort can be found in the Brewerton entry, Onondaga County chapter.

WOOD POINT

This point was named for Sam Wood, a former Oneida Lake fish pirate. Other titles have adorned it throughout history. Once it was called "Log Cabin Point," for a cabin Wood built. Some folk knew it as "Fitz's Point"; a Fitzgerald family had a cottage there. Mrs. Fitzgerald, according to Sam Wood's son, Warren, was fond of raising poodles and these dogs roamed her property. Boaters often called the point, "Poodle Camp Point."

MILTON POINT

Probably the most dedicated Oneida Lake historian of all time was J. Elet Milton. Milton spent years documenting aspects of the lake's past; Indian lore, genealogy, steamboat travel, piracy and even a bit of place name derivation found their way into his research. Without Elet's labors, this book's writing would have proved far more difficult. One of Milton's pet projects was obtaining official recognition for historic sites. Through his efforts, state markers were placed at the sites of Fort Brewerton and the Royal Blockhouse (Sylvan Beach), both French and Indian War era fortifications. Sadly, Elet never published much and only an occasional article emanated from his extensive research. His research files have been organized and are part of the collection of the Brewerton Free Library. They are truly individualistic files, with many notes recorded on scraps of paper or on magazine article margins.

The first Milton to come to Brewerton was William Tyler Milton, a War of 1812 veteran who resided in that village until his death in 1878. William and his son, Thomas T. Milton, owned land on Milton Point and, thus, gave it the name. William's grandson, Thomas M. Milton, was Elet's father. He was a famous Brewerton boat builder, owner of the T.M. Milton Boat Building Company. Milton built steamboats and canalboats of varying sizes; his business's location, on the Oneida River in Brewerton, made export of the boats convenient.

BIG BAY AND BIG BAY CREEK

This large bay is appropriately named; it is one of the most prominently indented bays of the Oneida Lake shore. Its greatest tributary is the creek bearing the same name. This creek and several smaller streams drain the Big Bay Swamp.

Big Bay is shallow, a site for thick aquatic vegetation and, thus, a productive fishing spot. Bullheads gather in its coves and "run" up its feeder streams in the spring. Bass and northern pike provide summer anglers with exciting gamefish action, but by far the greatest activity on Big Bay occurs during the ice-fishing season. The bay is Oneida's panfish "capital." Sunfish, bluegills, perch and crappies are the quarry for hundreds of locals who venture daily onto the bay's icecap. They fish with tiny "teardrop jigs" baited with maggots called "mousies" and "spikes." Seated on their five-gallon pails, these devotees fish for hours. For many, this angling provides an excellent source of side income as prices for panfish, live weight, have fluctuated from $.35 to $1.10 per pound in recent years. Such Big Bay notables as Bruce and Carl Stallknecht and Charlie Hackenheimer have reaped considerable financial, as well as culinary, rewards.

BIG BAY SWAMP AND DRY LAND POINT

The Big Bay Swamp is a large marsh surrounding that bay. It is thickest on the bay's east side and, like other Oneida Lake marshes, is a source of the lake's productive nutrient base. In many spots, the marsh is virtually impenetrable; its backwaters, devoid of human contact, are lush areas for spawning fish and nesting waterfowl. In the heyday of the Oneida Lake fish pirate, the marsh served as a hideaway from game constable searches. One local authority on fish piracy stated that the marsh was "a place where the wardens didn't go and where the pirates could practice their trade in security."

Dry Land Point, on Big Bay's eastern shore, was so named because it is one of the few dry spots in this wetlands area.

DEER POINT

Today, the pursuit of New York's whitetail deer is a popular, often expensive, sport involving thousands of hunters. In the Adirondacks, sportsmen roam the vast wilderness in search of its trophy bucks while in the state's Southern Tier shotgunners harvest the great percentage of New York's annual deer kill. Millions of dollars and an even greater sum of hours are spent in the whitetail's pursuit.

Deer Point takes its name from the whitetail. Legends vary as to the origin of the point's title. One story relates that deer came out of the Big Bay Swamp to feed on the nourishing lake vegetation that thrives in the shallows surrounding the point. Another saga has it that the point was the site of deer "drives" in which Indians chased whitetails to the lakeshore, frightening them into the water or onto the ice, rendering the deer extremely vulnerable. Whitetails are still common in the Deer Point area. A Brewerton observer has witnessed, in the last five years, two large bucks emerge from Deer Point, enter the lake, and swim to the south shore, over a mile distant.

WILLOW POINT

The willow tree is an ubiquitous feature of the flora near upstate New York's wet areas. Along trout streams it serves a valuable function, being both a source of cooling shade and of insects, which fall from its dropping branches to feeding fish below. The Oneida Lake shoreline has its share of these trees and Willow Point is named for them.

PODDYGUT POINT, BAY AND SHOALS

This strange sounding name intrigued me, not only for its uniqueness, but because for three years I could find nothing written on it and my interview questions concerning it produced little more than laughter. Finally, while discussing north shore history with Mr. and Mrs. Marvin Dunham of Constantia, I mentioned "poddygut." Mrs. Dunham laughed heartily and replied, "It's an old saying - he's got a poddygut - it means a beer belly!" Several other sources have since confirmed this place name's origin.

Why was "poddygut" used for an Oneida Lake name? It is physically appropriate. Poddygut Bay has a well-defined beer belly shape and Poddygut Shoals consists of a series of humps in the lake bottom that might favorably be compared to rotund stomachs. Poddygut was probably a fish pirate term, first used by this group in the early 1900's.

SHAW POINT AND BAY

These sites were named for Claude Shaw, who lived by this bay for three generations. Born in 1886, Shaw was descended from a family of farmers that worked the land surrounding the point. The 1892 census of Oswego County lists Claude and three agrarian Shaws: Albert, Francis and Lorenzo. Claude became a farmer but, according to those who knew him, made more money pirating fish than farming.

Jack Sauer of Constantia remembers Shaw well; Claude purchased lakefront property from Jack's uncle, Clint Smith. Claude's farm, according to Jack, was small, having chickens, pigs, a few milk cows, and some acreage under cultivation. Jack likens Claude to his Uncle Clint, another accomplished pirate. The latter once overheard that "undercover" game wardens were planning a sting operation to catch him practicing his beloved avocation. Approached by a suspicious person asking for a guided fishing trip, Clint readily agreed. Smith was a dynamiter and, after rowing to a productive fishing spot, immediately lit a stick and handed it to the shocked warden. The latter gave the explosive a mighty heave into Oneida, thus violating existing law. Mr. Smith had the last laugh.

FAIRCHILD POINT

This Oswego County point was named for Charles E. Fairchild, a Syracusan, who purchased land there in 1909 and 1913.

Fairchild, a salesperson by profession, bought the point as an investment and kept it but a brief time, selling it to Donald Wedgeworth (re: Wedgeworth Point, this chapter) on June 4, 1913.

ED NICK SHOAL

This shoal, directly south of Wedgeworth and Fairchild Points, was named for Edward Nicholson, an old-time fisherman who lived on the lakeshore directly north of Buoy 138 (in Brewerton). Nicholson supported himself through fishing and by doing the proverbial "odd jobs" around Brewerton. He was an excellent angler and the shoal was one of his favorite spots.

WEDGEWORTH POINT

Donald C. Wedgeworth owned the land on this point. Wedgeworth, a Syracuse native, operated a small farm here, only the barn of which remains. Don and Nancy Sheldon, owners of Gass's Toad Harbor Marina, recall the farm and its most salient feature - a beautiful field of daffodils. Wedgeworth was an engineer and used this talent to survey his lands for cottage development. Two maps of the Wedgeworth holdings, dated July 18, 1926 and June 25, 1927, are on file in the Oswego County Clerk's office.

JOHNSTON BAY

Hidden in a small wood, overlooking this bay, is the Johnston family cemetery. The graveyard's headstones tell the tragic story of this lakeshore farming family. David H. Johnston and his wife, Betsy, built a farm on the bay that bears their name. They raised four sons. Edgar became a fine boat builder with a reputation that spread throughout the lake area. Three Johnston sons, upon the Civil War's outbreak, enlisted in the Union Army; only one returned to Johnston Bay. Charles N. Johnston, the fortunate son, was a private in Company H, 148th Regiment, New York Volunteers. David and James Johnston were assigned to Company H of the 147th New York. Both were killed in 1864, probably in the Virginia theater of operations.

Life in rural New York was hard in those years; the rigors of existence took a physical and emotional toll on those who dared challenge the environment. Families were close-knit units in which every member performed essential tasks. This tragedy must have been devastating for the Johnston family. On a brilliant fall day of 1985, I sat quietly in their graveyard thinking of these people. My thoughts wandered to a Walt Whitman poem that portrays a similar tragic experience. The poem, "Come Up From the Fields, Father," ends with these two haunting stanzas:

> Alas, poor boy, he will never be better (nor maybe needs to be better, that brave and simple soul);
> While they stand at home at the door, he is dead already;
> The only son is dead.
>
> But the mother needs to be better;
> She, with thin form, presently dressed in black,
> By day her meals untouch'd - then at night fitfully sleeping, often waking,
> In the midnight waking, weeping, longing with one deep longing,
> O that she might withdraw unnoticed - silent from life, escape and withdraw,
> To follow, to seek, to be with her dear dead son.

TOAD HARBOR

A quick glance at this place name and one would expect to find amphibians galore in this north shore harbor. The name, however, is a corruption of Indian terminology. Elet Milton stated in the Oneida Lake Association Bulletin in May-June 1958 that the spot was called "O-De-Aba," meaning "harbor of refuge" in the Iroquois language. The Constantia column of the Syracuse *Journal* of June 27, 1892 states that the name given for Toad Harbor is "oadiarba," meaning a "place of safety." The minor discrepancies in spelling and translation do not distract from these sources' congruity. One can possibly imagine how a quickly pronounced Odeaba became Toad Harbor.

This lake port has a long and active history. Jack Sauer recalls stories of people cutting "jumper crooks," four to six foot poles used for sleigh runners, in the woods near Phillips Point. These crooks were drawn to Toad Harbor, which then contained water of sufficient depth to allow the entry of small export barges. The Harbor's shipping business and another of its place names found descriptions in the aforementioned *Journal* article.

> The form of the bay or harbor is a perfect key to the lake and shipping here can ride out the severest storm from any quarter, the anchorage being both gravel and sand. Since it has become a settlement of no small importance on the lake the place has assumed the more euphonious appelation of Little York. . . . The beauty of the scenery is unsurpassed around Oneida Lake. Among the shipping at anchor in the harbor were the steamers *Nancy Peer* and *Monette* and the sailing yacht *Bertha*. The boatyards owned by Edgar E. Johnson are one of the features of the place. Mr. Johnson's reputation as a builder is well known and attested on Oneida Lake, Onondaga Lake and elsewhere.

Elet Milton's description of Toad Harbor included this vignette concerning the cove's more distant past:

> In 1810 a company of fishermen from Cape Cod, having learned of the salmon fishing in Oneida Lake, came with their nets and boats to the present Town of West Monroe and settled at Toad Harbor. . . . For some reason the venture proved unremunerative and was not followed for many years. Among those who came from Cape Cod were Linus Walker and his five brothers, Enock Nickerson, and Jerry Boyington. Mr. Walker was subject to spells of insanity, and on December 10, 1836, he started to skate across the partly frozen surface of Oneida Lake. . . . He reached a point near Frenchman's Island when his family saw him disappear. . . . Two of his sons were to afterwards drown in the same waters where their father met his fate.

Today's Toad Harbor is a far cry from the shipping terminal-salmon catching endeavor that some called Little York. It is a peaceful spot, somewhat unique on Oneida Lake. Its shore is not overdeveloped. Unlike most lakeshore locales, no well-traveled road intersects it; the din of traffic is far from Toad Harbor. The first time I visited the Harbor, the loudest noise, save for an occasional motorboat, was the "honking" of the then migrating Canada geese.

NANNYBERRY POINT

Much local history is recorded in memory and story, filed in the thoughts of people that the local historians contact. Leonard Cooper, Constantia historian, has worked extensively in recording the oral traditions of his town. Although he specializes in the detailed history of the north shore manufacturing, Cooper has gleaned volumes of data about all aspects of his area's past. In the late 1930's, while talking with Lily Whiting, an aged Constantia resident, Cooper stumbled on the Nannyberry Point tale. Lily used to vacation at Frenchman's Island, a popular resort at the turn of the century. She recalled that the island's hotel had a cook who was fond of goats' milk and cheese. Knowing that a diet of berries produced richer milk, the cook maintained a small goat herd (his "nannies") at the point, a place abounding in blue and black berry bushes. The point is but a short boat ride from the island.

Nannyberry was also a haven for fish pirates. Fred Scriba of Constantia, remembers that the berry thickets and swamps surrounding the point made it nearly impenetrable from land, a perfect spot for pirates to store their nets.

PHILLIPS POINT AND BAR

The Phillips family was one of the original lakeshore settlers in the town of West Monroe. Jacob Phillips, the clan's patriarch, came to this town in 1819 from Massachusetts. He and his family were a part of the great migration of Yankees to New York during this era. Driven by the desire and opportunity to acquire rich, cheap upstate farmland, thousands of New Englanders emigrated here in the early nineteenth century.

With Jacob came his family, including son Peter. Peter's marriage produced Jacob's grandson, Elijah. The latter worked on the Erie Canal in his younger years, but eventually returned to the family farm. He amassed some four hundred acres, a large personal tract for that time. His son, William, was born in 1856; this is the Phillips from whom our place names emanate. In 1878 and 1883 William purchased land from David and Rubin Johnston (see Johnston Bay), in 1879 from Peter Coleman and, in 1881, from his father. He became one of the largest farmers in the area and built a new house in 1884, on a spot described by a contemporary as having a most "pleasant view of Oneida Lake." He and his wife, Emily, lived there with their five children, Leola, Lester, Leon, Lyle and Leland.

Upon retirement, Phillips sold his land to N. Ross McLoud, a state engineer on the canal system. The land was divided, as were so many of the lakeshore farm tracts, into cottage lots and marketed for its recreational value.

MUDTURTLE POINT

This little point, on the western end of Three Mile Bay, used to be much larger; wave action and ice have eroded its length. Ethel Hafermaltz Simmonds remembers the point well from her childhood. She and her friends used to journey there to dig up the eggs of the scores of mudturtles that mated at that spot. Ethel's father, William Hafermaltz, was an avid sportsman who maintained a camp across Three Mile Bay from Mudturtle, near Sand Point. Hafermaltz also owned Wantry Island and used that isle as a blind for autumn waterfowling.

THREE MILE BAY

Accurate measurement was not always the rule in past years and this bay is a fine example of that. Several of Oneida's veteran fishermen have stated that, for decades, everyone thought that Three Mile Bay was three miles across, measured from Phillips Point to Baker Point. While distance over water can be deceiving, the bay's width is much closer to two miles.

SAND POINT

Sand Point was characterized, in the early 1900's, by a large sand bar extending far out into the lake. The bar was a navigational hazard as was an artificial rock reef, built several hundred yards off the point in the late '20's. It was constructed to support duck hunting blinds and still gives trouble to errant boaters.

Legend has it that Sand Point was a source of sand for north shore Indians. Another early name for the point was Tanbark Point. Small barges loaded with tanning bark (hemlock or red pine) were towed to the point and unloaded at a waterfront tannery. Several of the barges met an aquatic demise and for years after the tannery's closing local residents found bark washed up along the shore.

BAKER POINT

The Oneida Lake region never produced a president or governor, but it can count one congressman, William H. Baker of Constantia, among its sons. He was born in Lenox on January 17, 1827, son of Samuel and Mary Baker; the family moved to West Monroe shortly after William's birth. His parents, like many New Yorkers of that era, were of Yankee heritage.

Baker's early education was typical of frontier instruction. He attended a one-room schoolhouse and studied briefly at an academy. He learned the trades of "salt-barrel" coopering and carpentry but, like Abraham Lincoln, engaged in extensive independent study. Winters were spent reading and teaching school while during the summer Baker practiced his trades. In 1849 he began studying law; he passed the bar examination three years later. In 1852 he established a law office in Constantia. Originally a member of the Whig Party, Baker joined the Republicans when that group gained power in 1860.

Baker's political career started in the 1860's when he was twice elected to the position of Oswego County district attorney. In 1874 he was elected to the forty-fourth Congress in the twelfth district (Madison and Oswego Counties); he was reelected in 1876. In Congress he sat on two committees, that of the navy and of the Centennial Exposition. His political career was evidence of America's social mobility. Here was a self-educated, small-time country attorney who once made barrels and pounded nails, serving in the country's highest legislative body.

After his second Washington term, Baker returned to Constantia. A history of that time stated that he "resides upon the north shore of Oneida Lake just west of Constantia village, on what he calls his 'swamp ranche' of about four hundred acres, and is now engaged in clearing up a part of it as a farm, being determined to have a provision for his old age, which the moths of caucuses cannot destroy, nor the tidal waves of politics overwhelm." Baker Point was once a part of this farm.

BULLHEAD BAY

Bullheads are a springtime Oneida Lake anglers' delight. This fish becomes active at ice-out, when thaws flush warmer, muddied water into the lake. Such tributary streams as Oneida Creek, Canaseraga Creek and Big Bay Creek provide excellent action for these bottom-feeding fish. It is not uncommon to see dozens of lanterns dotting the water at Oneida Creek's mouth when the bullheads are "in." Catches of several dozen of the big "laker" bullheads can be common. In the lake proper, the action warms a bit later. Shallow bays, like Bullhead Bay, produce excellent catches from shore, usually at night and after a hard, direct wind has riled the water. Pan-fried bullheads make for delicious eating and are featured on the spring menu of several lake area restaurants.

In pirate days, bullheads were caught by different means. Some were taken by set lines, long lines on which are attached scores of baited hooks. From 1915 to 1920, Harry Wing and his partner "Goodie" Gayle took hundreds of pounds of bullheads using the "schooling" method. Powered by an early "gas boat," which towed an extra vessel, Harry and Goodie would motor to coves like Bullhead Bay on calm days. Once at their destination, they would quietly row around the bay, looking for concentrations of foam on the water's surface. When such foam was found, they'd net a large area surrounding the spot. Harry recalls many days when this technique resulted in the filling of both boats, an achievement that netted each "schooler" approximately $20. May was the best month, as bullheads congregate then for spawning.

CONSTANTIA

George Ludwig Christian Scriba was responsible for Constantia's first significant growth. A German by birth, Scriba emigrated to Amsterdam, Holland, and later moved to the Dutch West Indies and reportedly thrived on those islands' American Revolution-induced prosperity. After two years there, he came to New York City. Charles Snyder, in his book *Oswego: From Buckskin to Bustles*, summarized Scriba's role in New York business:

> Scriba engaged in banking and insurance, was a founder of the Bank of New York, and a director of the Mutual Insurance Company. His office at number eight Wall Street was a landmark among the business community, and his substantial home at seventeen Queen Street testifies to his success.

But New York's economic magnetism could not contain George Scriba. In 1794, he purchased around five hundred thousand acres of upstate land from John and Nicholas Roosevelt. This territory, lying approximately between the north shore of Oneida Lake and the east shore of Lake Ontario, was a virtual wilderness. Scriba never inspected the tract prior to purchase, but his were dreams of empire development, of cities, villages and farms aplenty, and he was convinced that upstate held the potential for such a grandiose scheme's fruition.

He was grievously mistaken. Despite energetic promotion, the "Scriba Patent" met dismal economic failure. Factors such as incompetent local management, abundant competition from other, more fertile tracts, lack of sufficient development capital, the War of 1812, and Scriba's initial "absentee landlord" administration of the project from his New York City office, all contributed to his downfall. By 1820 he had mortgaged his holdings, owning little more than his home.

Scriba's name for Constantia was "Rotterdam," after the famous Dutch city. He started the settlement in 1793, even before closing on the property with the Roosevelts. French travelers visited Rotterdam then, observing "a sawmill and three log houses." Major Solomon Waring moved there in the same year and later, with Joshua Lynch, erected the first tavern. In 1795, the French Duke De La Rochefaucault-Liancourt came to Rotterdam during his American tour and, in his journal, commented on the settlement's progress:

> A dozen poor log houses, built almost entirely at Mr. Scriba's expense, constitute all there is of the city of Rotterdam.... The dams for the use of the mill that he has built have cost much money, and being always poorly built, he has been obliged to recommence them several times. The grist mill is not yet built, and the dam appears too feeble for the pressure it will have to sustain. Some work and considerable money has been expended at the mouth of the creek to make a landing, but the accommodation is very poor.

The Duke's account reflects George Scriba's misfortunes. The villages and farms of his patent were destined to grow and prosper, but not until years after financial burdens forced him to relinquish title.

In 1813, the name of Scriba's Rotterdam was changed to Constantia. Two theories exist as to the origin of this name. One story relates that George Scriba chose the name Constantia to honor a young girl in his family who had died in Europe. The name "Constantia" was five years old then, however, as the Town of Constantia was created in 1808 (from Scriba's old townships of Breda, Delft and Rotterdam). Contact with Otto Adolf Scriba of Monsheim, West Germany, the Scriba family historian, revealed that no "Constantia Scriba" ever existed in the family genealogy. Another version of the name's origin comes from Alice Kneeskern, now a Bridgeport resident. Mrs. Kneeskern taught in the old Constantia school for eight years. Prior to that, she often visited the village as a child during the 1920's, staying with her aunt, Georgianna Tanner Dunn. Mrs. Dunn's father was Otis B. Tanner, a Constantia resident then in his late 60's. "O.B.," as Alice recalls, refused to call Constantia by its contemporary name, always referring to the community as Rotterdam. Tanner, a lumberman and farmer in his working days, grew up in Constantia knowing people who lived through the Rotterdam-Constantia name change. When Alice asked him why the changing occurred, he replied that George Scriba selected the name for its classical background. "Constantia" is an adaptation of the Roman Emperor Constantine's name. This story is consistent with an upstate community-naming trend of that era. In the early 1800's, New Yorkers researched the classical world and emerged with names like Rome, Athens, Syracuse, Ovid, Euclid, and Carthage for their settlements. Directly across Oneida Lake from Constantia was yet another classical name, the Town of Cicero. Being an educated, world-wise businessman, George Scriba undoubtedly appreciated state cultural trends and it is easy to understand how classicism could influence him.

While not as industrial as its neighbor, Cleveland, Constantia in the nineteenth century nevertheless boasted a vital economy. An 1867 Oswego County Atlas shows numerous manufacturing concerns along Scriba and Frederick Creeks and adds, in a brief business directory, that Constantia contained two attorneys, two insurance agents, several boatmen, two blacksmiths, a commercial district along George Street (now Route 49) and a stage proprietor. In his brief history of Constantia, published in the North Shore *Citizen Outlet* in August of 1978, Leonard Cooper highlighted the village's prosperity of the 1880's, much of which emanated from the Erie Canal:

> Constantia was haven for canalers during the spring and summer months before the ice made traffic on the canal impossible in the late fall of each year.
>
> Two hundred or more mules were stationed in barns on the shore of Oneida Lake, which housed both tired and fresh mules on an hourly exchange basis. These mules were owned by different canal operators; thus it was a thriving business to board such mules on a year-round basis. . . . Constantia was a great horse-trading center in these days. Many farmers came to sell, trade or buy horses and mules.
>
> After the winter closing of the Erie Canal, hundreds of canalers would spend the off season in different hotels in Constantia and Cleveland. Fights and brawls were common most every night due to over drinking, losing a game of poker or being jealous of some call-girl who traveled from place to place during this season of the year.

Cooper ended by citing how the railroads, such as the Oswego-Midland (later Ontario and Western) eventually replaced the Erie, thus curtailing Constantia's canal-related economy.

Cooper's history also delves into Constantia's hotel business, a lucrative late-nineteenth and early twentieth century trade. Public houses have been a part of the Constantia fabric since Waring built the first in the 1790's. In 1849, on the site of Waring's "Stage Coach Inn," H.C. Champlin opened the Lake Side House Hotel, a four-story hostelry, containing a ballroom, banquet hall, dining room, accommodations for more than forty lodgers, and an apartment for the manager. This was, by far, the grandest hotel in Constantia's history; mahogany bannisters and plush red carpeting added a touch of class, while spacious porches afforded the tourist a commanding view of Oneida and pleasant exposure to the lake's cooling summer breezes. In 1913, the hotel was purchased by John Barnett of Syracuse and renamed the "Hotel Vanderbilt," after a Syracuse hotel of which Barnett had been manager. Barnett installed an elaborate barroom, hired wagon drivers to pick up his patrons when they arrived at the railroad station, and established steamboat connections with the Lower South Bay and Frenchman's Island resorts. The hotel had several other owners in its lifetime, among whom were "Bishop" Herbst and Fred "Stubby" Auth. The Vanderbilt endured until December of 1972, when fire destroyed it.

Leonard Cooper's history tells of three other major hotels that served Constantia tourists in the late 1800's. The Welder-Cole Hotel opened in 1870 and lasted until 1911, fire again causing the demise. The Dobson Hotel, owned by Frank and Ruth Dobson, was built on this site. The Prentice Hotel, located on the site of Constantia's Norstar Bank, operated from 1882 until 1890 when it was destroyed by fire. In 1892 the Empire Hotel opened its doors and lasted until 1905, when it was purchased by the Scriba Masonic Lodge. These hotels, like the Lake Side House, were constructed during the initial boom in Oneida Lake tourism, the era from 1850 to 1900, when railroad connections made the lake communities attractive summer alternatives for upstate's city dwellers.

A Constantia landmark since its erection in 1832 is Trinity Episcopal Church, built on land given by George Scriba. Set in a fine grove of shade trees, the church and its historical flair have been meticulously preserved. Trinity's rustic stained, rough lumber walls and plain, paned windows are reminiscent of its frontier beginnings. The churchyard contains the Scriba cemetery, a small plot in which the founder and his immediate family are buried. Here, weathered tombstones bear witness to the hardships the Scribas faced. Trinity Church, like many rural churches, was served by circuit riding preachers. Fred Griesmyer wrote that "the church, its clapboards stained with the years and its windows misted with age, was once the center of life in Constantia. Itinerant preachers rode down the corduroy road, their bible in the saddlebag and the communion service wrapped in rough linen." Once the church was almost abandoned, but in 1928 Frank Tallman, of Syracuse, contributed six thousand dollars to insure its restoration and preservation.

Constantia today is a bustling, vital community. Marinas, boat liveries and varied businesses line its Route 49 "downtown" area. The New York State Oneida Fish Hatchery, on Scriba Creek, annually rears millions of fingerling walleyes and, during early spring's walleye migration attracts scores of tourists to view the stripping/incubation process. The hatchery and its grounds are beautifully maintained. Constantia's main and side streets are lined with neat, well-kept homes, many of recent construction. In contrast, buildings like the William H. Baker house, the Scriba Masonic Lodge, the restored Scriba mansion and the aforementioned Trinity Church provide historical balance. Although it never attained the "Rotterdam" ideal of his dreams, contemporary Constantia would most certainly please George Scriba.

SCRIBA CREEK AND FREDERICK CREEK

Scriba Creek was named for George Scriba, businessman and land developer, whose life in the Oneida Lake region is described in the preceding article. The stream was first called "Bruce's Creek," for an early settler. Cited as a "Mr. Bruce" by nineteenth century Oswego County historians, the man lived near the stream in 1791 but, having no land title, left shortly thereafter. Francis Adrian Van Der Kamp met Bruce and wrote that he was once a "Connecticut merchant" but, in the wilderness, led a hunting/fishing subsistence life. Frederick Creek acquired its name for Frederick William Scriba, son of George Scriba and his second wife, Maria Dundas Starman. Both streams provided water power for Constantia's first industries. An 1867 map shows several mill dams along the creeks, with two sawmills and a grist mill located by Scriba Creek and a sawmill and tannery by Frederick Creek.

Although its bordering factories have long since vanished, Scriba Creek remains important to the Oneida locale. The stream is the site of the Oneida Hatchery, a state-owned walleye fry (young) producing facility that is, to a great extent, responsible for maintaining healthy walleye populations in Oneida. New York State began experimentation in walleye reproduction around the year 1893 and, in 1894, built a hatchery at Scriba

Creek's mouth. During the following year, this operation boasted production of fifty million walleye fry. The original hatchery was replaced in 1897, when the "Oneida Fish Culture Station" took form on Frederick Creek. A local paper mentioned the new facility.

> The New York State Fish Commissioners have located the hatchery long talked of for the propagation of pike and other food fish on the site of the old tannery at Constantia, through the generosity of Romain (Romayne) C. Robertson of Parish, who donated the site to the state. This will be a great industry at Constantia, as every spring from $500 to $1000 is paid out (to workers). George Scriba has been appointed head of the hatchery.

The Scriba mentioned was the grandson of Constantia's early developer.

The Frederick Creek hatchery endured until 1942, when it was replaced by the present building on Scriba Creek. The latter site was preferable to Frederick Creek, as it was much nearer the lake. Today, there is discussion concerning construction of a new hatchery though, at this writing, nothing concrete has materialized. Groups like the Oneida Lake Association have zealously lobbied legislators to keep the new facility at Constantia. The Association's paper, the Oneida Lake Association *Bulletin*, ran an article by Cornell biologist John Forney (re: Shackelton Point, Madison County Chapter) that highlighted the hatchery's role in Oneida Lake ecology. In the article, Dr. Forney wrote:

> The contribution of stocked fry and natural spawning to the fry population was evaluated in the late 1960's and early 1970's by stocking Oneida in alternate years. Abundance of fry in these years was estimated from numbers of fry caught and the volume of water strained by fine mesh nets towed from a boat. In 1968, 1970 and 1972 when fry were stocked, the population of recently hatched walleye averaged 39 million. In 1969, 1971 and 1973, when all young originated from natural spawning, the population averaged 9 million. Subsequent studies confirmed that a large proportion of the walleye fry in the lake were of hatchery origin.
>
> Hatchery stocking could maintain the walleye fishing in Oneida Lake at near current levels, even in the absence of any natural reproduction. In effect, the Oneida Hatchery assures an adequate supply of fry which is independent of weather conditions and other factors which influence the success of natural spawning. How many of these fry survive

to catchable size is governed by another set of variables, but stocking does add some needed stability to the walleye fishery.

SUNSET BAY

This bay's magnificent view of Oneida Lake's sunsets brought about its title.

CLOUGH POINT AND PINNACLE

George Clough, from whom these place names originate, ventured into several aspects of the north shore's economy. Born in 1837, Clough became a farmer, owning lakeshore land now encompassing Clough Point. Assisted by his wife Francis, his daughter Addie (who was also a local teacher), and his four sons, John, Howard, Ralph and Hubert, Clough operated a modest farm and, when not "choring it," fished Oneida extensively. George Clough was also an adept boatman who knew the lake well. He had to - he and his family owned a barge business that drew "bog iron" across the lake, from the south shore to a Constantia foundry. One false course by Captain Clough and a ship could easily have been lost on the shoals and reefs that punctuate Constantia's waters. George Clough had another daughter, Marion, who married Frank Winn of Bernhard's Bay. Their son, Courtney (Corky) has been one of my finest sources of data about the North Shore.

Today, many know Clough Point as "Will's Point." Louis Will, once a Syracuse mayor, was mentioned in a local history publication in 1926, citing that he "has done much for Constantia in the way of village improvement of which the public is given free use, like the beautification of the waterfront in the line of terrace, lawn, park, pavilion and dock." Will donated five hundred acres north of the village for the Boy Scouts' Camp Woodland, and, on land he owned across from the Hotel Vanderbilt, kept a small herd of tame deer. Louis's son, Eric, was President of the Will and Baumer Candle Company in Syracuse. He purchased land on Clough Point in 1939; his son, Richard, currently lives on the point.

DAKIN'S BAY, POINT AND SHOAL

The Dakin family for whom this bay, point and shoal are named, emigrated to Constantia from New Hampshire around 1835. George E. Dakin was a prosperous farmer who lived on Dakin Bay with his family and a servant. Dakin supplemented his agrarian income with profits from a lumber dealership; great rafts of logs were exported, via Constantia and Oneida Lake, in the early 1800's. George's brother, Timothy J. Dakin, operated a blacksmith shop and, during the 1850's heyday of the Oneida Lake and River Steamboat Company, was the seasonal tender of that company's beacon on Little Isle (called "Lighthouse Isle" at that time). The latter Dakin exhibited wit in a written report to the company in which he explained a fire at the lighthouse on July 27, 1855. Rationalizing the issue, Dakin wrote, "Unless some evil disposed devil had a hand in it, there must have been some defect in the fluid." Timothy Dakin, like brother George, prospered in Constantia and, in his commodious home, found ample space for wife Eliza, five children, two local teachers and a servant. Timothy's son, George, followed in his father's lake-oriented interests and became a boatman.

GRASSY ISLAND

This tiny island, lying just south of Dakin Point, is appropriately named for its vegetation. Several other grassy shoals and islands exist throughout the lake.

TAFT POINT AND BAY

In a modest home on the north side of Route 49, overlooking the bay that bears his family name, lives Elden Taft. For fifty years Elden farmed the lakeshore land surrounding his home. He is descended from generations of Tafts that lived on the bay in the 1800's. An atlas and a gazeteer for Oswego County, both published in the late 1860's, list Stephen Taft, a farmer with fifty acres, as living on the bay.

NORTH SHORE IMAGES
CONSTANTIA, BERNHARD'S BAY AND CLEVELAND

Ira Brown opened the Lakeside House in Constantia in 1849. In the 1890's the business's name was changed to the Vanderbilt Hotel, after a popular Syracuse hostelry. Demolished in 1972, the Vanderbilt was synonymous with years of Constantia tourist joy.

Begun as the Welder-Cole Hotel in 1890, the Dobson House was a noteworthy Constantia landmark until it was destroyed by fire in 1925.

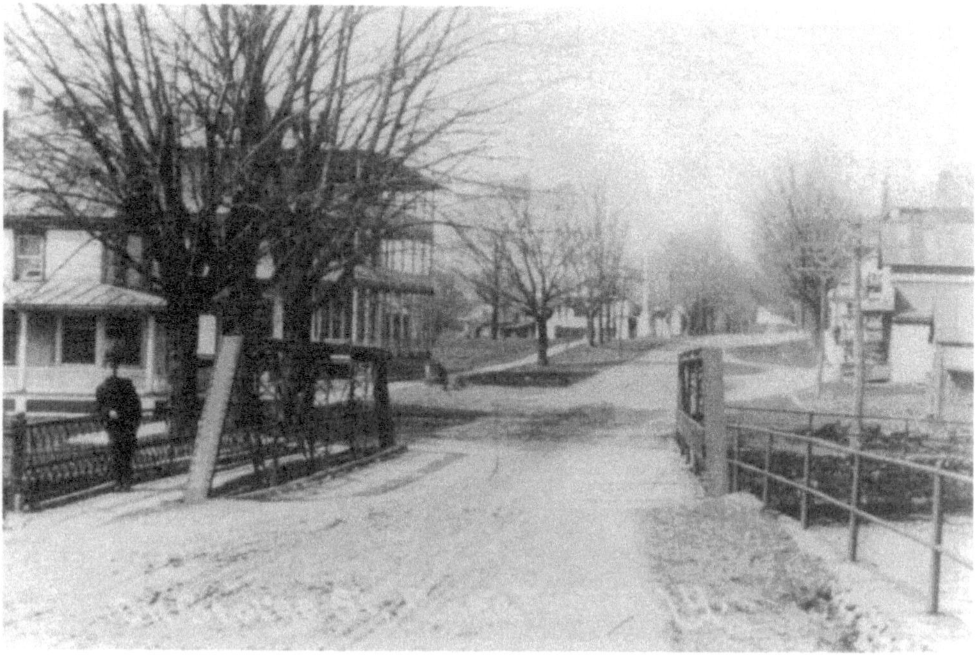

Corky Winn

George Street, now Route 49, looking west from the Scriba Creek bridge, around 1900. The Dobson House is on the left and the Vanderbilt is the taller right-hand building.

Corky Winn

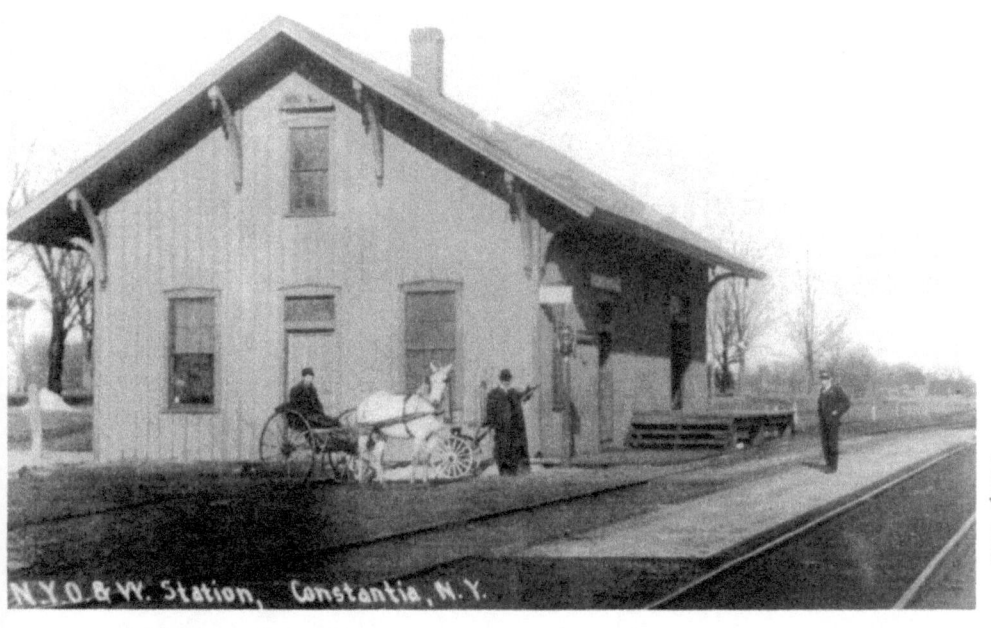

Originally named the Oswego-Midland Railroad, the Ontario and Western served the north and east shores of Oneida Lake and connected with the New York Central at Oneida Castle Station.

Taken in 1911, this photo shows Constantia's Sunset Bay. Much of Oneida's shore was nearly devoid of trees by that date, the result of intense 19th century logging, home builidng and farming.

Such small tourist facilities as this boat house were common around the lake in the early twentieth century. Typically, they catered to city "sports" and often provided picnic facilities and refreshments.

Built in 1832 on land donated by the Scriba family, Trinity Episcopal Church still serves the north shore faithful. The structure's frontier rustic architecture has been preserved.

Artist M.E. Barber painted this portrait of George Scriba in 1898, basing the likeness on an earlier drawing.

William H. Baker, the north shore's most successful politico, served in the United States' House of Representatives from 1874 to 1878. Below is a print of the Baker home, headquarters for what the Congressman called his "swamp ranche" along the lake shore.

On a slight knoll just east of Scriba Creek, George Scriba built his "mansion" in the early 1800's. The home remains and has just recently been restored. Pictured below are some of Scriba's furnishings.

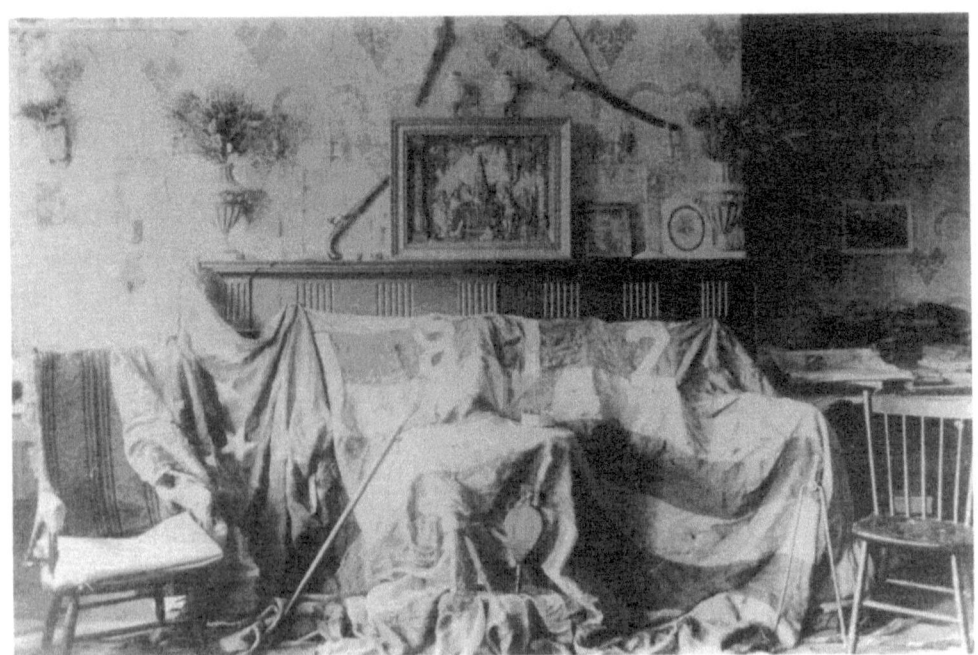

The first Constantia fish hatchery arose on the banks of Frederick Creek, a Scriba Creek tributary, in 1897. It was used until 1942, when the present facility was completed.

State hatchery workers proudly pose with the Oneida Lake fish trap net. This device was designed by Constantia personnel and received national use.

Walleye holding pens on Scriba Creek, 1921. Fish destined for "stripping" of eggs and milt were kept here. Note the Vanderbilt Hotel in the upper right corner.

Activity at the Oneida Hatchery in the 1940's. Hatchery superintendent Frank Yeomans (right) checks the progress of walleye fry.

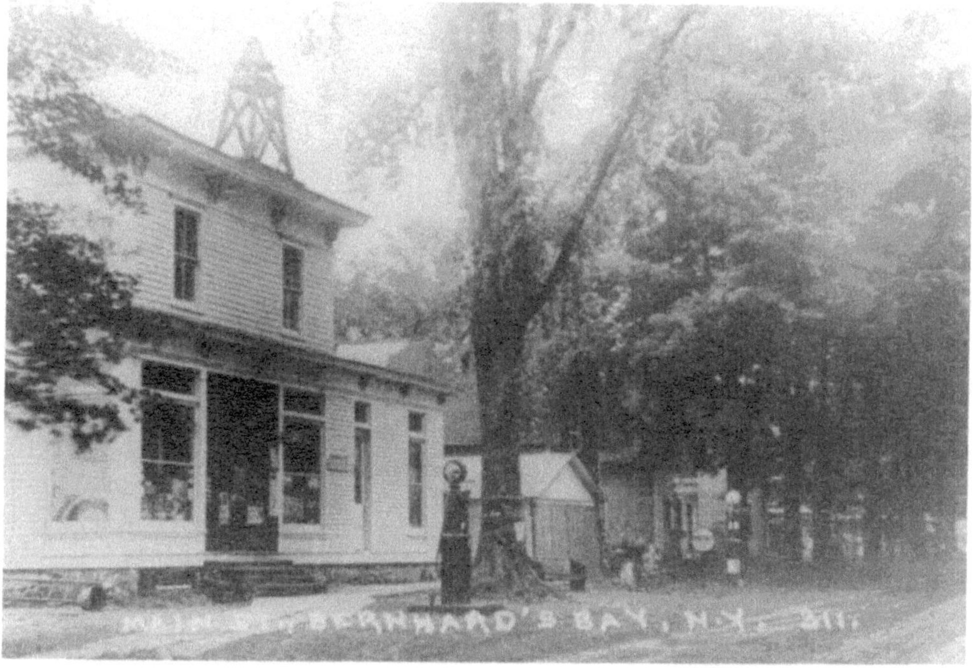

Corky Winn

George Davis's "Trading Post," a Bernhard's Bay landmark, occupied the building on the left of this photo. The bucolic essense of Bay existence permeates the scene.

Corky Winn

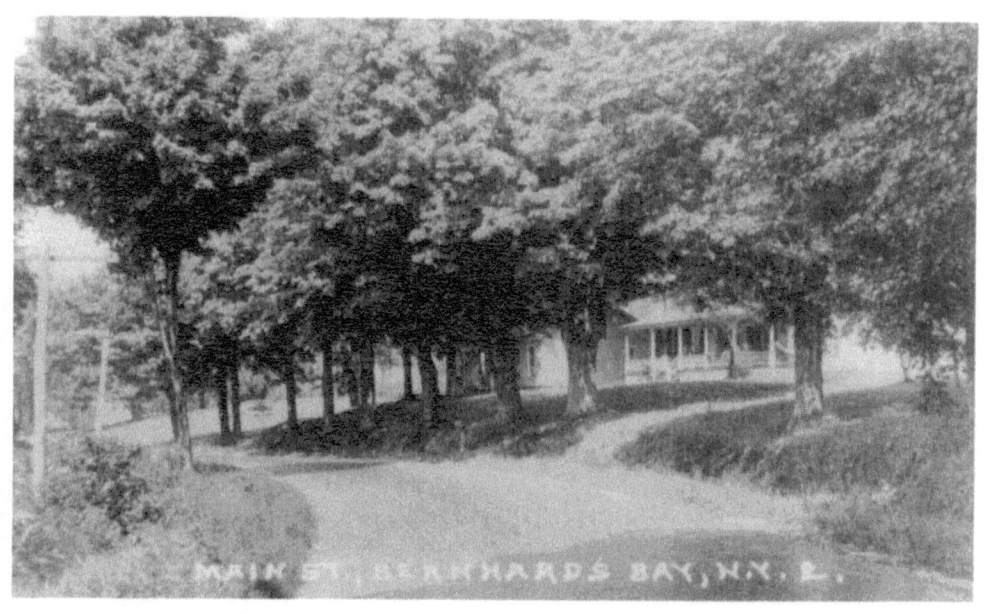

More than any Oneida Lake resort, Bernhard's Bay offered tourists a break from the bustles and annoyances of everyday life. This picture depicts Route 49, going west.

Bernhard's Bay boasted a small glass works, started by Henry and Dennis Winn in 1847 and enduring until 1895. This print was taken from one of the company's bill-heads.

Upon arriving at the Bay in the 1790's, John and Elizabeth Bernhard suffered the hardships of wilderness life, but their determination prevailed and Bernhard's Bay grew around their homestead.

Nature has surely been kind to Oneida Lake and its environs. An early photographer captured Bernhard's Bay's dramatic panorama while, in contrast, the lower shot of the Bay's Winona Park projects a "life on the Mississippi" doldrum quality.

For decades the Cleveland House provided shelter for sportsmen, tourists, loggers, canal workers, glass makers, et. al. The pluralistic clientele often blended rather raucously.

Later day alterations transformed the Cleveland House facade. In the 1930's, the inn was called Gilbert's "Hotel Cleveland."

"Downtown" Cleveland was vital to the village economy. The King Block, above, was a commercial-residential section while the Joe Bitz General Store, crammed in the photo below, sold "everything a household needs." Bitz's store was located on a Route 49 site, across from what is now "lighthouse park."

Route 49, then Main Street, in 1890's Cleveland.

The ice house on this photo's left was used by Cleveland fishermen, who would stop each summer morn to fill their "lard-tub coolers" with its catch-preserving commodity.

An early view of Cleveland's Saint James Episcopal Church and the factory mill pond it overlooked. This gothic revival "English country type" house of worship was designed by Richard Upjohn, who drew plans for Trinity Church, New York City.

The now-demolished Cleveland Methodist Church was once a large congregation, boasting a Sunday School with over 150 pupils. The beautiful, ornate sanctuary was a monument to Cleveland's prosperity during the glass-making era.

Corky Winn

Pictured here with his altar boys, Father John B. Mertens was appointed pastor of the north shore Roman Catholic parish in 1894. His primary congregation was Cleveland's Saint Mary's, but his ministry entailed the arduous tasks of the "circuit rider."

Two Cleveland shore vistas. Above, anglers savor success in the weed-beds off the village, around 1910. Below, Oneida's shoreline's starkness at ice-out.

The "Three Day Blow" was a summer-ending Cleveland holiday. Named for a common Oneida Lake wind condition, the celebration featured the "Rube Band," a becostumed musical group that paraded their "talents" down Main Street.

Frances Houser was another attraction to the Three Day Blow. Her gaudy paper attire complimented the "Rube Band spirit" of the occasion.

Clarence Bitz

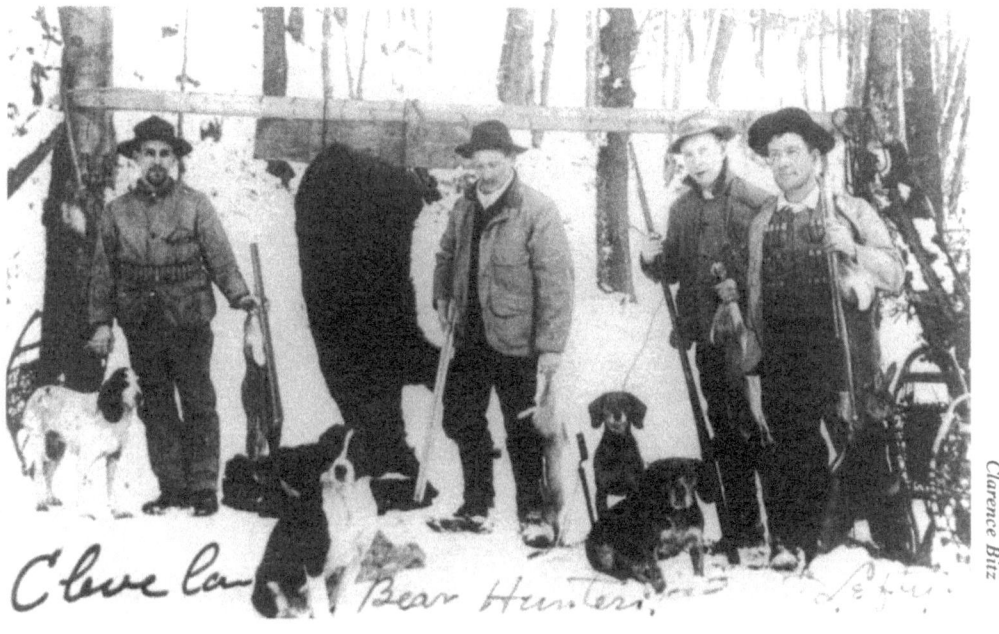

Bears and panthers were once common around Oneida Lake. As late as 1905, hunting success was possible, as evidenced by Cleveland hunters (left to right) Emery LaVancher, Anthony Houser, Arch Beely and John Fitzpatrick.

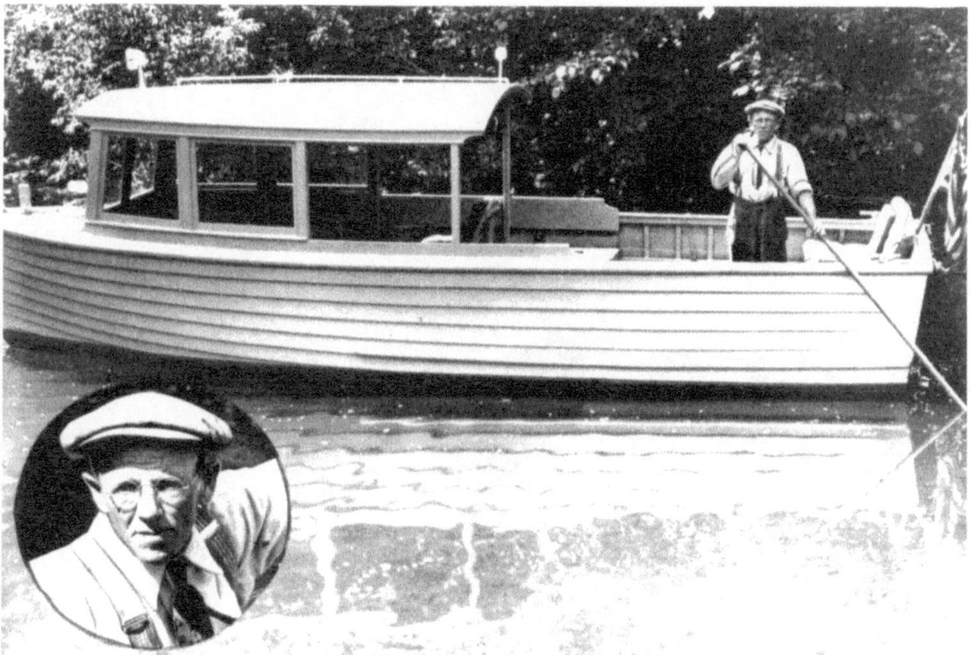

Onondaga Historical Association

Pictured here with his 22-foot "pirate catching power launch," Harry Best of Cleveland was, at one time, Oneida's most renowned game warden. The photo was taken in July, 1936.

Started by German immigrant Anthony Landgraff (below), the Cleveland Glass Works was the first glass operation in the village. The factory continued production until 1901.

Charlie Griesmyer

Crawford Getman was, perhaps, the most prominent figure in Cleveland's glass history, owning companies there from 1863 to 1910. Among his properties was the modest "Getman Cottage."

Charlie Griesmyer

Charlie Griesmyer

Getman Glass workers were paid in "script," redeemable only at the company store.

Glass workers revel in a Getman factory picnic-campout, 1908.

Charlie Griesmyer

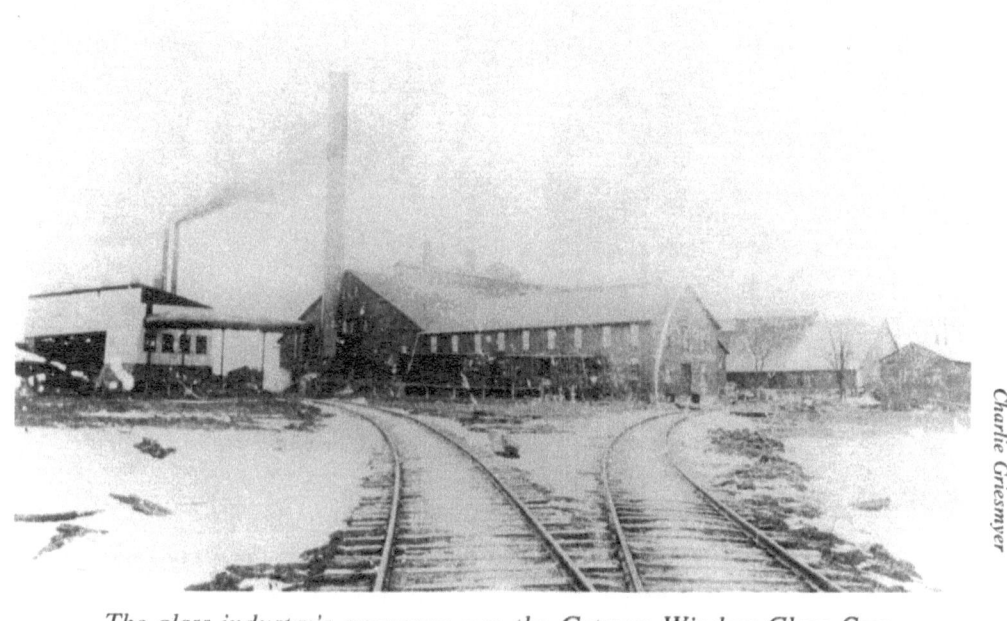

The glass industry's swansong was the Getman Window Glass Company, which opened in May 1902. The factory was forced to close by 1910.

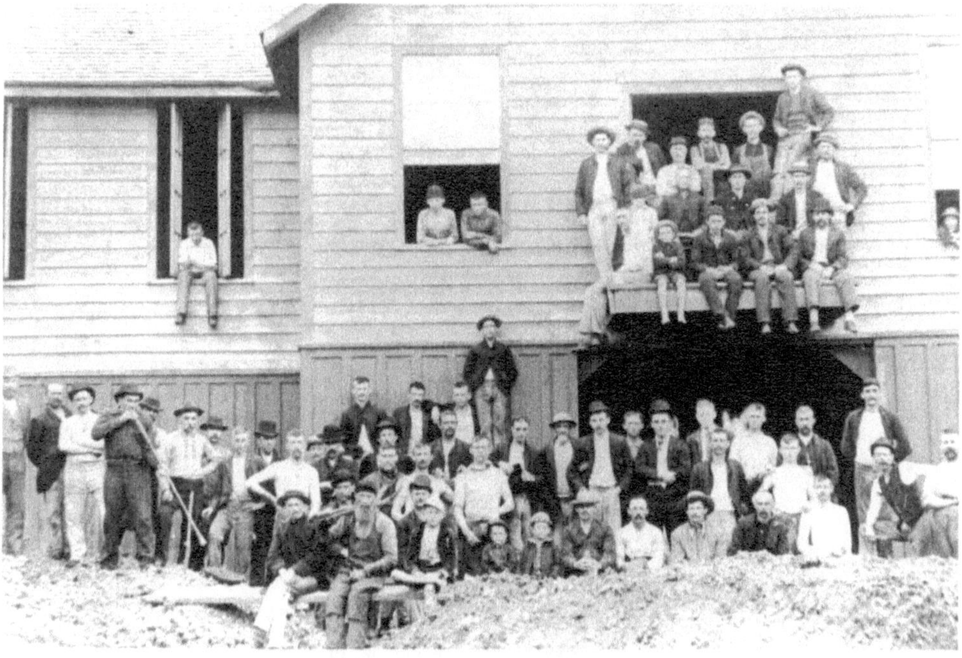

Charlie Griesmyer

Union Glass workers pose proudly for the photorapher. Note the glass "blower" in the lower left corner.

A detail of the Getman Glass Works' interior, showing the art of glass "blowing."

Examples of Cleveland glass survive today. This captioned creation is from the Charles Griesmyer collection.

Mill dams like this backed up the waters of Oneida's north shore tributaries, providing power for 19th century factories.

The convent-school of the Sisters of the Presentation Order of Nuns was erected in 1875, east of Cleveland, at Nunnery Point. This New York City order used the building for about fourteen years.

William Taft, Elden's father, was a canaller ("canawler" to the folklorist), as was William's brother, Hiram. Both men owned barges that they piloted on the Erie Canal. The Dickinson family of Bernhard's Bay built barges for the Tafts (see "Dickinson Isle and Point" entry in this chapter). Elden recalled the day when many canal boats were towed to sites along the lake to pick up cargo. Among the most important area exports were wood, sand, iron and glass. Several of the lake's points were created in this era; stone was drawn to the shore, the point was extended outward and piers were built on the point's tip. Tugs towed barges to berths along these piers. Once filled with cargo, many barges were drawn to Three Rivers, an important dispersal point in upstate trade. Many of these barges were brought into the lake on the Oneida Lake Canal, an economically disastrous venture that connected the Erie Canal at Durhamville with Upper South Bay (see that bay's entry in the Madison County chapter).

Elden Taft's memories take the writer back to an Oneida Lake of commerce, of small industry, of hard-working lakeside communities bound together by common economic bonds. Elden's home and his land transport one to the turn of the century, when small farms dotted Oneida's periphery. Here rests a weathered farmhouse, a tired yet dignified building with a view commanding a broad hayfield, stretching from Route 49 to the lakeshore. On the day I visited Elden Taft, the hay was fully grown, the sun brought out its golden yellows and browns, the wind swayed it, almost in rhythm with the waves that formed its backdrop. A tractor and mower replaced the scythes that once harvested this field. But nothing replaced the field itself - no camps, no restaurants, no marinas or neon. It was good to be there.

BERNHARD'S BAY AND POINT

Few white men settled on Oneida Lake's shore during the eighteenth century. The region was a wilderness, haunted by vast forests, wild animals such as panthers and bears, and the memories of Indian violence, still fresh from days of the American Revolution. Furthermore, adequate transportation was lacking. A journey from Albany to the lake took days, weather permitting. One family that did brave these travails was that of John Bernhard, a Dutch emigrant who came to the United States in

1790. Bernhard, his wife Elizabeth, and their son, John, lived on Staten Island from 1790 until 1795, when they made the great trek to Oneida. Arriving at the bay that bears their name, they discovered a crude cabin, built two years earlier by a man named Dayton. The cabin was not suited for winter habitation and Bernhard's neighbor, Francis Adrian Van Der Kemp, invited the family to spend the frozen season in his home. John Bernhard, to his extreme misfortune, was an argumentative person. After a short time at the Van Der Kemp house, Bernhard and his host engaged in a heated political discussion culminating in Bernhard's blustering that he "would not live with such a man." The family returned to Dayton's cabin, filled gaps between logs with blankets and clothing, and prepared as best they could for a wintery evening. On the first night a blizzard struck. Bernhard awoke to find that his cabin was part of a gigantic snow bank! Dining on the proverbial "humble pie," John Bernhard asked Van Der Kemp for shelter and the latter consented. The home of "such a man" was infinitely preferable to a rustic cabin during the harsh upstate winter. At spring's advent, Bernhard returned to the bay, cleared land, and built a comfortable farm house. He and his descendants farmed the bay area for several generations thereafter. Francis Adrian Van Der Kemp, by the way, gave Bernhard's Bay its first recorded name. In his letters he refers to the bay as "fisher's bay" and raved over the quality of fish caught there and elsewhere in Oneida Lake.

Throughout history, Bernhard's Bay has been a quiet retreat community, though never approaching Cleveland, Bridgeport or Sylvan Beach in size or bustle. An Oswego County historian described the spot in mid-nineteenth century with these words:

> The little hamlet at this point, a station on the New York and Oswego Midland Railroad, had in 1865 a hundred and sixty inhabitants. It has a general country store in connection with the glass works, which are owned by Stevens, Crandall and Co. These works employ about sixty men and manufacture nearly thirty thousand boxes of glass per year.

Another Bernhard's Bay industry was Ezra Dickinson's boat yard, a business that employed about thirty. The hamlet contained a school, several craftsmen's shops, a Society of Friends' congregation, and was surrounded by small farms. It fit well into the mold of the nineteenth century upstate "age of homespun" community.

As the twentieth century approached, Bernhard's Bay experienced the transition felt by other lake communities as farmland was divided into cottage lots and old-time business faded. The hamlet maintained its bucolic air, however, and does to this day. Route 49, the north shore's "Main Street," borders the water for several hundred yards as the highway winds through Bernhard's Bay. Camps line the shore, looking out onto the bay's often placid surface, a sheltered sheet of water accented by aquatic grasses, a few boats and two small islands. Crowds and noisome traffic are largely absent as the emerald hues of bordering woods and Oneida's azure tones dominate the image.

In the 1970's, a highlight of my visits to Bernhard's Bay was George Davis's "Trading Post," a general store-post office combination. This enterprise was a uniquely preserved example of bygone America. Two large windows, each filled with a greenhouse of flora, complimented the building's faded clapboard exterior. A weather-worn sign bearing the title "The Trading Post" hung over the door. Inside, stuffed birds and animals, antique post office boxes, and a cash register that rang up a harsh, yet fitting tune, greeted the shopper. At the top of the walls, surrounding the entire inner store, was painted a mural depicting the Bernhard's Bay scene. The Trading Post marketed such merchandise as bandana handkerchiefs, safety pins, life's grocery staples, finger nail clippers, assorted hardware, humorous Bernhard's Bay post cards, and even copies of a young author's first attempt at history. George Davis enjoyed reminiscing the lake's past and talks with him helped me research several north shore place names. At conversation's end I'd always buy some item, listen to the cash register's song, then thank George for his help. As I left, the floor creaked with each step and the old door closed hard as its entry bell bid me time's goodbye.

WILLARD'S ISLE AND POINT

The Willards of Bernhard's Bay were active in that settlement's commercial sector. Henry Willard was a wood dealer, selling logs to sawmills such as Jacob Dickinson's. Henry's son, Henry Jr., also operated a sawmill at the Bay. The Willards' products were probably exported, via barges, to points around the lake. The family owned land on Willard Point, opposite from Willard Isle.

DICKINSON ISLE AND POINT

Very often a family fills a community leadership niche, active in civic affairs and prominent in the commercial sector. So it was with the Dickinsons of Bernhard's Bay in the 1800's. In 1826, Jacob Dickinson moved from Greene County, New York, to Constantia Township, settling on the old Van Der Kemp farm west of Cleveland. In addition to agricultural activity, he established a sawmill, a significant business in this expansionist era. Jacob's burgeoning lumber business was taken over, in 1853, by his sons, Jacob and Ezra. The partnership lasted until 1856 when Ezra withdrew, moved to land on the east side of Bernhards' Bay, and set up a boat building company. The business's sustenance was canal boats, produced for use on the Erie and its feeder canals. It was an important local employer, having over thirty workers on the payroll. The Tafts of Taft Bay were among Ezra's customers.

Ezra Dickinson, for whom the Isle and Point are named, was a man of many talents. In addition to his lumbering and boatbuilding skills, he was an accomplished blacksmith and wagon maker. He once served as railroad commissioner of Constantia and purchased the Society of Friends meetinghouse in Bernhard's Bay, converting it to use as a public hall. Undoubtedly, his commercial and civic enterprises made him a community leader.

Dickinson was a common nineteenth century north shore name. An 1867 atlas lists an Isaac P. Dickinson as being a sash, blind and door manufacturer in Cleveland. Concurrently, Almon Dickinson was a Cleveland boatman who also owned a 150-acre farm. Charles, Samuel F., William P. and Henry W. Dickinson were farmers in Bernhard's Bay, owning over 300 acres among them.

A touch of folklore surrounds Dickinson Isle. An early county history states that the isle was a punishing site for Iroquois squaws who broke tribal rules. They were canoed to the isle and forced to swim to shore, some three hundred yards distant.

POTTER BAY

This bay, nestled in Cleveland's center, was named for Asher Smith Potter, an early village settler. Potter's parents, originally from Camden, moved to Cleveland around 1823. Young Asher was born with a restless spirit and left Cleveland for eighteen years, living in New York City and the South. In the early 1840's, Potter returned home. Cleveland then was a bustling lake village, sustained by the glass industry and other small family factories. The village's population and economy were steadily growing and Potter, business-wise from his experiences, determined to capitalize on this, and opened a tavern and general store. He became a popular community figure and was elected to several village offices, including a seat on Cleveland's original board of trustees.

CLEVELAND AND THE CLEVELAND BAR

Cleveland was named for James Cleveland, who emigrated to Oneida's north shore from Peterboro, Connecticut, in 1826. In partnership with Samuel Stevens, Cleveland built the village's first hotel and general store. Upon establishment of the infant settlement's post office, a conflict arose between the partners. Stevens wanted the office to be named "Stevensville," while Cleveland pushed for his name. The two reached a compromise, which was approved by popular referendum, that the post office would become "Cleveland" and Stevens the first postmaster.

Two other names have been associated with Cleveland. The northern part of the village was sometimes called "Unionville," for the Union Glass company located there. Elden Taft recalled that old-timers once referred to Cleveland as "Black Creek." This stream, named for its dark-hued water, flows through the village and, as shown on an 1867 map, provided energy for four sawmills and a grist mill. Several dams in the village impounded Black Creek, creating power-generating waterfalls.

Whereas most lake communities' economic vitality centered around either agriculture or tourism, Cleveland boasted an industrial economic base. The village became renowned for its glass industry and the fine workmanship that characterized it. In 1840, Anthony Landgraff, a German glassman, moved to Cleveland and built the first glass factory. Landgraff initially imported sand from Verona township (James D. Spencer, Sylvan Beach's founder, was the dealer at Fish Creek hamlet), but soon discovered that Cleveland sand, upon which his factory rested, was superior. Others took advantage of Cleveland's potential in glass manufacturing. Landgraff's company, the Cleveland Glass Works, acquired competition in 1851 when the Union Glass Company opened. Originally organized as a stock company financed by several local citizens, this corporation came under the ownership of Forest Farmer and Charles Kathern.

Crawford Getman and Henry J. Caswell purchased the Cleveland Glass Works in 1863. Getman assumed full control of the plant upon Caswell's retirement in 1877. Despite a disastrous New Year's Eve fire in 1880, which totally engulfed the factory, Getman rebuilt his company and operated it until 1889, then selling out to the United Glass Company. The latter corporation ran the factory until 1893, at which time the building was sold and razed. In 1897, however, the United Glass Company bought and remodeled the old Cleveland Glass Works. United's venture lasted until 1900, when American Window Glass Company purchased the plant. American's Cleveland tenure endured for but one year; the factory closed in 1901 and was never reopened.

Crawford Getman's influence in the Cleveland glass industry was not over, however. Under Getman's and Eugene Morenus's leadership, a workers' cooperative formed the Getman Window Glass Company, completing its new factory in May of 1902. Skilled Cleveland glassworkers such as the Schmidts, Bonneaus, Griesmyers and Bernets zealously supported this welcome economic stimulus, purchasing stock and working in the factory. The latter Getman enterprise, initially prosperous, soon found increased fuel costs and competition from more automated Pennsylvania mills to be overwhelming. The plant shut down in 1910, thus terminating Cleveland's glass making era.

While glass factories constituted Cleveland's largest industry, their positive economic impact was supplemented by other manufacturing concerns. A paper delivered by Francis Eggleston to the Oswego Historical Society in 1943 described Cleveland's industrial heyday:

> The forty years from 1834 to 1874 covered the most prosperous days of Cleveland. With its large tannery, two glass factories, numerous sawmills, its brickyards, chair factory, wagon shops, lake and canal traffic, it was a busy and

hustling place, full of picturesque life and incident. The tannery and glass factories consumed great quantities of bark, lumber and wood and mingling with the residents of the village, with its businessmen, canal men, tannery and glass workers, were the men of the farms and woods, lumbermen, bark peelers, wood choppers and hunters, forming a motley population of various races and occupations. But one by one these various industries dropped out or were abandoned and finally nothing remained but the glass industry.

Eggleston also cited an interesting item about Cleveland sand. Local sand was of such high quality that it was used by Steuben Glass, Corning, in making the famous Mount Palomar telescope, located in California.

One of the first examples of American labor unionism occurred at Cleveland. James Gallagher, who experienced Cleveland's glass industry era, was a primary source for Eggleston's paper. Based on Gallagher's recollections, Eggleston wrote:

> Frank Putney, a veteran of the Civil War, was secretary of the Cleveland Glass Company. He evolved the scheme of a secret organization of workers.
>
> It was then against the law for workers to organize - but they did at Cleveland, and seemed to have controlled firing and hiring and wages - by secret methods. They held their meetings outdoors in a nearby ravine - where they couldn't be seen from any point.
>
> Mr. Samuel Gompers - who was then a young cigar worker - learned of the scheme and spent some days visiting Frank Putney in Cleveland and secured complete information as to the organization and methods of the glass workers' union. He returned to New York and organized the Cigar Workers' Union - his first.

The economic vitality engendered by Cleveland's industries is directly reflected in the number and diversity of other businesses there. A late nineteenth century Oswego County historian wrote that the village had six general dry goods stores, two of which were operated by the glass companies. Crawford Getman paid his workers in certificates redeemable at his personal store, a practice that perhaps abetted the early union movement. Three hotels, the Marble House (by far the most important), the Cleveland House and the Globe Hotel catered to the village's business-related trade, as well as to a few sportsmen. There were, in addition, two druggists, two butchers, one hardware merchant, one harness maker, two shoe stores, a tailor, a barber, two physicians, two attorneys, a jeweler, three saloons (in all likelihood extremely colorful spots), a photographer, and a village newspaper, the *Lakeside Press*. Numerous craftsmen, such as blacksmiths and carpenters, thrived in Cleveland's heyday, as did many enterprises not mentioned above.

Cleveland is now a peaceful, largely residential north shore community, much contrasted to its industrial past. Harmon Landgraff, in *Oneida Lake - An Historical Sketch*, published in 1926, defined an initial cause of this change. Landgraff wrote:

> ... Now the lake villages are quiet and prosaic. The tanneries are gone, the saw mills are gone, the boat yards are gone, for gone are the great primeval forests which made this busy variegated life possible. ...

Urbanization in American society and the transportation revolution engendered by the auto hastened and eventually finalized the transformation of industrial villages like Cleveland. Reminders of its past, though, live on in Cleveland today. Plain, functional homes of former glass factory workers stand side-by-side with revivalist architecture dwellings of the village's once-prominent businessmen and factory owners. Saint James Episcopal Church, a beautiful gothic structure, overlooks a picturesque mill pond. Crumbling concrete breakwaters still guard the Cleveland canal harbor, while a small, red lighthouse continues to flash its regular warning. History permeates the air in the venerable Apps' boat yard; aged wood and scarred metal hoists speak to the years. And, in springtime or after a heavy rain, Black Creek flows with ancestral force, exhibiting a power that once made capitalists dream and a village prosper.

ONEIDA COUNTY

Oneida Lake ... the view from the north side of the lake is truly beautiful, the hills of Madison and Onondaga rising in the distance, with their waving fields of yellow grain and green forests, with the clean sheet of water intervening, now calm and motionless, now lashed into fury by the winds and storms. . . .

—Pomroy Jones, 1851

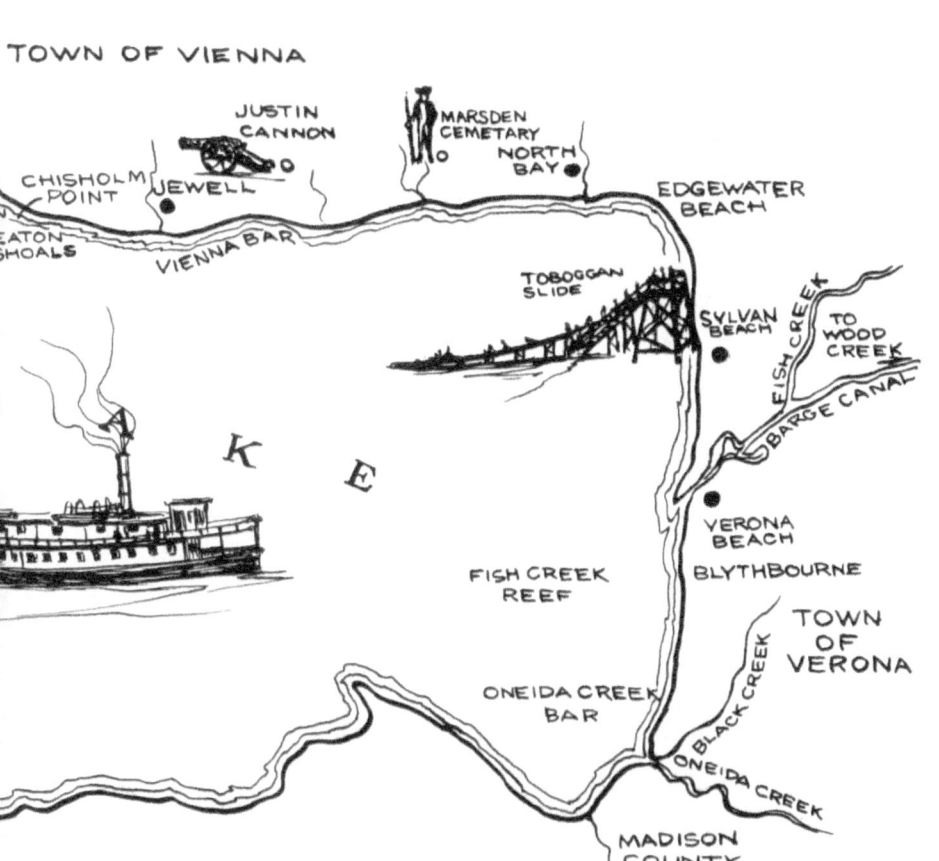

"Oneida," in the Iroquois language, translated to "people of the stone." Two Oneida County townships border the lake. Verona, named for an Italian city, was separated from Westmoreland township on February 17, 1802. Vienna has had three names in its history. In 1807, it was called "Orange," but that title was altered to "Bengal" the following year. In 1816 the town became Vienna, after the Austrian capital city. This chapter opens with Wells Bay, near Cleveland and includes all place names eastward to North Bay and then south to Oneida Creek. Summative histories of Jewell, North Bay, Sylvan Beach and Verona Beach/Fish Creek hamlet are included.

Order of topics reads as follows:

Wells Bay	Wood Creek and River
Nunnery Point	Fish Creek and
Colon Bay	Fish Creek Reef
Godfrey Point	Barge Canal
Eaton Bay and Shoals	Verona Beach,
Chisholm Point	Fish Creek Hamlet
Jewell	Blythbourne
Vienna Bar	Black Creek
North Bay	Oneida Creek and
Edgewater Beach	Oneida Creek Bar
Sylvan Beach	

WELLS BAY

This small bay, just east of Cleveland, is bisected by the Oswego-Oneida County boundary line. Its title comes from the Wells family, landowners whose property once bordered the bay. Albert, Judson and William Wells owned a boat building business, constructing canal boats and steamers in the middle to late 1800's. The lumber of north shore forests made location of such businesses on that shore convenient. Albert Wells was also a captain who brought vessels to the lake from distant points. In 1886, for example, Captain Wells brought the steamer *Wide Awake* from Newark to Brewerton. The voyage had to be rather dull for Wells as the *Wide Awake's* lethargic speed soon earned her the nickname "Fast Asleep." Another Wells family member to reside on the bay was Wesley Wells, listed in an 1869 Oneida County directory as being a "horticulturist and farmer."

NUNNERY POINT

In 1874, Father Donnelly of Saint Michael's Roman Catholic Church, New York City, bought several acres of land approximately one mile east of Cleveland. Donnelly was acting on behalf of the Sisters of the Presentation Order of Nuns, a group desiring a country retreat. This order staffed the faculty of St. Michael's

Parish School in New York City, an academic institution instructing over three thousand pupils. Fred Griesmyer's "Cleveland - Past and Present" historical series described these sisters' Nunnery Point experience:

> Work on the convent started on November 20, 1875, under the direction of Daniel Santry, the contractor for the building, which was of wooden structure, 63 by 23 feet on the ground and two stories high, with a full sized cellar. For over ten years this property was used by the Sisters for their annual retreat, which consisted in devoting a great part of the day in prayer and meditation. . . . Here also a school was opened, where the hours left unoccupied by devotion and necessary recreation were devoted to the education of the children of the vicinity, whether these children were Catholic or Protestant. On July 26, 1889, the convent property was leased to a woman from Frankfort, New York, to be run as a hotel. This plan was abandoned shortly thereafter and (the building) was left unoccupied for years. Finally it was torn down.

One of the school's students was George App, father of Clarence App, long-time proprietor of Cleveland's App's Boat Livery.

COLON BAY

"Colon" is a corruption of Cole, the name of the 19th century family who resided on this bay and for whom the water was named. Thomas Cole, an Englishman by birth, came to this area in the early 1800's. Cole was a farmer; he and his wife, Ann, had four children: Thomas, Charles, Ellen and Ann. The younger Thomas and Charles followed their father's vocation but, in 1854, branched out into the boat building industry. Their business was a significant one. The Oneida County Directory for 1869 stated, "Mr. T.G. Cole carries on boat building quite extensively, on the lake shore, about two and one-half miles west of West Vienna (now Jewell). He employs about 30 hands." This was a considerable number of workers for a rural area. Cole's economic importance was cited in Fred Griesmyer's writing. The lake historian wrote, "In 1854, a man by the name of T.G. Cole started boat building. In twenty-two years he built one hundred and eighty-one canal boats. The first sold for $1,600 and gradually the price increased up to $4,000. Nine million feet of lumber, at an average price of $20 per thousand (board feet) was used. The total costs of all these boats in wages, materials, etc. amounted to $365,561. Many people benefited by this enterprise."

GODFREY POINT

This north shore point was called "Nine Mile Point" by colonial travelers, the nine miles referring to its estimated (and incorrect) distance from Wood Creek's mouth on the east shore. Like many other lake locales, this point was named for a farming family that once owned it. William Godfrey, a Vermonter, was the family patriarch. The 1835 Oneida County census lists William, his wife, Mary, and six children. His farm was small then, having but sixteen acres. By 1869, however, Godfrey had expanded his holding to 180 acres and his son, Hiram, owned a neighboring farm of 138 acres. The assessed valuation of William Godfrey's farm was $3,500 in 1870, an average sum for the era and region. The family worked their land well into the twentieth century. On March 3, 1932, a map was filed with the Oneida County clerk that depicted the surveying of "Godfrey's Shady Point" into cottage lots. Later, New York State purchased land on the point and constructed a public boat launch.

EATON BAY AND SHOALS

Several families of Eatons lived in the bay area during the 1800's. The 1835 Oneida County census lists Samuel Eaton and family occupying a forty-acre farm. In this small enterprise were five cattle, eleven sheep, seven hogs and two horses. The sheep's wool was used by Samuel's wife, Martha, to make cloth, seventy-three yards of which was produced that year. By 1870, three Eaton families inhabited the shores of the bay. Alexander and his wife, Mary, ran a large farm valued at $9,000. Henry and his wife, Julia, were prosperous enough to afford a "domestic" (servant) and a farm laborer. Martha Eaton, then Samuel Eaton's widow, owned a farm that was worked by her son, William.

Henry Eaton served as election inspector for his Vienna township voting district, a position that was later filled by Alexander's son, Anson. The latter was also the first station agent-operator at the Ontario and Western Railroad station at Jewell.

CHISHOLM POINT

On August 2, 1834, Robert Chisholm purchased eighty acres of land from Caleb Knight for approximately $1,500. Chisholm's land holding, which included this small point, was expanded in 1862 when he purchased additional acreage from Henry Godfrey, William Godfrey's son. Like his neighbors, the Godfreys and Eatons, Chisholm was a farmer.

JEWELL

This pastoral north shore hamlet was originally called West Vienna, it being in the western part of Vienna Township. The name was changed to Jewell in 1921 to honor the hamlet's pioneer, Eliaphat Jewell. Eliaphat came to this spot prior to 1817, clearing and farming the land and building the settlement's first grist mill. In 1817, Silas Jewell came to the area from Massachusetts, and subsequently moved to Constantia. His Constantia sojourn lasted about five years and, in 1822, he returned to the Jewell area. In 1826-27 Silas built the Jewell House, the hamlet's first hotel. He also served as the community's first postmaster, eventually moving the post office to his hotel.

Like Bernhard's Bay, Jewell has historically been a small, quiet community. Boat building occurred there to a minor extent in the 1800's, but all business and industry have been limited family operations. The greatest "noise" in Jewell's history occurred in 1896 when Dr. Joel G. Justin, of Syracuse, sponsored a test of cannons he had invented. These innovative artillery pieces were nineteen and thirteen feet long, respectively. They were transported via railroad to Jewell in April of 1896 and mounted on a point overlooking the lake. The guns were innovative in that their shells were more powerful than previous loads and boasted greater range. The tests attracted a large crowd, described by

Fred Griesmyer:

> About 300 people, mostly from Syracuse, went down by special train over the Ontario and Western from Oneida, and excursions from Oswego and Norwich contributed about 200 more to the eager throng. They rushed pell mell across lawn, wheat field and wood to the shore of the lake where the big guns stood pointed out across the water, waiting for the experiment of the day.

The United States Army was represented at the tests, as were the governments of Cuba, Russia and China. The first test failed due to shell malfunction, but the second try on July 11 was a great success, demolishing a barge anchored far out in the lake. A third experiment was even more successful, delighting Justin and his backers. Their plans to manufacture and sell the ordnance went astray, however, as better weapons surfaced and gained market preference. For years, Justin's cannons remained at Jewell, hidden by overgrown vegetation. During World War II most were cut up for scrap metal, but the heavy sections were never moved. Surviving cannons can still be seen; one at the Constantia VFW and the other on the lakefront at Bernhard's Bay.

Lifestyle in Jewell during the 1880's and 1890's received excellent documentation in a series of Syracuse *Post-Standard* articles written in the late 1940's. The articles, contained in the "Just Around the Corner" column authored by one "Bertrande," described Jewell as viewed through a young boy's eyes during his life in that community and his companionship with "Uncle Noel" (Noel Gardiner). "Bertie" loved Jewell and, through his keen memory and skilled pen, preserved the joy and reality of those days.

The fair weather scene at Jewell was a relaxing experience. Again, like Bernhard's Bay, Jewell was more of a retreat than a busy resort. Bertrande wrote of this time:

> My Uncle Noel sat in the big barroom of the Jewell House in West Vienna. Mrs. Jewell, the friendly proprietress, stood behind the bar with her head between her hands and her elbows resting on the polished surface.
> In was mid-afternoon in May and, in the little hamlet on Oneida's north shore, activity was at low ebb. Thru the big open door blew a gentle breeze off the lake and the wrens chattered merrily in Widow Myers' balm-o'-gilead tree next door. A bevy of house flies hovered hopefully above the screen-covered bowls of crackers and cheese at the far end

of the bar, and there was a pleasant odor of old-fashioned malt in the air.

At the moment, no customer was imbibing, although the town drunk, Ceph Adams, was anxiously awaiting such an event. In addition to my uncle, Mrs. Jewell, and Ceph, the room was further peopled by Old Man Palmer, who lived across from the depot but spent most of his waking hours at the Jewell House, Dick Bevan, the blacksmith, Dell Candee and Bill McArthur.

And there they sat, surveying the slow scene, with conversation, a cold brew, and an occasional attempt at fly assassination to highlight the day.

Religion played an important part in the life of these nineteenth century lake communities. Jewell's church occupied a central role in the hamlet's social life. Bertrande, who attended the "white church" (still a Jewell landmark) and its Sunday school, wrote of a religious revival there:

> In 1891, there came to Jewell an evangelist named Britton. He was a famous exhorter of his time and was noted thruout the country for his uncanny ability to inspire mass conversions - to bring sinners 'forward' to the altar. At the moment, he was conducting a series of meetings at Cleveland and he and his trombonist and his male quartet branched out to Jewell for a few days for some extra inspirational work.
>
> When Uncle Noel heard of the evangelist's impending visit, he was to some extent impressed but not too enthusiastic.
>
> 'I dunno,' he confided to LeRoy Page, 'this here feller, Britton, has got quite considerable uv a repytachun fer cookin' up quick religion - but I misdoubt me if he's got any way fer to make it stick!'
>
> On the evening of the first meeting the little church was filled to the doors. The kerosene lamps on the wall brackets threw a mellow glow over the assembled audience and the chandelier above the pulpit glittered with a thousand points of irradiance. On the bench, directly beneath the altar, sat the church dignitaries - the trustees - of which Uncle was the chairman, and beside him were 'Squire' Parker, Jane Dunham and Levi Hoag. A long-standing edict of the board of trustees allowed Uncle Noel to smoke his pipe at church services - a privilege of which he always took full advantage.

Winter brought degrees of isolation to Jewell, but hardships were braved with a stoicism common to country folk back then. Bertrande wrote of one memorable storm:

> It was January, 1899. For four days and nights the snow had fallen heavily and continuously along Oneida Lake's north shore. Between our house and Uncle Noel's was a solid bank of snow rising nearly to the tops of the first floor windows and at the back there was a drift so high that our barn, not more than 200 feet distant, was invisible from the woodshed door.

The family gathered at Bertrande's home on the storm's fourth night. Several neighbors trekked through drifts to visit.

> So we sat there and ate dried apple pie, washed down with home-made root beer. Presently, little old Aunt Cyrena came briskly thru the tunnel holding her spotless apron over a big tin of hot gingerbread. 'Sakes alive, folks,' she laughed, 'why wasn't I invited to the party too?' And she passed the cake around. My Uncle Noel's keen wit and apt repartee as usual dominated the talk and he was in his glory.
> We popped about a half bushel of popcorn, we ate Pound-sweets and Northern Spies, while the cheerful glow of the big oil lamp and the bright flicker of the wood fire thru the open grate cast beneficient haloes about the room.

There were many Bertrande columns. He wrote of fishing trips with Noel, the old man oaring a heavy wooden boat through Oneida's choppy water. A sailboat journey across Oneida to visit Sylvan Beach for the 1892 Hop Growers' Picnic, during which he met New York's Governor Roswell Pettibone Flower, was described in vivid detail. Bertrande wrote of the common, the happy and sad, and the fictitious, once citing Noel's "encounter" with an Oneida Lake "sea monster." At one article's conclusion, he mused about his writing's focus:

> Yes, life was simpler in the old days. We were, I believe, closer to earth in some ways and nearer to Heaven in others - or is it, perhaps, only that the mellowed memories have gained added sweetness thru the dim years?

VIENNA BAR

This North Shore bar, running from Jewell to North Bay, is located by a steep drop-off between shallows and depths to thirty-five feet. Both on the bar and along the deep side of the drop-off are highly popular east-end fishing spots. Like Vienna township, the bar was named for Austria's capital city.

NORTH BAY

North Bay's name is of obvious directional derivation, the bay being nestled in Oneida's northeast corner. This village has a long history as a lake resort. Durant's 1878 *History of Oneida County, New York*, described the village's tourist appeal:

> North Bay is the largest and most thrifty village in the town (Vienna) and is located on the shore of a bay of Oneida Lake bearing the same name. It has a commanding view of the lake and has become a noted summer resort. Its hotels are filled during the season and plenty of sport awaits the fisherman who shall launch his boat upon the silvery waters of the noble lake, for it has won golden fame as the home of the 'finny tribe,' which abound in vast numbers. A large number of boats are kept here for hire and the business of canal-boat building has in former years been extensively carried on, the product of a single season having reached as high as 35 boats. During the winter of 1877-78 five canal-boats were manufactured here, the material used being hemlock lumber. Picnic-parties in great numbers resort here for pleasure during the summer.

Durant summed up North Bay's commercial-professional sector by saying the village had "three hotels, five stores, two churches, a school-house, two saw-mills, a planing-mill, a shingle-mill, two small potteries, a blacksmith-shop, a harness-shop, a wagon-shop, and two physicians."

The North Bay hotel business was well capsulized in Daniel Wager's Oneida County history, *Our County and Its People*. In his work, published in 1896, Wager wrote:

> ... One of the most active founders of the place was Henry J. Myer, who erected the first hotel there on the site

of the late Phalen House. This hotel was burned. He also built the later Tremont House and many other of the early structures in the place. The Myer hotel was changed to the Frisbie House and subsequently burned. James A. Wooden built the Phalen House in 1873. . . .

The present North Bay Hotel was built by Josiah Cleveland and is owned and kept by Peter Cole. The property was in the Cleveland family for many years. Since this place has become somewhat noted as a summer resort, a number of hotels have been built at the beach. Among these are the Butler House, built and kept by George Butler, the Brayton House, by Michael Brayton, and a house kept by John Fiddler.

Daily life in North Bay received good coverage in the *Vienna Amateur/Vienna News*, a small weekly paper published in the 1870's and 80's. Reading that tabloid's issues gives one a small-town, homey feeling concerning North Bay and surrounding Vienna Township communities. Entries about Peter Flanagan building a canal boat, about steamboat excursions from Bay hotels to Frenchman's Island, about a New Year's Eve community party at the Phalen House and about life's everyday matters allow a reader to feel this village's pulse. Humor was a trademark of the paper. One March 1878 issue contained the item, "Fishing through the ice is played out. Ward and Satterlee are preserving their fishing holes for next winter." That same issue printed that "North Bay boasts of a man who was bred a Methodist, yet lived as a Baptist and died a Catholic." For a penny a copy, the *Vienna Amateur/Vienna News* was a great bargain.

Approximately one and one-half miles west of North Bay, on the south side of Route 49, is a tiny, yet very significant cemetery. Marked at roadside by a state historic plaque, the graveyard contains a monument to the last resting place of Captain Adjutant George Marsden, a staff officer to George Washington during the American Revolution. Marsden resigned from the British army at the war's advent and enlisted in the colonists' Massachusetts forces. He served with distinction through several campaigns, culminating in his promotion to Washington's command in 1779. After the war's conclusion, he married Wilmuth Lee, sister of Virginia's Richard Henry Lee, a signer of the Declaration of Independence. The couple moved to the Bernhard's Bay area in 1783 and, that same year, were visited by Washington. Ironically, Marsden and his wife are interred almost six miles east from the site of their pioneer log cabin home.

Today's North Bay is a serene residential community, with a population that swells in summer as camp owners return. Gone are the resort days, the excursions, the picnics. Reminders of that past endure, however. On Route 49 stands the vacant North Bay Hotel, once a village watering hole. Saint John's Roman Catholic Church, founded by Father J. B. Mertens around 1900, remains a landmark and its building's interior, although slightly altered, radiates historical flair. Many older dwellings rest peacefully along the Bay's shaded avenues. And at Lake Street's crest the visitor may park his car, take a stroll, and luxuriate in a grand view of Oneida, the rolling Alleghenies to the south, a grand view that brought people to North Bay in the first place.

EDGEWATER BEACH

Lake Shore Drive runs along Oneida's edge at this appropriately named North Bay beach. The beach area is active year-round. Swimmers and boaters frequent the area and sightseers enjoy the fantastic sunset vistas afforded there. Ice fishermen take walleyes and perch in large quantities in the bay and the spring and fall seasons find many anglers wading the beach area, casting jigs and rapalas, luring pike to their offerings. Springtime also heralds the beginning of an old-time fishing custom at Edgewater - that of "set-lining." The laws of New York State allow a properly licensed person to operate an unattended setline, a long, heavy line to which a maximum of 500 baited hooks may be attached. The line is anchored on each extremity and the hooks, sweetened with large nightcrawlers, are kept on or close to the bottom. Every day, sometimes twice per day, the set-liner checks his line, hook-by-hook, carefully removing the catch and rebaiting empty barbs. Large fish, such as channel catfish, are often gaffed before being flipped aboard. The majority of the catch consists of bullheads, smaller catfish, and white and yellow perch, fish that are legally marketable in New York. Set-liners remove their apparatus from the lake before walleye season's opening to avoid conflict with the many pike anglers that fish near Edgewater.

SYLVAN BEACH

"The Coney Island of Central New York." Sylvan Beach has filled this role for thousands of upstaters throughout its eleven decade long history. The village has evolved from a cottage owned by the Oneida Community amidst a towering oak and sand pine forest to an active resort, boasting an amusement park, regionally renowned restaurants, great fishing, swimming and boating facilities, and a summer population that exceeds five thousand. Today, on peak weekends such as the July Fourth holiday, Sylvan Beach commonly hosts over ten thousand people. Autos line Main Street and fill the beach-front parking lot. Bathers bronze their bodies on public sands. Scores of vessels ply the canal and lake waters. Strollers fill the sidewalks, browse in flea markets and play "skee-ball" and "fascination" at the Midway. Contemporary Sylvan Beach presents a dramatic contrast to its serene, frontier roots.

"The Beach," as aficionados know it, has had several names during its history. In colonial times, it was occasionally referred to as the "Old Scow Place." Treacherous sand bars combined with nasty storms to create wreck-causing hazards at the junction of Wood River and Oneida Lake. The Beach's second title was "Joppa." In 1873, Sewell Newhouse, a representative of the Oneida Community in Sherill, negotiated a property lease with James D. Spencer, Sylvan Beach's founder. The utopian-minded community members wanted a secluded spot on Oneida and the then unsettled Sylvan Beach lands offered ideal isolation. The Community's newspaper, the *Circular*, explained Joppa's origin:

> ... Joppa was suggested (for a name for the lake cottage). We like this name because it was short, unique and scriptural; and no sooner had she appropriated it than Augusta found from the books that the word Joppa signifies comely, pleasant, so it seems we had unwittingly made another good hit. A reference to Robinson's Calmet gives the following items of interest concerning Joppa: 'Joppa, lying on the southeastern Mediterranean coast, is one of the most ancient seaports in the world.'

Even after the Community disbanded around 1880 and abandoned their cottage, "Joppa" still referred to Sylvan Beach. The *Vienna Amateur/Vienna News* of that era makes repeated reference to persons visiting "Joppa."

Sylvan Beach acquired several names in the 1880's. "Joppa" faded during that decade and the title "Beacon Beach" emerged. Newspapers such as the *Rome Sentinel* and the *Utica Herald* wrote of "Beacon Beach" in terms such as the following:

> The Utica Herald says: 'People of good taste who live in the vicinity of that portion of Oneida Lake now called Fish Creek propose to change the name to Beacon Beach, a pretty substitute. It is a historical tradition that one of the two old trees used by the Indians and traders as a landmark in navigating the lake yet remains standing.'

Another story had it that the "beacon" was a bonfire that the Oneida Indians lit at Wood River's mouth to mark the spot for their night spearfishermen. Clarification of the "beacon" title's origin comes from Hector Gale's *Oneida Free Press*, in the August 30, 1882 issue:

> The only time the place has ever been used for a beacon is when the elder Mr. Spencer was shipping sand by canal boats and built a fire on the point in order that tug boats could get in when they arrived after dark.

Other appellations applied to the Beach in the "pre-Sylvan Beach" 1880's. Some called the place "Spencers" or "Spencer's Beach," for its founder. Others used the geographic titles "Wood River" and "Fish Creek," the latter being distinct from Fish Creek hamlet in Verona Township. The resort certainly suffered from an identity crisis, what with six quasi-official names.

All this came to an end around May 8, 1886. The Ontario and Western Railroad finished its "loop" line running down Main Street (then Railroad Avenue) in the village. A station was built approximately on the site of today's Eddie's Restaurant. The company named the station "Sylvan Beach." This title endured.

The legitimate question arises, "Why was 'Sylvan Beach' chosen?" Several reasons emerge. First, it was appropriate. "Sylvan" derives from the Latin adjective "sylvanus," meaning "wooded," and the village had long prided itself in its great groves of trees. "Beach," of course, was synonymous with Oneida's east shore, an area that boasted "five miles of the best bathing beach in the world." Thus, the name was logical. Someone had to choose it, though, and I believe that James D. Spencer did. He was the resort's father, a respected community leader, and his life had involved favorable exposure to the word sylvan. Before moving to this area, Spencer lived in West Monroe on Oneida's northwest corner. There, one of his close friends was a man named Sylvanus Allen. An early Oneida Lake resort was the "Sylvan House," built on Frenchman's Island in the 1850's. Spencer's sand business at Fish Creek hamlet gave him close contact with the total lake community and he was well-acquainted with this hotel. Furthermore, near Spencer's Fish Creek home, the Lehigh Valley Railroad named its local station "Sylvan Junction" and a picnic area called "Sylvan Grove" arose across the track from the station. Although I have never found specific writing saying that James D. Spencer gave Sylvan Beach its name, in my opinion the evidence in support of this is convincing.

Throughout its history, Sylvan Beach's economy has centered around the resort business. Unlike other lake communities, it was devoid of the sawmills, boat building shops, and small family industries upon which those locales' financial lifeblood was dependent. Sylvan Beach's initial growth as a resort began in the late 1870's. In 1879, Lyman Spencer built the Forest Home, the Beach's first commercial hotel. Five years later the Stoddard and Garvin partnership, of Oneida, constructed the Algonquin Hotel, a larger facility on Wood River, just west of Spencer's inn. Steamers began to stop at this new place. Sylvan Junction station served as a debarkation point for railroad-traveling tourists. Picnic groves were built in the forest. Lindley's Boat Livery catered to the angler. Many cottagers built personal summer spas. Despite the activity, Spencer's town was billed more as a "retreat" than a resort. An advertisement for the Algonquin echoed this image.

> Upstream you see the encottaged banks, the mingled yellow and green of willow fringe and hickory thicket along the shore, the quaint ferry above, the widesweeping, silent stream, so like that flood of Tennyson's, down which floated fair Elaine to the imploring Lancelot.
> Rounding the sunny side bend, the full life of this new river town bursts upon him (the traveler). The picturesque cottages hang upon the banks or look out brightly from the hickory copses along the stream. The river is alive with pleasure boats ... the scene is restful as well as active; there is diversion, quiet interest, healing for tired brains, in the liquid clamor of propellors, in all the 'quiet noise' about you.

SYLVAN AND VERONA BEACHES
THE "INLAND CONEY ISLAND"

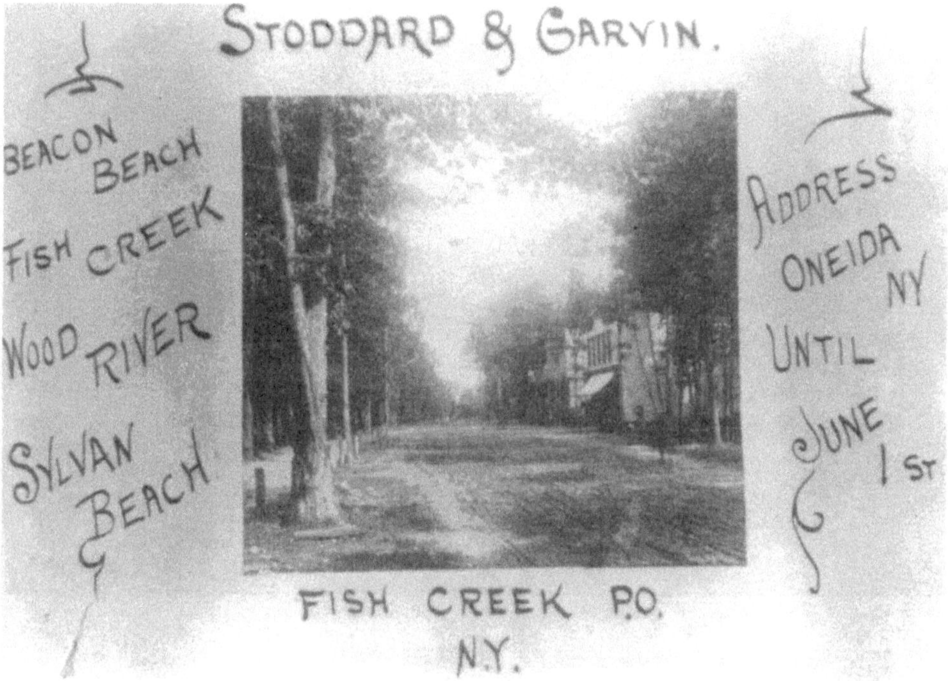

Oneida Historical Society

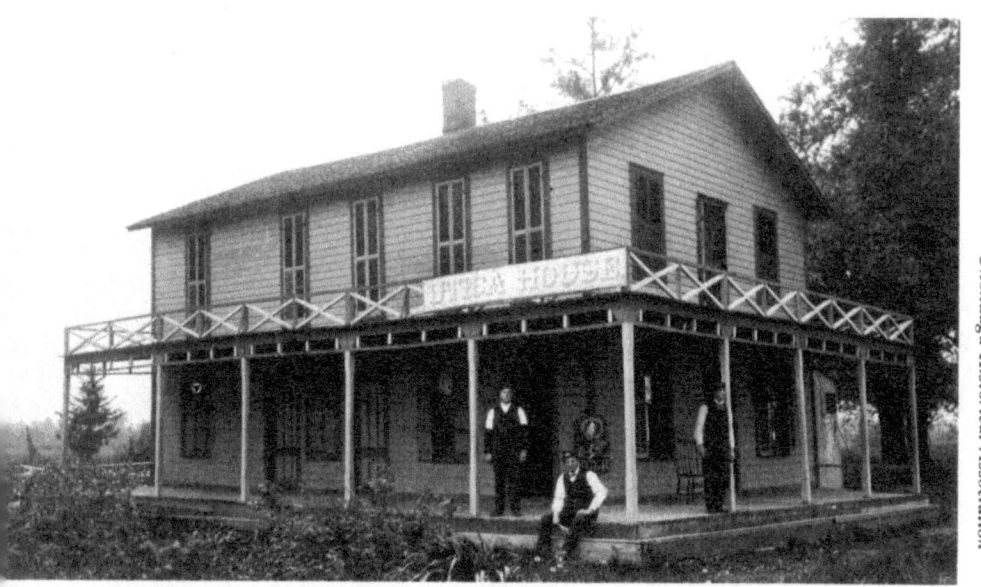

Several early names for Sylvan Beach are shown on this photo, taken from an advertisement for the Algonquin Hotel. Fish Creek, the post office reference, was the Beach area's first settlement. It was a tiny community but had a hotel - the Utica House.

Onondaga Historical Association

The Utica House and staff. Among the inn's regular customers were boatmen on the first Oneida Lake Canal, which connected the Erie Canal at Higginsville with Fish Creek.

BARGE CANAL from the N. Y. O. & W. R. R. Bridge, Sylvan Beach, N. Y.

The Barge Canal flowed under the Fish Creek hamlet bridge. A dredger, right, cleans silt from the canal bottom while two couples enjoy rowing on the waterway's placid surface.

Activity from the 1880's on a Sylvan Beach dock. The site of the British 1759 outpost known as the Royal Blockhouse was directly behind the small ferry. The white-bearded gentleman is Joseph Cottman, builder of the Beach's Cottman's Carousel.

Constructed by Stoddard and Garvin of Oneida in 1884, the Algonquin Hotel occupied a site where today's Canal View Restaurant stands. The rope-powered ferry was one of several that carried people across Wood River/Fish Creek in the pre-bridge days.

A waiter serves cooling drinks. A sport pauses from a game of billiards. Tourists summer on the Algonquin's veranda, 1885.

The pastoral 1880's - an oarsman glides his craft up Wood River, just east of Sylvan Beach.

In 1879 Lyman Spencer established the Forest Home, Sylvan's first resort hotel. It operated until the early 1980's, when fire destroyed the landmark.

The diverse attractions of the Forest Home and vicinity were depicted on this 1880's post card advertisment.

Two glass plate prints bring outstanding clarity to early Beach life. Byron Scoville's Leland Hotel (1905) was located on the site of the Algonquin. Construction of the village's second bridge (1906), a part of the Barge Canal project, is shown below.

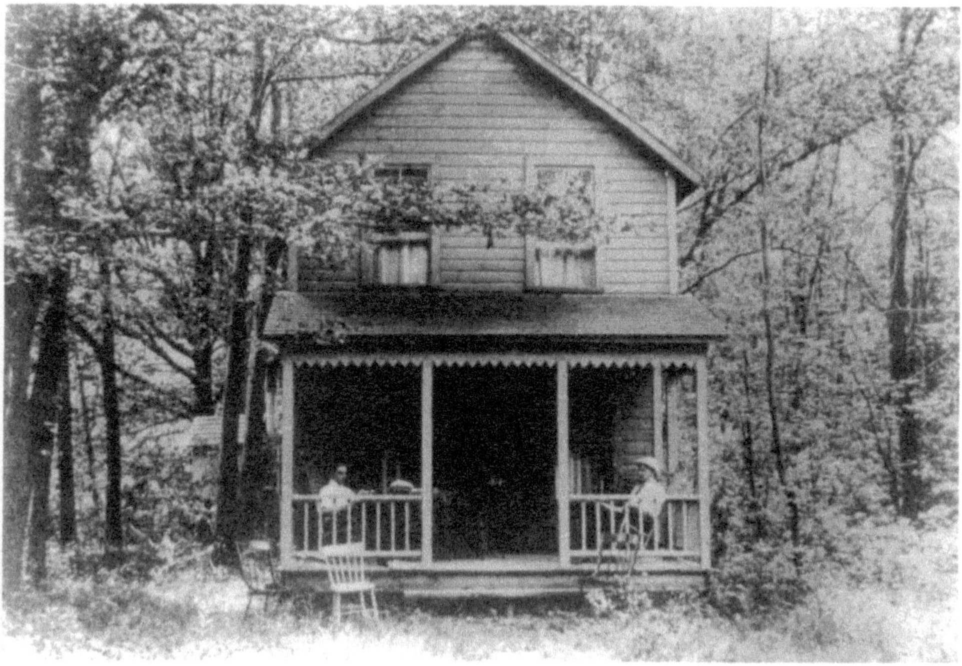

The sylvan "retreat" aura of the late 1800's. This cottage was typical of the plain, functional structures which developers built in the village's heyday.

This was Sylvan Beach's first bridge over Wood River/Fish Creek. The Barge Canal straightened this meandering waterway and provided control for spring floods, which often inundated the resort.

"Five Miles of the Best Bathing Beach in the World!" - so advertisements boasted Sylvan Beach. Here we view that sandy expanse, the Rowe Brothers' Bath House and the "toboggan slide."

A close-up vista of the slide and its patrons. The adventuresome, for five cents, could board a sled and speed down the slide into Oneida's choppy waters.

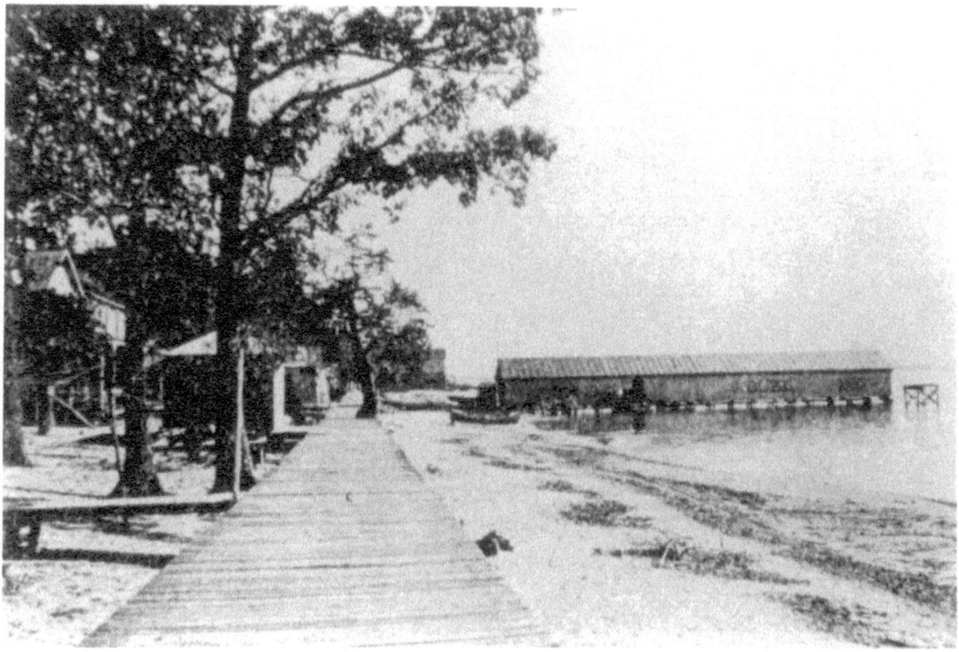

Ruth Weimer

Sylvan Beach was no Atlantic City, but it had a boardwalk. This promenade stretched from the Barge Canal to approximately 16th Avenue.

Brewerton Historical Society

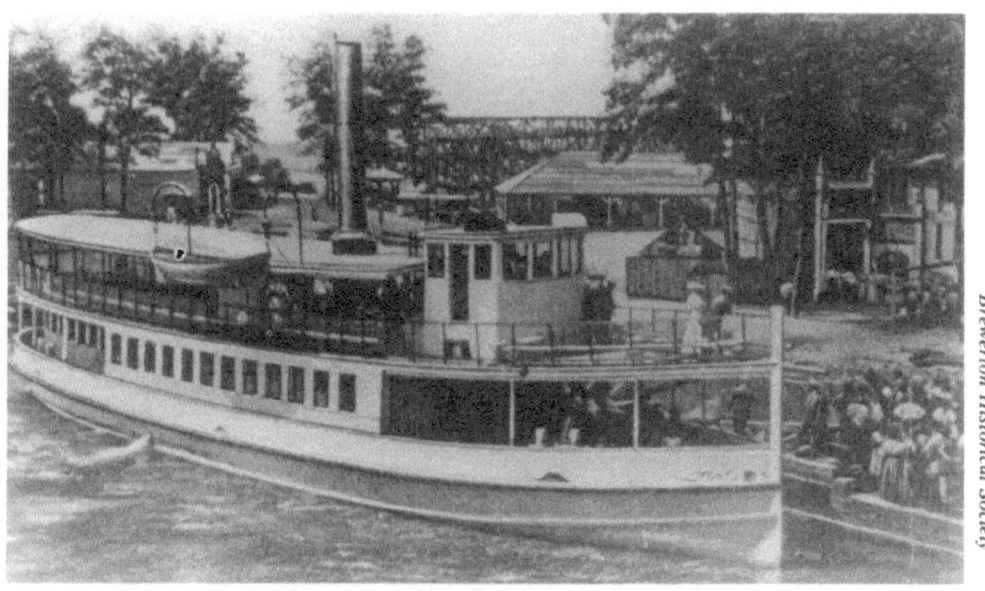

Clifford Beebe's Sagamore *awaits its touristy cargo along the Beach's canal front. This large steamboat called on all major Oneida Lake ports.*

In the golden Cavana years, Sylvan Beach was often crowded - up to fifty thousand visitors per day. Both beach and boardwalk teemed with humanity.

During the Cavana Era, Sylvan Beach boasted two amusement areas, Carnival Park and Luna Park. This small roller coaster of the former midway was a popular attraction.

Dr. Martin Cavana's "sanitarium and private hospital for nurses" was located at the corner of 13th and Park Avenues. Cavana, Sylvan Beach's leader during its golden era, persuaded Louis Chesebrough to build the Saint Charles.

A composite post card depicting Sylvan Beach's lake front activity was created by Martin Cavana, who sits on the sea wall in the lower right corner, comtemplating the scene.

The Saint Charles Hotel was the Beach's grandest establishment. Built by Louis Chesebrough of Vaseline fame, the hotel catered to patrician tastes, holding "balls" and providing carriage service. Above is an architect's plan for the inn while the lower shot shows the Saint Charles in reality. The hotel was where the Sylvan Sands Restaurant is now located.

"People" post cards were favorite souvenirs of Oneida Lake resorts around the turn of the century.

Founded by Cleveland's Father John B. Mertens in 1899, Saint Mary's of the Lake was a quaint, gothic revival church. This edifice was replaced in 1965 by a modern brick structure in Verona Beach.

Upstate fishermen smile when they recall the Beach's old fishing "pier." Built as a canal harbor breakwater, the pier gave anglers access to fantastic fishing. Safety concerns prompted its closing in the 1960's, but a united Oneida Lake Association-Sylvan Beach Village Board effort is now promoting reconstruction.

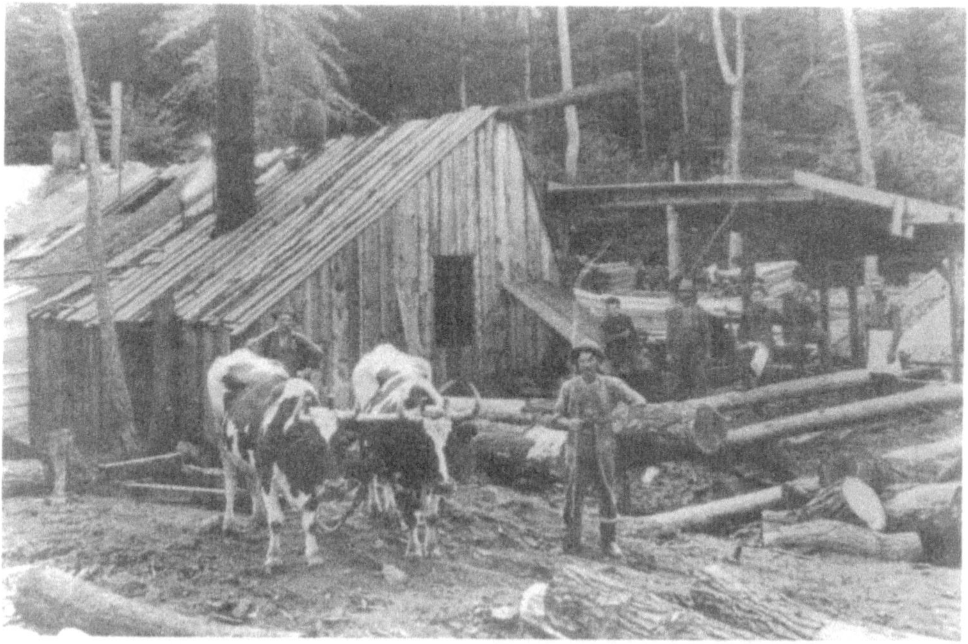

Logging provided a living, albeit a hard one, for many early settlers. Clear-cutting practices decimated much of the area's forests in the 19th century, though much restoration has occurred since then. Pictured here is a logging camp near Verona Beach, 1908.

Connecting with the New York Central at Canastota, the Lehigh Valley Railroad transported vacationers to its Verona Beach station.

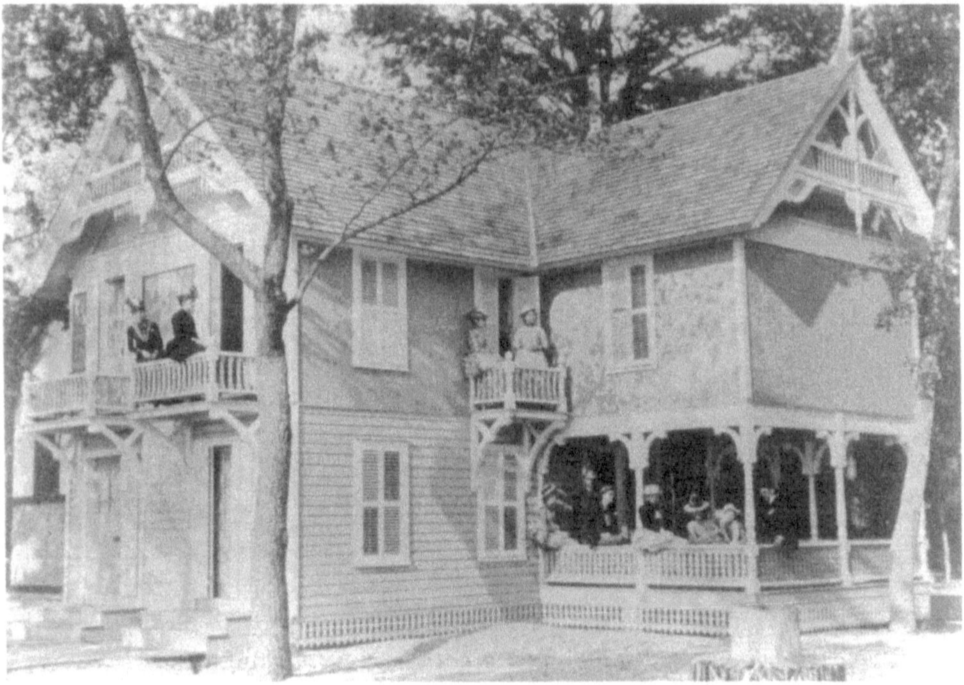

Many of the Beach area's first cottages were of the "gingerbread" gothic revival style. This particular camp was near the lakefront at Verona Beach.

In the Beach's heyday, hundreds of thousands experienced this card's sentiments.

Sylvan Beach experienced its "golden age" in the period from 1891 through the early 1920's. This was the "Cavana Era" at the Beach, so named for Dr. Martin Cavana, the village's leader and tireless community promoter. Cavana established a private hospital-nursing school on Park Avenue that served patients from throughout the northeast. Cavana encouraged his friend Louis Chesebrough, owner of the Vaseline Company, to build the Hotel Saint Charles in 1899. This upper-crust inn lent a patrician air to the otherwise plebian Sylvan Beach. Cavana promoted his village through the newspapers, by encouraging business to locate at the Beach, and by organizing local merchants to partially fund train tickets for "picnics," mass gatherings of factory laborers, farm workers, and such for a day of rampaging fun at the "Inland Coney Island." The annual hop growers' picnic drew in excess of 20,000 tourists. On peak summer days, scores of Ontario and Western cars emptied their eager human cargo at Railroad Avenue station. The "Ever Glorious Fourth" lived up to its billing at Cavana's Sylvan Beach. The doctor's name became synonymous with his village and its success.

From the Cavana Era to 1971, Sylvan Beach's economic fortunes resembled an American business cycle curve, with periods of prosperity and recovery alternating with those of recession and depression. The late 1920's and early '30's were tough years as passenger trains were replaced by the auto, giving tourists mobility and reducing the village's exclusive position as the most convenient Central New York resort. Many Beach hotels faded during this time. The Great Depression, of course, subtracted leisure funds from personal incomes and resorts consequently suffered. An upturn occurred in the late '30's and '40's as Russell's Hotel and Danceland, home of the "Big Bands," attracted great crowds. Sinatra, Ellington, the Dorseys and Glenn Miller charmed packed houses at Russell's. For the Dorsey concert on August 9, 1939, cars were backed up from the Beach to the intersection of Routes 13 and 31, three miles south.

America's post-war boom made the late 1940's and the 1950's prosperous Beach years. Thousands came to tour Emory Sauve's and Francis Money's Midway. Parking facilities were expanded and business grew. The 1960's, however, witnessed a great downturn in village fortune. Crowds went elsewhere, a myth that Oneida Lake was severely polluted cast a damaging stigma, and building deterioration scarred the once neat Beach facade. The situation became so critical that the *Utica Observer-Dispatch,* on August 9, 1970, ran a front page article entitled, "Sylvan Beach - A Last Resort." This article, a culmination of the preceding decade's events spurred Sylvan Beach citizens to action. A committee to incorporate the village organized and succeeded, in March of 1971, in winning a public referendum. Sylvan Beach became a separate political entity.

While incorporation has received criticism, objective eyes are forced to conclude that it has brought tremendous positive change to Sylvan Beach. The "Last Resort" of 1971 is now a mirror of its Cavana years. Millions of dollars have been invested in new Beach businesses such as Captain John's, the Canal View Restaurant, the Midway Mall, Harpoon Eddie's, Ada MacGee's, and Yesterday's Royal. The Village Board has succeeded in obtaining hundreds of thousands of federal EDA urban renewal dollars that financed a commodious bath house, a lake-front park, a village park bandstand, brick sidewalks and simulated gaslights. The Board formulated financing and construction of the East Oneida Lake Sewer District, with treatment facilities just north of the village. Today, the Oneida Lake East Shore Merchants Association (OLESMA) engages in successful "Cavanaesque" promotional plans. Sylvan Beach ads fill newspaper pages, occupy television and radio spots, and each summer weekend a crowd-attracting event is brought to the village park. The Association even sponsors "tram" service and, with the village board, is spearheading a drive to rebuild the Beach's fishing pier. Today's Sylvan Beach projects a healthy optimism.

WOOD CREEK AND RIVER

Old maps label the stream formed by the joining of Fish and Wood Creeks as "Wood River." This river meandered west from its source a distance of approximately one mile and flowed into Oneida at Sylvan Beach. When the Barge Canal was excavated, Wood River received a re-channelizing and its sweeping bends became "backsets" as the river's current was directed through the canal's straight course. Three of these backsets remain and each is named. On the canal's south side, by Sylvan Beach's Route 13 bridge, is Cottman's Backset, named for William Cottman, a Beach businessman who owned the backset's marina and built the large white home that still stands at the harbor's mouth.

Cottman operated Sylvan Beach's noted "Cottman's Carousel," a merry-go-round that featured hand-carved horses. East of Cottman's is Holmes' Backset, named for James Holmes, who constructed that harbor's marina. On the canal's north side, across from Cottman's, is a backset referred to as Skinner's Harbour, named for Harold Skinner, who started a large marina-mobile home complex on the property.

Wood Creek, a small stream whose source is near Rome, has played an important role in upstate history, being an integral part of the great colonial trade and travel route through New York. Travelers bound for Oswego from Albany would journey to Schenectady and voyage up the Mohawk to Rome, a trip requiring several portages. At Rome, a mile-long portage would be made from the Mohawk to Wood Creek. The Wood Creek-Mohawk River portage was known to colonials as the "Carry," "Carrying Place," and sometimes the "Great Carry." Upon reaching Wood Creek the traveler would, high water permitting, canoe downstream to Oneida Lake, cross the lake (usually following the more sheltered North Shore), enter the lake's Oneida River outlet, sail down the Oneida to Three Rivers' Point, embark into the Oswego River and take the latter waterway to Oswego. This journey was arduous, but it was the most convenient route across upstate until the canal and turnpike era.

Wood Creek, according to legend, received its name during the French and Indian Wars. The French captured Oswego in August of 1756. At that time the British General Daniel Webb was marching to the fort's aid and, upon reaching the Carrying Place, learned of the French victory. Before retreating down the Mohawk, Webb directed his men to drop trees into Wood Creek. When the French advanced, they were compelled to clear the stream of obstructions and, so the story goes, gave the creek the title "Riviere du Chicot" - River of Stumps.

Several attempts have been made to improve navigational qualities of Wood Creek and the Carrying Place. Colonials constructed sluice dams on the creek's small feeder streams and released water to propel grounded vessels downstream. In 1796, the Western Inland Navigation Company built a small canal across the Carry, but the waterway did not prosper. Most people chose to portage their belongings alongside the canal. Wood Creek's importance as a thoroughfare amounted to nil after the Erie Canal's opening in 1825.

As in the case of Wood River, the Barge Canal de-channelized much of Wood Creek. The streams' backsets and oxbow lakes border Verona Township's country roads. From Rome, downstream, the creek has current and, above its guard gate-waterfall west of Barge Canal Lock 22, it bears resemblance to the past. Here the stream flows amidst a dense forest. Sunlight filters through the high canopy of leaves. Many trees have toppled into the water. In spring and summer the air is impregnated with the fragrance of rich vegetation. Avian calls enhance the image. One can imagine an Iroquois canoe or French batteaux in this primeval setting.

FISH CREEK AND FISH CREEK REEF

This stream, largest of Oneida's tributaries, originates deep in the Tug Hill Plateau. Until it reaches Blossvale, the creek is primarily trout water and fine water it is. A steep bed gradient produces in Fish Creek a seemingly endless series of rapids, waterfalls and plunge pools (endless, that is, if one tries to wade the creek). Highlighting this stretch are gorge-like banks, formed over centuries as the creek eroded its bedrock base. From Blossvale south to its Barge Canal mouth, the creek takes on a tamer personality, meandering through cornfields and haylots, winding its way to Oneida. Indeed, this stretch inspired the Oneida Indians to call Fish Creek "Ta-ga-soke," meaning "forked like a spear."

Fish Creek was named for the abundant fish life that thrives within it. Today, a variety of warm and cold water species inhabit the stream. In spring, Oneida's walleyes and perch make a significant spawning migration up the creek. It is not uncommon to find fishermen lined elbow-to-elbow along the stream on opening day of pike season. In summer, anglers take numerous walleyes, bass, bullheads, and panfish from the stream. Trout from the headwaters are often transported downstream at spring flooding, providing a bonus for lower creek anglers.

Up to the early 1800's, landlocked Atlantic Salmon came each year to Fish Creek. These salmon, some of which surpassed thirty pounds in weight, lived in Lake Ontario and migrated, up the Oswego and Oneida Rivers, through Oneida Lake, and up Fish Creek to spawn. The fish were an important food staple for the Oneida Indians who would trap them in Fish Creek, using brush weir dams. After the salmon were corralled, the Oneidas entered the water, clubbing and spearing fish en masse. Countless salmon were harvested in this manner; many were consumed immediately and the rest were dried and salted for future use. One turn of the century historian described the affair as being the "piscatorial picnic of the Oneidas." In the early 1800's, dams were constructed on the Oswego and Oneida Rivers. These barriers stopped the migration, effectively eliminating Oneida's salmon run.

BARGE CANAL

This cross-state waterway was approved by New York's electorate in 1903 and opened in 1918. Named for the cargo-carrying barges that use it, the Barge Canal once saw heavy commercial traffic. In the '20s and '30s it was common to see twenty-five barges a day passing through Sylvan Beach harbor. Today, commercial barge traffic is minimal and the canal serves primarily as a pleasure boat course.

The Barge Canal brought tremendous benefit to Oneida Lake. Flooding on the Oneida River and on Wood River-Fish Creek is largely controlled by the canal's Caughdenoy Dam gates. Previously, spring rains often inundated large sections of Sylvan Beach and Brewerton. The canal also opened Oneida Lake to pleasure boat navigation from afar. Via the Canal, the lake is accessible to the Great Lakes and the Atlantic Coast and vessels from Canada, Delaware, Michigan and Illinois can often be viewed on the lake during a pleasant summer's day. These boats sometimes dock at Sylvan Beach and Brewerton, enriching those village's economies.

VERONA BEACH AND FISH CREEK HAMLET

As in the case of Verona township, this place was named for the city of Verona, Italy. A long, wide sandy beach once graced Oneida's shore here. Except at low water and in the Verona Beach State Park, most of the sand is now submerged.

Verona Beach's first settler was Asahel Jackson, a Yankee who emigrated there from Berkshire County, Massachusetts, in May of 1796. Jackson and his family settled near the ruins of the Royal Blockhouse, a British frontier outpost constructed in 1758. This small fort was located on the south side of Wood River near that stream's mouth. Jackson established a public house for the accommodation of the many travelers who journeyed through the water highway at his doorstep. DeWitt Clinton once stayed at the Jackson Tavern. Upon Jackson's death, his wife assumed ownership of the enterprise. Mrs. Jackson was reported to be a very competent innkeeper and, above all, a tough frontierswoman. Christian Schultz, a German sampling America's wilderness (1807-08), met the lady and recorded his impressions:

> There is a tolerably good tavern kept at this place by a Mrs. J. . . . and her sister, a young woman who, you may be assured, displays no ordinary degree of courage in dealing out whiskey to thirty or forty Indians who generally rendezvous at this place, especially as there is no other white settler within sight or call.

The first major settlement at Verona Beach occurred during the 1840's. This took place not in Verona Beach proper but at what is now known as the hamlet of Fish Creek, one mile east of today's Route 13, on Oneida Street. Fish Creek was often referred to as "Sylvan Junction," it being the spot where the Ontario and Western and the Lehigh Valley Railroads met and crossed Wood River. At the river bridge was the Sylvan Junction Station, a hotel called the Utica House, a picnic grove, and houses belonging to the Roberts family, pioneering settlers. Before the Ontario and Western constructed its "loop" line into Sylvan Beach (1886), steamboats from the Beach would meet tourists at the Sylvan Junction Bridge. Fish Creek hamlet itself had one hotel, first called the Sylvan House and later the Hamilton House. The hamlet also had a post office, a general store, and several homes.

James D. Spencer and his family arrived at Fish Creek in the 1840's. Spencer and his four sons, Reuben, Houghton, Lyman, and Bruce Lamott, purchased large tracts of land, cleared the timber, built fine homes and had their holdings surveyed by Peletia Leete (re: Dutchman's Isle). Spencer and sons acquired hundreds of acres on each side of Wood River, promoted the land's sale, and are credited with marketing the first cottage lots in Verona and Sylvan Beach. Indeed, Spencer is considered to be the founder of Sylvan Beach and it was largely through his family's efforts that the village first grew.

Verona Beach was directly served by the Lehigh Valley Railroad, originally called the Elmira, Cortland and Northern Railroad. The line ran through this community on its route to Sylvan Junction. In 1888, the first bridge linking Sylvan and Verona Beach was built. Prior to that year, Sylvan Beach hotels such as the Algonquin and the Forest Home sponsored ferries to carry patrons across Wood River.

Verona Beach has boasted several hotels in addition to those already mentioned in connection with Fish Creek hamlet. Mabel Myer, James D. Spencer's great-granddaughter, wrote a short Verona Beach-Fish Creek history in 1967 and discussed these hostelries:

> There was a hotel known as the Stevens House on the west side of the highway, just before crossing the bridge into Sylvan Beach. It was there at the time the ferry was in operation. It outgrew its usefulness as a hotel and burned in 1922. A new building was erected on the site and today is known as the Verona Beach Hotel.
>
> I have a post card view of the first bridge with the Riverside Hotel on the Verona Beach side. It was close to the river where a gas station for boats is located today (by the Verona Beach side of today's Route 13 bridge).
>
> Another hotel known as Brietensteins was located up the lake front toward Oneida Creek. This was a thriving and lively resort hotel.

Several other notable events belong to Verona Beach's history. When the Barge Canal was finished, New York State constructed a lighthouse at the lake front on the Verona Beach side of the canal. This beacon is both a landmark and a useful aid to Oneida Lake navigation. For years, the Sylvan-Verona Beach school occupied a small structure on Oneida Street. In 1957, a new building for the Sylvan-Verona Beach Common School District took form at Verona Beach. The district serves elementary students. New York State replaced the narrow, cast iron Sylvan-Verona Beach bridge with a spacious span in 1960. And in 1965 Saint Mary's Roman Catholic Church, a Sylvan Beach landmark since its founding in 1899 by Father J. B. Mertens, was razed and a new edifice built at Verona Beach.

BLYTHBOURNE

This is a defunct place name that was given to a railroad stop on the Lehigh Valley Railroad between Upper South Bay and Sylvan Beach. Marshall Hope, former historian of Oneida City and a columnist for the *Oneida Dispatch*, wrote of Blythbourne in May of 1963. Hope discovered the place name on a 1906 railroad map and, upon researching it, found that cottage owners in the area of the Verona Beach State Park used the station frequently. Several of Hope's sources related that Blythbourne "was the name of a lake front camp whose owner provided the small station building used at the stop." The station had seasonal importance,' discussed by Hope:

> Canastota people who traveled on the Lehigh Railroad to Sylvan Beach probably are more familiar with Blythbourne than Oneida people are. The state road from South Bay to Sylvan Beach was not built until the 1920's. Prior to that time it was necessary to drive along the sandy beach front from Oneida Creek bridge at Willow Grove along the lake shore to within a short distance of the canal bridge between Verona Beach and Sylvan Beach.
>
> In the spring when the lake water level was high the beach could not be used, and it was then necessary for Canastota people to drive to State Bridge then into the Beach over the Jug Point Road, as Oneida people did. Under these circumstances, it was almost necessary for Canastota people to ride through Blythbourne to get to Sylvan Beach.

Taking the Lehigh Valley through Blythbourne would have saved Canastota motorists time and aggravation. Roads were poor, ruts abounded, and the train offered a smoother, more sheltered way of travel.

BLACK CREEK

This stream, which drains the Verona Beach State Park marsh, flows into Oneida Creek just east of its Route 13 bridge. The stream merits the name "black" because of its dark waters, a condition rendered by the mineral content of the soil through which it flows. Two additional Black Creeks are lake tributaries, one at Maple Bay and the other at Cleveland.

ONEIDA CREEK AND ONEIDA CREEK BAR

This important lake tributary derives its name from the Oneida Indians, one of the six nations of the Iroquois Confederacy. The Oneida tribe settled throughout this stream's valley, as evidenced from archaeological excavations and colonial journals. For these native Americans, this creek was an essential supplier of fish and drinking water; the stream's mouth at Willow Grove to the Route 31 bridge was fine angling territory and the Oneidas, throughout history, established several fishing camps along this stretch. Elkanah Watson, in the 1790's, wrote of sending a member of his expedition to the Oneida Creek mouth to obtain fish from the Indians. The stream, which traverses through agricultural land for much of its length, collects a significant nutrient supply and thus contributes to Oneida Lake's fertility and productivity.

CONTEMPORARY ONEIDA LAKE SCENES

Sunrise over the eastern shore, as viewed from Lewis Point.

The lake in its full fury, raging wildly during a spring storm.

The Oneida Lake Congregational Church, built east of Lakeport circa 1830, is a fine variation of the Greek Revival style.

"Orchard Cottage," on Route 31 east of Lakeport, was designed like an English country home and was once the hub of John Chapman's estate, (re: Chapman's Point).

Italianate revival architecture is evidenced in this Lakeport building, formerly the home of Elmer Johnson, (re: Johnson's Bar).

Night life excitement at the Sylvan Beach Midway.

Beach front relaxation on a mellow summer's day.

The tomb of George Marsden, an aide to General George Washington during the American Revolution, is in an extreme state of disrepair. The grave is located in a small cemetery on Route 49, west of North Bay.

A replica of the Oliver Stevens' Blockhouse houses the Brewerton Historical Society's museum.

The site of Fort Brewerton, a British French and Indian War fortification, is exceptionally well maintained.

Sailboats at rest in the harbor of Oneida Lake Marina, awaiting . . .

. . . the time for a cruise on the lake's broad, often windy, surface.

My grandfather, Stanley Osterhout, holding an Oneida Lake angler's pride - a five-pound walleyed pike.

The Oneida Hatchery at Constantia annually rears millions of walleye fry (young) for stocking throughout New York State.

Buoys mark the navigational channel of the lake. This one, 113, notes Messenger's Shoal (sometimes called Blind Island), a large reef in the lake's east end.

Constructed on land donated by the Scriba family, Constantia's Trinity Episcopal Church retains the rustic quality of its frontier birth.

Morning sunlight illuminates Trinity's interior.

The lake's two largest islands are Dunham's, on the left, and Frenchman's. New York State maintains a lighthouse on the latter isle.

Route 81 rumbles across the lake at the Oneida River outlet. In the distance, on the right, is Frenchman's Island.

Dutchman's Island, viewed from Cornell University's research station grounds at Shackelton Point.

Wantry Island, south of Constantia, is the summer home to a large colony of cormorants and gulls. The isle is popular with autumn's waterfowl hunters.

The Alexander Brown estate "Xandria," at Shackelton Point, was donated to Cornell University and transformed into a biology research center. Invaluable studies of Oneida Lake's environment have been conducted at this facility.

Constantia has more preserved historic buildings than any other lake community. This is the Scriba Masonic Lodge, Route 49.

"Kempwyk," home to Francis Adrian Van Der Kemp, is located on Route 49, west of Cleveland. Van Der Kemp served as an advisor to Governor DeWitt Clinton and, in the 1790's, wrote extensively of the Oneida Lake area's potential.

Saint Mary's Roman Catholic Church, Cleveland, maintains this picturesque shrine.

Architect Richard Upjohn designed Saint James Episcopal Church, Cleveland. This beautiful gothic revival sanctuary is currently undergoing restoration.

Productive wetlands such as this one on Hamilton Brown Road, Town of Sullivan, are essential to the lake's environment but . . .

. . . development, particularly around the lake's western end, threatens to engulf some of these rich areas. The creek in this lower photo is a tributary of Big Bay, near Brewerton.

A movement is now underway to restore the delapidated Sylvan Beach fishing pier.

One major cause of the pier's erosion is the force of Oneida's ice at spring break-up. This photo was taken along Sylvan Beach's lakefront park.

Boats await their rental customers at the venerable App's harbor, Cleveland. Since this picture was taken, the facility has been considerably refurbished.

It is still possible to enjoy cropland vistas along the lake's developed shore. This field is located just west of Lakeport.

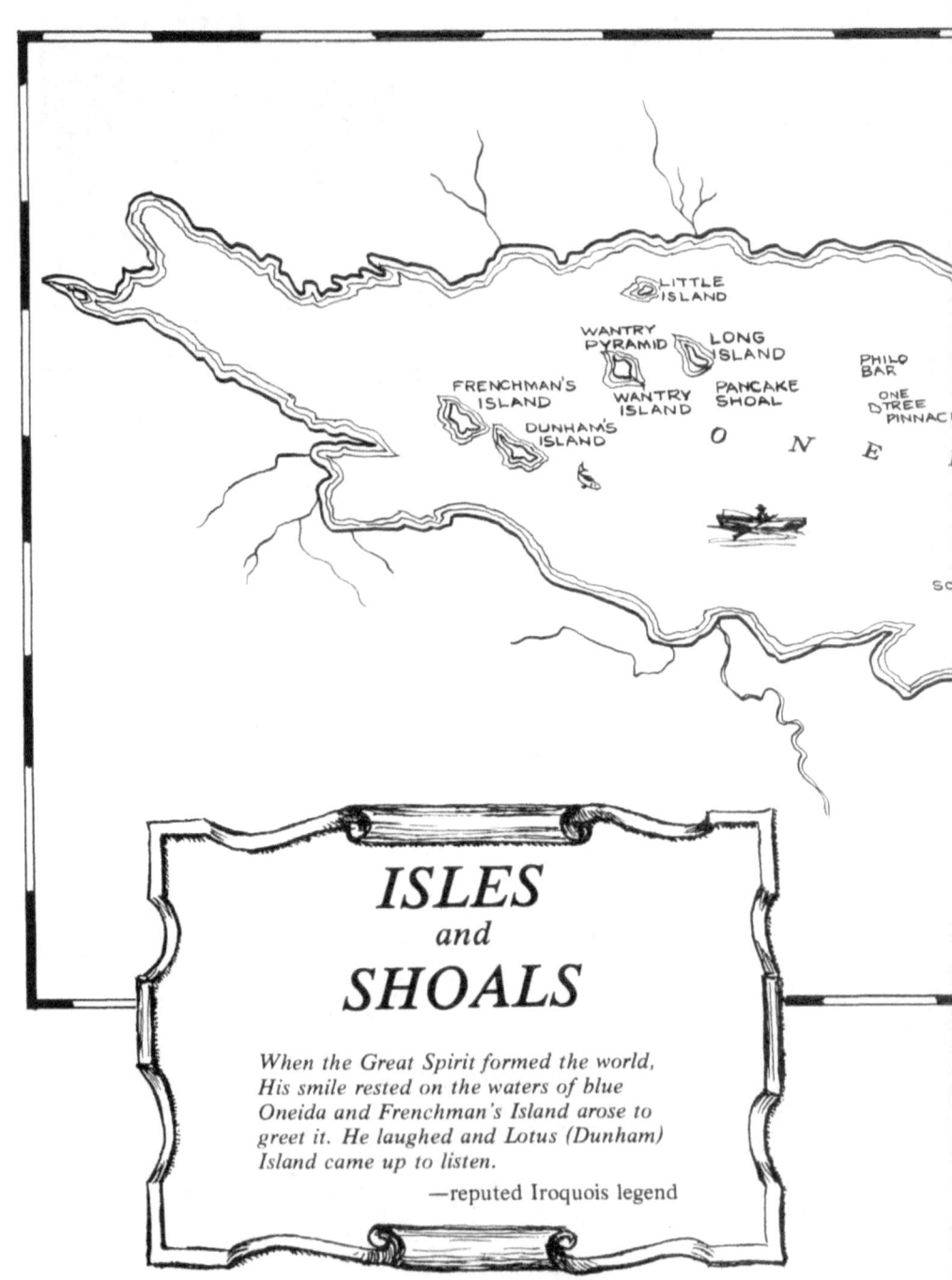

ISLES and SHOALS

When the Great Spirit formed the world, His smile rested on the waters of blue Oneida and Frenchman's Island arose to greet it. He laughed and Lotus (Dunham) Island came up to listen.

—reputed Iroquois legend

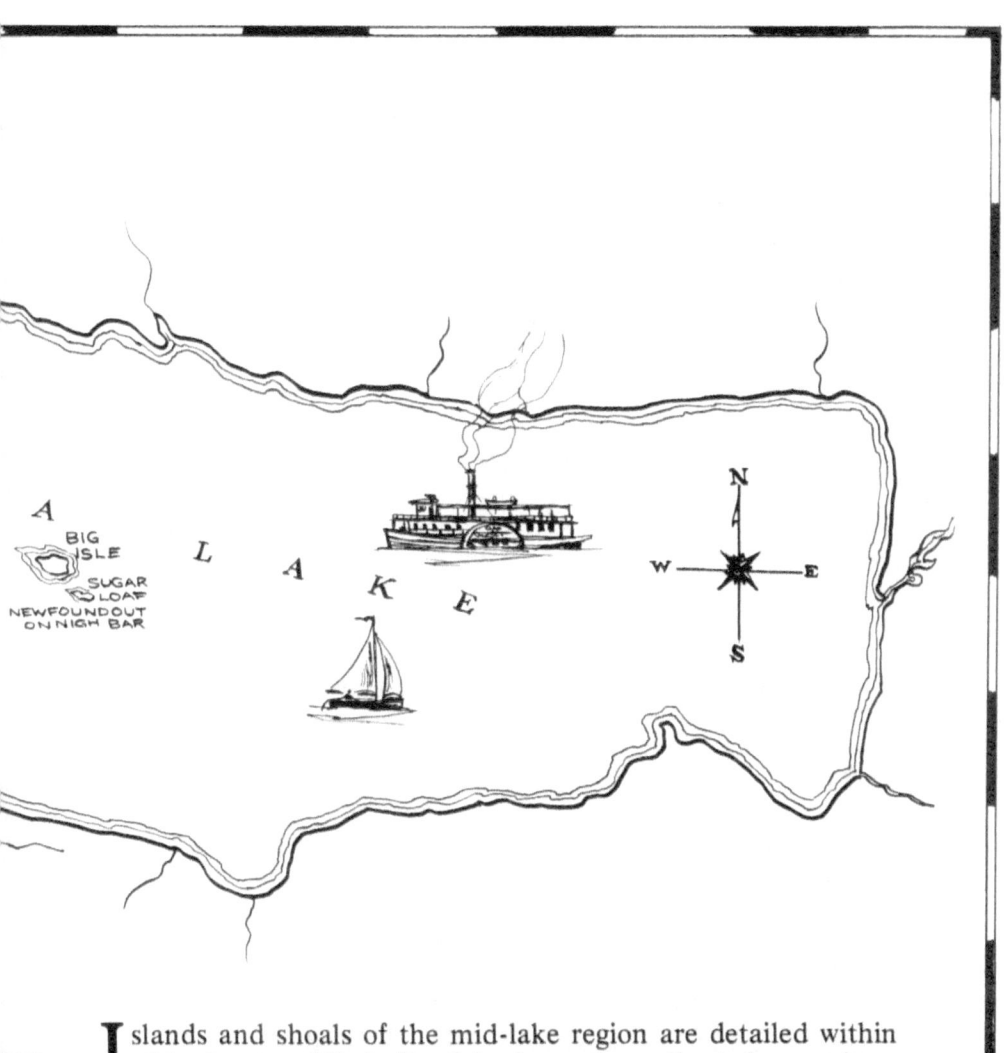

Islands and shoals of the mid-lake region are detailed within this chapter. All similar lake formations situated near shore are discussed in the chapter relating to the county to which they are in closest proximity. In addition, if a mid-lake isle or shoal bears the same root place name as a shore locale, it is included in that locale's section. For example, Shackelton Shoals is listed with Shackelton Point in the Madison County chapter and Fish Creek Reef with Fish Creek in the Oneida County section.

210   *Oneida Lake*

Subject arrangement for this chapter reads:

Frenchman's Island	Philo Bar
Dunham's Island	Pindle Stone Pile
Wantry Island	Schoolhouse Bar
and Pyramid	Newfoundout on
One Tree Pinnacle	Nigh Bay
Long Island	Sugar Loaf
Little Island	Big Isle
Pancake Shoal	

FRENCHMAN'S ISLAND

Romance, intrigue, deception and development - all these elements form integral parts of the Frenchman's Island saga. This isle has inspired the imagination more than any other Oneida Lake site. Writers have composed flowery tales of the Frenchman, his wife and their "undying love." Other authors have marveled at the island's mysteries, the Frenchman's identity, and his mysterious past. Unabashed lies about the island's history have gushed forth from some historians' pens, stretching even the limits of historical "faction." Objective writers have documented the island's post-Frenchman history, citing details of its resort story - the names of developers, hotel construction dates, and accounts of those who experienced the island in its vacation heyday.

Several names have applied to Frenchman's Island. Early lake boatmen called the isle "Hoger Bust," a Dutch term meaning "high breast." In 1783, Captain Alexander Thompson of the Continental Army journeyed through Oneida Lake on his way from Fort Rensselaer to Fort Oswego. Thompson's purpose was to inform the British commander at the latter fort that an armistice had been signed, ending the American Revolution. The Captain kept a journal of his travels and noted the point when he sailed past the "Six Mile Islands, as the two largest islands, lying side by side, are called." Four years prior to Thompson's trek, Colonel Goose Van Schaick and his troops camped overnight at Frenchman's Island. In his writing, Van Schaick referred to the island as "Seven Mile Island." Each officer's name for Frenchman's originates from his estimation of the distance between the isle and Fort Brewerton on the lake's western extremity. A further name for Frenchman's was "DeZeng's Isle," a title found on a 1790 lake map. The Baron DeZeng was a friend of the north shore's Francis Adrian Van Der Kemp and George Scriba.

Our Frenchman was a man named DesVatines. In France, he was reputed to have belonged to the aristocracy. The Duke de La Rochefaucault Liancourt, on his American tour, met the Frenchman after he had moved from the island to Rotterdam (Constantia) and reported that the man claimed that "he possessed a viscount's estate in the neighborhood of Lisle." Assuming that this is accurate, the French Revolution might have forced DesVatines to flee to America. The exile's identity has best been described in T. Wood Clarke's book, *Emigres in the Wilderness*. Clarke wrote:

> Concerning this early settler of what is still known as Frenchman's Island in Oneida Lake, there are many romantic traditions, most of them probably untrue. M. Devatines was certainly a French gentleman of culture and learning. One rumor had it that he was an aristocrat who had escaped the Reign of Terror. Another is that he was a noble who had eloped with a nun. He himself said he was a seigneur from near Lisle who, having lost most of his fortune, had come to America in the hope of regaining it. He had brought with him a charming young wife and two small children. After wandering aimlessly for some months and squandering most of his small capital in foolish land speculation, he was advised by the Chevalier de Goyen to go to an island in Oneida Lake. He sold his furniture, but not his library, and set out. Shortly after, he turned up at Oneida Lake, landed on his isolated island, unpacked his family silver and his truly fine library and settled down as a farmer.

DesVatines came to Frenchman's in 1791 and resided there until 1793. In 1792, DesVatines' wife gave birth to their daughter, Camille, the first white child born in Oswego County. DesVatines was merely a squatter and he left the island, going to Rotterdam after having been informed that New York State had sold his isle to John and Nicholas Roosevelt (re: Constantia, Oswego County chapter). In Rotterdam, Adam Mappa gave DesVatines a farm. Rochefaucault reported that the Frenchman had the "reputation of being a very skillful gardener." He disliked Americans, however, thinking most to be "extremely dull and melancholy." Rochefaucault's DesVatines was an unhappy individual and Madame DesVatines was "as little pleased with America as her husband, especially the environs of Lake Oneida."

Writers swayed by the romantic tradition have expounded with vigor on the Frenchman's saga. Such authors may have been influenced by accounts such as Francis Adrian Van Der Kemp's description of the isle:

> This island might in ancient days have been the happy seat of a goddess, in the middle age that of a magician, or a fairy's residence in the times of chivalry. Proceeding on one after another through the stately trees, through which we perceived yet the last glances of the setting sun, we were at once, after a few yards, surprised with an enchanting view, of which it is not in my power to give you an adequate description. All that the poets did sing of the gardens of Alurions, all the scenery of those of Arneida, so highly decorated by Virgil and Aristo, could scarce have been made upon me, who was captivated unaware and bewildered, a more deep impression than this spectacle of nature. We did see here a luxuriant soil in its virgin bloom, we did see industry crowned with blessing, we did see here what great things a frail man can perform if he is willing. It seemed a paradise which happiness had chosen for her residence.

Had DesVatines read this, his reaction might have proved interesting. Other writers characterized the Frenchman as being persecuted by government, rejected by a family displeased with his marriage, yet retaining most traits of nobility. DesVatines has been named the "Count Saint Hillary" and the "Count Whitien de Wardenou." His friends were reputed to include Robert Livingston and Robert Fulton. The list of romantic speculation, often stated as "fact," is lengthy. Were it not for competent historians like T. Wood Clarke, who set the record straight, the DesVatines legend might have been expanded to make our Frenchman half-brother to the decapitated Louis XVI!

Frenchman's Island remained under state control until 1835 when New York granted it to Christopher Lansing. In 1836, Lansing sold the isle to Leonard Hoadley for $1,000. Hoadley did nothing with Frenchman's for fifteen years but, in 1851, in partnership with his brother-in-law Larmon Dunham, he built the "Sylvan House," a two-story frame hotel on the island's southwest corner. Oneida Lake sportsmen's resorts were becoming popular then and the hotel was constructed to profit from this trade. An advertisement for the Sylvan House read:

> If you seek a fashionable resort, do not go to these Islands. If you need rest, healthful recreation, pure air, water and milk, a liberal table of wholesome food, and an appetite to enjoy it - in short, if you wish to 'laugh and grow fat,' here is the spot for you.

Rates were $1.50 per day and $7.00-$8.00 per week, typical for similar lake inns.

Ellen Birdseye Wheaton, of Boston, visited the Sylvan House in 1854. Her diary's entry for August 21 described the hotel and its isle:

> After breakfast we took 'The Glide' for the Island, and as the wind had freshened by this time, we had a delightful sail, only too short. Where we landed was the beginning of a broad gravel way, that sweeps round the border of the Island, up to the hotel, which is a plain, unpretending building, but very handsomely furnished and with a fine toned piano. The Island is nearly covered with a noble growth of forest trees, many of them very tall and large. Among them I noticed several magnificent oaks. There is a romantic legend of the first discovery and settlement of the Island that will doubtless add greatly to its charms in the eyes of many visitors.

Wheaton's "unpretending" comment is significant. Nineteenth century Oneida Lake hotels were not luxurious. They catered primarily to the middle-class and, in the case of sportsmen's inns, were often as rugged as their clientele. Only the Saint Charles Hotel at Sylvan Beach and the Sagamore Inn at Lower South Bay aspired to meet patrician tastes.

The Sylvan House had numerous owners during its history. In 1876 the hotel burned, but it was quickly rebuilt. A dancing pavilion, picnic groves, a large pier, a bowling alley, and a children's playground were, over the years, added to the resort. The hotel was last occupied from 1898 to 1901, under the management of "Cronk" Rogers. The inn was sold to the South Bay railroad in 1904, buildings were razed and salvaged material was taken to Lower South Bay to aid in hotel-cottage construction. Clifford Beebe's syndicate purchased Frenchman's in 1907 and constructed a new dock in 1910. Beebe relinquished ownership in 1915. Eventually New York State acquired the island and, as a part of the Barge Canal navigation system, built a lighthouse on the island's north side in 1917. The state still owns Frenchman's and maintains a public dock there. As a consequence of state ownership, the island is now heavily forested. Nothing remains of colonial military encampments, of the Frenchman's meager dwelling, or of a once thriving resort. Nothing, of course, save memories.

DUNHAM ISLAND

Dunham Island's first owner was Peter Smith, land baron of Peterboro, Madison County, who bought the island from New York State. Hazael Dunham, a hotel proprietor from Hamilton, New York, purchased the island from Peter Smith's son, the prominent abolitionist Gerrit Smith, on November 9, 1838. Like many early upstate immigrants, Dunham was a Yankee, hailing from Colchester, Connecticut. He kept the island until 1853, then sold it to Dean Hawley, William Willard and Patrick Lynch. Hazael Dunham's son, Captain Valentine Dunham (re: Lower South Bay, Valentine's Beach entries of Onondaga County chapter), purchased the island in 1859 and briefly resided there. Dunham moved to the mainland and established a lucrative boat rental-fishing guide business. Valentine's son, William, assisted with the family livery and later got involved in Lower South Bay's hotel industry, building the splendid Sagamore Inn in 1901. Valentine Dunham sold the island to James Cutler of Cambridgeport, Massachusetts, in 1868. From that point until today, the island has had many owners.

French's map of New York State, published in 1860, labels Dunham Island as "Harvey's Island." The nomenclature is in error and should have read "Hawley's Island," for former owner Dean Hawley. Another name applied to Dunham's was "Grape Island," used by the *Syracuse Post-Standard* on September 14, 1854. Sampling the island's tasty wild grapes highlighted early excursions. The *Madison County Times* of the summer of 1885 stated that the island's owner, then a Joseph Baker of New York City, had renamed it "Lotus Island." None of these names endured.

Tragedy haunted the Dunhams during their occupation of the island. During Hazael's tenure one of his children died. Asa Eastwood of Lower South Bay, in a diary entry dated November 25, 1846, wrote: "I went to the Island to the funeral of Dunham's child. Dreadful snow and blow. Fuller preached." In 1956 a man and his two young daughters were walking on the island when they discovered a plain gravestone with the name "Ambrosia" on it. The *Post-Standard* reported the mysterious find and Elet Milton wrote to the paper, explaining the stone. It marked the grave of Valentine Dunham's first wife who died on January 1, 1853. Ambrosia Dunham was twenty-seven years old.

WANTRY ISLAND AND PYRAMID

From 1792 until 1889, one tree stood on this island and it was appropriately called "One Tree Island." Around the latter year, Oneida's ice cap uprooted and carried off the tree. The United States' government lake survey in 1913, which mapped the lake for Barge Canal navigation, renamed the island "Wantry Island." The surveyors state that the "One Tree" name would confuse persons not familiar with the lake, thus creating a potential navigational hazard.

Wantry is a part of a group of Oneida Lake islands long famous for their waterfowl hunting. A Syracuse newspaper on August 24, 1872, referred to the islands as the "Duck Islands" and stated that passenger pigeon shooting there, "is said to be in its prime." Waterfowl hunters have built duck blinds on the islands for years.

Wantry Pyramid is a small shoal north of Wantry Island.

ONE TREE PINNACLE

One Tree Pinnacle, on the eastern end of the Duck Islands, once supported a tree. Francis Adrian Van Der Kemp described the isle as a "one tree adorned rock."

LONG ISLAND

This is a long, narrow island. It provides a summer home for gulls, terns, cormorants and other waterfowl.

LITTLE ISLAND

The Oneida Lake and River Steamboat Company maintained a lighthouse on this isle from 1850 to 1860, during which time the isle was called "Lighthouse Island." Some persons have referred to it as "Constantia Island," it being the nearest of the Duck Islands to that village. It was named Little Island, a title denoting its size, by the United States government surveyors in 1913.

PANCAKE SHOAL

Oneida Lake "pancakes" are small, circular rocks, sometimes likened to petrified cow manure in appearance. Cornell biologist Edward Mills discussed these strange rocks in "Oneida Lake Profile." Mills wrote:

> Concentrations of iron and manganese termed 'Oneida Lake Pancakes' cover large areas of the lake's bottom. Some sites are literally paved with these deposits. Scientifically referred to as ferromanganese nodules, these deposits are found not only in freshwater lakes but also in bogs, brackish water, and the deep sea. Concentrated deposits of these nodules in Oneida Lake are generally found in aerated offshore areas in depths of less than 30 feet. Some nodules approximate the Age of Oneida Lake (10,000 years) accumulating iron and manganese at a rate of less than .04 inch per 100 years. Factors responsible for their formation and growth remain speculative; however, the presence of these unusual deposits in Oneida Lake provide a unique field laboratory for continued scientific study.

Two Pancake Shoals are found in Oneida, one near the Duck Islands and the other north of Lakeport. Pancake rocks, however, are present in other areas of the lake. Ten years ago, I was trolling for walleyes east of Buoy 109. Working the line by hand, I felt the spoon catch bottom, then release, still imbedded in a dead weight. Reeling in quickly, I expected to pull out a branch or other lake flotsam, but instead I caught a pancake. The rock was filled with tiny crevices and holes, from which emerged scores of aquatic insects. Considering that these rocks shelter a base of the Oneida Lake food web, it is easy to understand why fishing on the Pancake Shoals can be superb.

PHILO BAR

A deep shoal north of One Tree Pinnacle, Philo Bar was named for the Philo family of Constantia, who regularly fished there. George Philo was Superintendent of the Constantia Fish Hatchery during the 1930's. Both he and his father, Henry, spent numerous hours on "their" shoal.

PINDLE STONE PILE

Located on Shackelton Shoals' south side, this small reef was entitled for Michael Pindle, a Bridgeport area farmer and fisherman. Earl Lee Pindle, Michael's grandson, recalls that his grandfather and father, William Pindle, "fished all the time" in the Shackelton locale. The Pindles packed their catch in barrels and shipped the fish to Syracuse markets. They were veteran lake anglers and located Pindle Stone Pile through alignment with shore points.

SCHOOLHOUSE BAR

Shore bearings are the key to understanding this place name. For years, the old barn on the Isaac Delamarter farm was used as a reference to locate this reef. Slightly east of the barn was a country schoolhouse and for this the bar was named.

NEWFOUNDOUT ON NIGH BAR

Nigh, of course, means "near" and Nigh Bar is the closest reef of Shackelton Shoals to the lake's south shore. Undoubtedly, some old-time angler happened upon the spot, "newly finding it out" so to speak, experienced substantial success and named the place appropriately.

SUGAR LOAF

The title of this eastern Shackelton Shoals' reef refers to its shape.

BIG ISLE

This is a large, shallow shoal, having but one foot of water in some places. Located just south of Buoy 121 on Shackelton's, Big Isle rose above water in pre-Barge Canal days. The canal project elevated lake levels, submerging Big Isle, Messenger's Shoal (Buoy 113) and Dakin's Shoal. A 1790 lake map, on file with the Oneida County Historical Society, clearly shows these three areas as being above water.

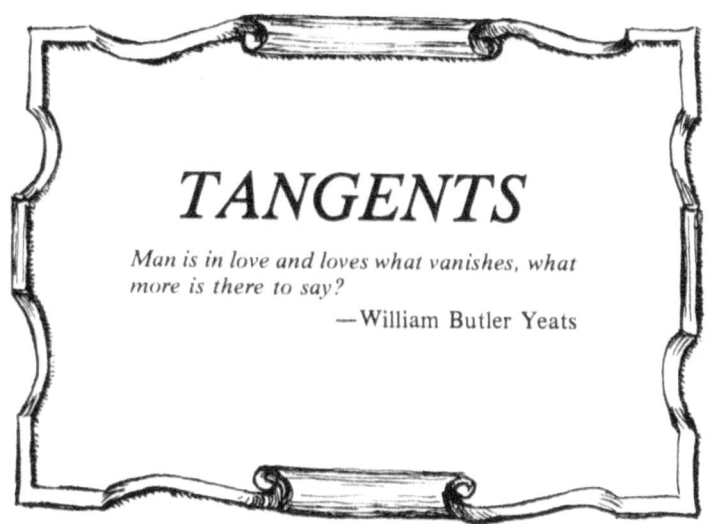

TANGENTS

Man is in love and loves what vanishes, what more is there to say?

—William Butler Yeats

In researching Oneida Lake's place names I encountered some interesting topics which, though possessing strong local history value, did not fit in well with my place name chapters' organization. These subjects are discussed in this section. In order, they are: Ice Fishing, Eel Fishing in Oneida's Past, The Steamboat Era, Fish Pirates, Ice Harvesting, Waterfowl Hunting and My People.

ICE FISHING

Oneida Lake in mid-winter. The wind always seems to howl, the temperature hovers around fifteen degrees, and snow squalls drift in from the neighboring Lake Ontario precipitation factory. When the storms subside, the lake's center appears to be dotted with numerous small, darkened figures. Ice fishermen, the hardiest of Oneida Lake anglers, are enjoying their winter avocation.

Danger is inherent in this sport. Times when ice forms at winter's advent or thaws in early March are particularly threatening. Even in mid-winter, safety must be a prime concern of the angler. Air pockets, locally referred to as "gas holes," are created when the ice separates; some of these openings are large enough to swallow a snowmobile. Cracks can materialize quickly and, on occasion, large masses of ice break loose from shore (usually when part of the lake is still ice-free). Those who venture to the lake's middle, two or more miles from shore, must constantly be aware of heavy snow (whiteout) conditions which could prove disorienting, especially towards evening. The ice fishermen must be concerned with exposure; hypothermia arrives quickly to winter's unprepared.

Oneida Lake's ice has claimed many lives throughout history and caused innumerable scares. Early settlers found the ice to be a convenient winter thoroughfare but some of these pioneers, driving their ox-drawn wagons, met an untimely demise. Today, nearly each year witnesses a state police helicopter rescue of anglers stranded when the ice cap separates from shore. Ice is a powerful force, as evidenced in its erosive qualities at Sylvan Beach during spring break-up, and it must be respected. One cardinal rule needs constant repetition - if you have any doubt whatsoever as to the safety of Oneida's ice - stay off it.

For decades, the standard fish catching device used by ice anglers was the tip-up. These contraptions involve a spool of line which is suspended underwater at the end of a metal or wooden rod. An opening in the rod allows for placement of a stick, which prevents the device from falling into the fisherman's hole. A minnow is baited on the line's hook and lowered to just off the lake's bottom. The tip-up can be set so that, when a fish strikes the minnow, a "flag" (a small piece of cloth or plastic attached to fairly stout wire which, in turn, is further rigged by light wire to the spool) pops up. Older tip-ups could also be set with their line attached to an underwater release "clip" which, when the fish hit, would release line allowing the fish to ingest the minnow. Enough line was placed on the spool to let the fish swim off with the bait and, eventually, be solidly hooked. Tip-ups rigged in the latter fashion were used by fishermen who left their devices in the lake overnight. Walleyed pike are active night feeders. Anglers would often keep their tip-ups aligned in this way and check them once or twice a day, harvesting the "hangers" (walleyes that hooked themselves and stayed on the line).

Old-time ice fishermen used axes and "spuds" (heavy chisels attached to a strong metal rod) to bore their holes. This was often arduous labor, as Oneida's ice cap can exceed twenty inches in thickness. As winter progressed, holes had to be drilled farther out in the lake to keep the tip-ups in the vicinity of the walleye schools. Winter water temperatures are the opposite of summer's, with the warmer, pike-attracting water being the greater depths. Anglers were allowed fifteen tip-ups and each rig had to be tagged with the fisherman's name and address. Buckeye minnows were the most effective bait in the waters from Cleveland eastward, while an Oneida Lake "chub" worked well in the Brewerton to Constantia area. Smaller versions of each minnow were used to catch large perch which could be also taken with hooks baited with fish eyes.

In the era of commercial fishing, until walleye sale was banned in 1961, ice fishing provided a nice supplementary income for many lake anglers. For the most part, a code of ethics stating "thou shall not steal thy neighbor's pike" existed among the fishermen. Exceptions to this honored rule occurred, however, and the consequences to such violations were often sanguinary. Three brothers operated forty-five tip-ups in Lower South Bay during the 1940's. They noticed a severe decline in their catch and, being suspicious, decided to stage a night watch. One evening, around eleven o'clock, they spotted human activity near their fishing area. The brothers skated to the spot, chased down the walleye thieves, and exacted extreme physical retribution on the violators.

A great change occurred in 1973, when the leaving of tip-ups in the lake overnight was banned, the walleye limit dropped to five fish and a fifteen-inch size limit instituted. "Hanger" fishermen found themselves limited. The action by New York's Conservation Department was taken in response to a precipitous decline in the walleye population but, in doing this, the department also addressed a poaching problem, as tracking night fishermen was very difficult for game protectors. Several other changes in Oneida's ice fishing scene have taken place since that time. "Jigging," the use of spoons such as the "Swedish Pimple" and "Sidewinder" has become a very popular pike-catching technique. Panfish anglers have discovered that tiny (half the size of a dime) jigs baited with maggots such as "mousies" and "spikes" (fly larvae) are very effective fish catchers. Snowmobiles and ATV's have replaced skates and hiking as the methods for Oneida's fishermen's mobility. Power augers now facilitate the heart-pounding labor of hole drilling. Modern technology has overtaken the lake's most popular winter sport.

EEL FISHING IN ONEIDA'S PAST

Caughdenoy, a small community west of Brewerton on the Oneida River, was once the Oneida Lake eel industry's hub. Beauchamp's 1908 book, *Past and Present of Syracuse and Onondaga County, New York*, states that the name Caughdenoy means "where the eel is lying down." Large eel "weirs," V-shaped funnels that led to a cage, stretched across the river at Caughdenoy. Each side of the "V" was long and the porous weir was wide enough to intercept hundreds of migrating eels. The latter, making their spawning run to the Atlantic, wanted to swim downstream and thus, once caught in the trap at the V's end, would not reverse their direction to escape fate. The quantity of eels in the river dictated the amount of times per day that the trap would be emptied.

Long before eeling became a commercial endeavor, the Oneida Lake eel had gained a reputation as a gourmet delight. In 1792, Francis Adrian Van Der Kemp wrote to his friend, Adam Mappa, praising the fish's qualities, saying: "The eel of the Oneida Lake is equal to the best of the Holland market, and far surpasses every kind which I have ever tasted here, in size, in fatness, in tenderness of the fish." In later days, the fish were salted or smoked for export; their skins were used to make livestock whips and the oil extracted from their flesh was sold for its purported medicinal value.

Eel Island, off the Chittenango Creek mouth, was a prime spot for finding this fish. Harry Wing of Brewerton recalled that a fisherman could walk around that island, spot eels in the shallows and spear them with ease. Wing and a pirating partner once speared five hundred pounds of eels in the immediate island area. The *Roosevelt Wildlife Annals* volume entitled "The Ecology and Economics of Oneida Lake Fish" (C.C. Adams and T.L. Hankinson, 1928), contained the following passage concerning the Eel Island locale:

W. H. Weston and J. D. Black inform us that Eels are often speared on Eel shoals, at the mouth of Chittenango Creek, where the water is 5 to 10 feet deep. This is done early in July in the 'eel fly season,' when the Mayflies (Ephemerida) float in windrows. (Note - these aforementioned insects, once a big part of the Oneida Lake food web, are now virtually gone.) As the Eels congregate among these Mayflies they are speared during the day or at night with what is called a 'top water spear.' This is a long-handled implement about 16 feet long with a nail-like spear at the end to which are lashed two flexible tines (of ash or tamarack root) which compress the Eel and cause it to coil around the fork and handle. The coiled Eel is pulled off in the boat by means of the feet of the operator.

Before the Barge Canal construction altered the Oneida River's channel, massive runs of eels kept weir operators busy around the clock. Catches of three thousand fish per night were common. Canal construction limited fish migration and eventually killed the business, but as late as 1928 the Brewerton-Caughdenoy fishermen were marketing 100 tons of the fish. The last weir on the Oneida River made its swan-song harvest in 1938.

Early twentieth century eel prices corresponded with those for other lake species. In 1928 live eels sold for twenty cents per pound, with the smoked variety bringing thirty-five cents. Twelve years earlier, the same products brought twenty and twenty-six cents, respectively. Eels are occasionally caught by anglers today, usually when bottom fishing for bullheads, but these occurrences are rare.

THE STEAMBOAT ERA

The history of steamers on Oneida Lake stretches from 1835 to the early 1900's. Brewerton's Elet Milton did prodigious research on this topic and my data comes from his well-documented work. The first steamboat to navigate Oneida entered the lake in 1835. Asa Eastwood, an early resident of Lower South Bay, wrote in his diary, "On November 27 last (1835) a small steamboat came from Baldwinsville into the Oneida Lake, went to Rotterdam (now Constantia) and next day returned and left the lake. She came up the Oneida River." This boat was owned and built by Stephen W. Baldwin, son of Dr. Jonas Baldwin, founder of

Baldwinsville. It was a sidewheeler, approximately forty feet long. Though it never returned to the lake, it profited from the cargo and passenger trade from Baldwinsville to Syracuse. The boat's appearance caused a bit of a stir among lake residents. A public meeting was held at Constantia to discuss the economic impact steamboating might have on the lake communities. The thrust of the meeting's discussion centered around improvement of Oneida River navigation to permit steamers from Syracuse to easily enter the lake. Rifts at Brewerton and rapids at Oak Orchard and Caughdenoy made navigation hazardous; the first steamboat had to wait for high water before attempting its journey. Public agitation from meetings such as this one brought results. Locks were built on the Oneida River at Oak Orchard and Caughdenoy, in 1840 and 1841 respectively. These events, coupled with completion of the first Oneida Lake Canal in 1835 (connecting Wood Creek, an east end tributary, with the Erie Canal at Higginsville), greatly increased commercial boat traffic.

To take advantage of the lake's economic potential, the Oneida Lake and River Steamboat Company was incorporated in 1838. Founded by George A. Hoyt of New York, and Henry Fitzhugh and DeWitt Littlejohn, both of Oswego, the company operated two docks, a large warehouse, a dry dock, and four "horse boats," vessels which carried tow horses belonging to the barges which were pulled through the lake by the company's steamers. Of the latter vessels, there were four; the *Oneida* and *Oswego* were launched in 1849 while the *Onondaga* and *Madison* first sailed in 1851. These boats were named for the four counties which border Oneida Lake. The corporation prospered until the late 1850's, when the Erie Canal was enlarged, permitting heavier freight transportation. The Oneida Lake Canal was not similiarly altered and bigger barges could not reach the lake. Faced with financial ruin, the company's directors voted to disband. *Oneida* was broken up and sold for parts, *Onondaga* and *Madison* were marketed to a Hudson River company, but *Oswego* remained on the lake. It was sold to William H. Carter and later renamed *Manhattan*. Primarily used for tourist excursions, the vessel plied Oneida's waters until its destruction at Caughdenoy in 1901.

Oneida Lake's steamboats served a variety of purposes. A previously mentioned boat, Joseph Norcross's *Twins*, was a passenger ship named for its builder's twin children. Sold in 1861, the boat was later renamed *Teaser* because its size and speed "teased" its competition. In addition to the excursion business, it was used for towing barges, for hauling logs, and in the construction in the 1870's of the second Oneida Lake Canal, which connected Upper South Bay with the Erie at Durhamville. The *Annie Laurie*, a vessel built for John Greenway of Syracuse and named for his favorite child, was used in the late 1870's and early 1880's to transport beer and pleasure parties around the lake. The *Ice Trader*, built for Louis Henley in 1898, brought ice from J.W. Sniper's ice house on Lower South Bay to Syracuse. The *Canastota*, constructed by Robert Simpson for William Lindley of Canastota, was used by the latter in his game protector's work. Lindley, according to Elet Milton, was a crafty warden. Said historian Milton, "He frequently would leave Brewerton at night on his way to Onondaga Lake, would turn about a few miles down the river and return to reap a rich haul of nets, which had been set by unsuspecting fishermen, who had not anticipated his return until the next day."

The excursion trade, though, was the Oneida Lake steamers' lifeblood. Several of the lake's hotels maintained boats to entertain their patrons. In the 1850's the *Queen of the Lake*, a Norcross work, and the *Island Hotel* were among the steamboats that brought vacationers to the Frenchman's Island Hotel. On July 4, 1857, the *Queen* and three other vessels brought over eight hundred tourists to that island. Another steamer serving Frenchman's was the *Island Queen*, built by Toad Harbor's Edgar Johnson for George Crownhart of Lower South Bay. The *Lottie* accommodated customers of the Leland Hotel, Sylvan Beach, while in the same village the more fashionable clientele of Louis Chesebrough's St. Charles Hotel sailed on the *St. Charles*. One of the larger hotel steamers was the *Fred B. Randall* which ran in connection with Sylvan Beach's Forest Home. Originally christened the *Oneida* (not the previously cited *Oneida*), the ship carried a maiden voyage passenger total of over four hundred. The boat was so large that in 1889 Simon Denniger, the "jolly Frenchman" of Brewerton, exclaimed as the steamer came into view, "My God, Tommy (Thomas Milton), she looks bigger than Frenchman's Island!" Eleven days after the initial cruise, the steamboat's steering mechanism jammed. Out of control, the *Oneida* slammed into the Brewerton bridge, heavily damaging the boat. It was sold to Fred Randall, reoutfitted, used for Sylvan Beach tourism, and resold in 1902 to a Staten Island business.

Grandest of the lake's steamboats was the *Sagamore*. This

vessel was owned and operated by the Syracuse to South Bay Railroad Company, an organization that, in the early 1900's, attempted to develop Lower South Bay's resort potential. Having room for six hundred, the *Sagamore* was approximately one hundred feet long and twenty-two wide. It served the tourist trade from 1909 until 1915, its demise paralleling that of its parent company. In its day, however, it provided vacationers with a veritable bargain; a round trip cruise, from Lower South Bay to Sylvan Beach, cost a mere fifty cents.

The maiden voyage of the *Sagamore* generated prodigious excitement around Oneida Lake. Frederick Griesmyer, author of "Cleveland - Past and Present," captured this emotion in the following:

> When the boat got within view of the Lewis Point, it was greeted by nearly a score of motor boats with flags flying. Long before the boat was due at Sylvan Beach the big Barge Canal bridge and the docks were lined with people. Along the bridge was hung a 25-foot banner, three feet high, inscribed 'Welcome Beebe.' (Clifford Beebe, the ship's owner.)

In their day, steamboats served a useful purpose. They were working ships, towing barges, hauling cargo, stimulating the lake villages' economies. Their construction and maintenance provided needed employment. They gave boat builders, caulkers, dock tenders, captains, crew and ticket sellers a livelihood. But above all, I think, their primary function was to provide fun. The average upstater's life in the nineteenth century was mainly a time for labor. Working hours were long, wages relatively low, and amusements few. Imagine the welcome diversion an Oneida Lake steamboat ride must have provided these people. A moonlight cruise amidst a summer night's cool. A dancing party miles from shore. A chance to picnic on Frenchman's Island or to circumnavigate the lake. The anticipation felt by children sailing to Sylvan Beach with its "Midway" and "Carnival Park." The opportunity to just "get away" from life's melancholy routine. Steamboats brought these pleasures to their patrons. The wonder and joy surrounding these grand vessels were great feelings, as much a part of this era as the steamers themselves. Ah, for a ride on the *Manhattan*, the *Sagamore*, the *Fred B. Randall*! Antiquity's joy sailing on Oneida.

FISH PIRATES

Fish pirates have been, and are, an influencing factor in Oneida Lake's ecology. Operating with various forms of nets, explosives, traps and hooks, commercial fishermen have harvested tons of fish from the lake. The economic value of these fish has been nothing short of tremendous. In 1927, the *Roosevelt Wildlife Annals*, published by Syracuse University, stated that the 1902 sucker catch marketed at Brewerton weighed 617,000 pounds. In that same year, 13,400 pounds of yellow perch were marketed. A former Brewerton fishmonger, C.F. Davison, deemed to be the "best informed fish dealer on the lake," once estimated a yearly take from Oneida to be 250 to 300 tons. The Oneida Lake whitefish (tullibee), now decimated by parasitic lampreys, once provided fishermen with four to five tons of export each year. Fred Griesmyer, former historian of the lake's north shore, wrote that close to a ton of fish was shipped weekly to New York City, in addition to local trading in upstate cities. Griesmyer stated that some pirates could make nearly $100 per week, a tidy sum in those years.

At one time, commercial fishing for all species on Oneida was legal; the state went so far, in 1885, as to issue netting licenses to over one hundred Brewerton men. Later, however, netting was banned and only fish caught on hook and line could be sold. Those ignoring this law became the Oneida Lake fish pirates; the law heralded the advent of a long battle between pirates and their age-old nemeses - the game protectors.

Violence marked some early encounters between pirate and warden. In 1890 Charles Shackelton, George Crownhart and some deputy game protectors made several productive raids on pirate netting grounds. The confiscated nets were taken to Clinton Square in Syracuse and subjected to a public burning. Pirate retaliation was swift. Two of Shackleton's horses were bloodily de-tailed and Crownhart's Hotel, a Lower South Bay landmark, was burned to the ground. Game wardens fared better in other years. In 1901, constables seized 803 fyke nets, 433 trap nets, 416 gill nets, 76 squat nets, 30 seines, 335 set lines, 7 spears, 16 eel weirs, 8 wire nets and 2,637 illegal tip-ups. Total value of this devious equipment ran into the thousands of dollars.

Harry E. Best, a north shore game protector, knew the pirates well for, indeed, their existence justified his job. George W.

Walter, an *Oneida Dispatch* writer, interviewed Best in 1966 and recorded some of the veteran warden's thoughts on piracy.

> Netting fish was a big business, and many of the farms along the shores of the lake were paid for from the proceeds of these illegal catches. The pirates used to haul in fish by the boat load and the catches were sold in certain markets in Syracuse for 10 to 15 cents per pound. We caught the pirates one after the other, but you couldn't stop them. They would pay an average fine of $100 or more and then would be released. Many have told me they could go out in one night and catch enough fish to pay for their fines.

Best related that the increase in both net costs and in fines combined with better law enforcement techniques, crippling the fish pirate business. This decline in piracy was reflected in the number of nets seized by Best each year. This statistic fell from forty-nine in 1945 to eight in 1954.

Increased law enforcement was not the sole factor that curtailed fish pirating. Over the years the number of boats on Oneida Lake has multiplied astronomically. Millard Rogers, whose father Jack was an accomplished pirate, recalled that around 1930 there were less than fifty boats in Brewerton; today that total has swelled to eleven hundred. The same phenomenon occurred throughout the lake. More boats meant more observers, more vigilance and thus greater difficulty for the pirate. The spinning reel's invention contributed to the pirate's demise. Before, most Oneida Lake anglers would "still-fish," lowering their lines from the side of anchored boats. Spinning reels made casting an elementary operation. Casters covered infinitely more water in their fishing than did the old-time still-fisherman and their angling style resulted in the snagging of pirate nets. Nets, too, were a factor in pirating's descent, as rising cost for nets lost to casters or wardens put many an outlaw out of business.

Much has been said against the Oneida Lake fish pirate and this is, in itself, unfair. Pirates had several positive impacts on the lake region. As Harry Best stated, scores of lakeshore farms were financed by their owners supplementing milk checks with fishing income. Two Brewerton churches' mortgages were paid off, by in large, through fish pirate contributions. Pirates also engendered advantageous biological effects on the lake. Hook and line fishermen, decades ago, could not possibly harvest enough Oneida Lake fish by themselves to keep populations from exploding, a condition which would result in stunted fish growth.

Pirates, by keeping everything they caught (except bass), filled the niche that legions of modern, efficient Oneida anglers now occupy.

The Oneida Lake Association has a long history of opposition to fish piracy and promotion of a sound conservation policy at the lake. Largely through the Association's lobbying efforts, New York State passed a law in 1961 banning the sale of walleyes from Oneida. In effect this curtailed most commercial fishing for the popular walleye and halted many local restaurants' selling "lake pike" dinners. It was a giant step in maintaining a sizeable walleye population for the sportsman, but it did not stop pike poaching entirely. That activity, in the spirit of the pirate, shall never cease so long as a lake as bountiful in fish as Oneida coexists with some of the more avaricious aspects of human nature.

ICE HARVESTING

In the days before refrigeration, a significant industry in Oneida Lake communities was ice harvesting. Needed for family "ice boxes" and the large ice houses in which hotels and restaurants kept liquid refreshment, ice was an extremely important commodity. Trains carried tons of lake ice to upstate cities and beyond and, after warm winters which limited freezing, the product commanded a top dollar. The Ontario and Western Railroad extended its Main Street line at Sylvan Beach to reach the Barge Canal just for the purpose of facilitating the ice loading process. In ice harvesting, workers cut ice with cross cut saws and the blocks were then slid out of the water. By using inclined planes and eventually conveyor belts, cutters then transferred the ice chunks to wagons. The latter vehicles brought the ice to railroad cars for shipment. Sawdust was used as an insulator in ice houses during warm months. The sawdust proved very effective and ice that was cut in February could be counted on to retain its chilling qualities well into September.

Weather influenced the ice harvest tremendously. One particularly warm winter in the early part of this century witnessed little ice formation on Oneida. Fortunately, a late freeze solidified Big Bay to sufficient thickness and the ice houses of Syracuse were filled. An account of the 1890 ice harvest in the *Madison County Times*' March 7 issue revealed the rather tenuous nature of the business. The paper reported:

> The coldsnap that set in the latter part of last week has continued this week and people who had been nervous about being able to fill their ice houses have been able to secure all the ice they wanted. Monday morning the business started with a general rush, every team available was secured, and it is estimated that 325 loads were delivered that day at Chittenango and the Station from Oneida Lake. There were fears that it would not last, and everybody tried to secure all they wanted that day. There has been plenty of ice since, however, and some thoroughly cold weather, with prospects of more (arrived). A few filled their ice houses during the cold weather of two weeks ago. The ice brought from Oneida Lake this week costs about $1.80 a load, but is first class.

WATERFOWL HUNTING

A lake the size of Oneida is an obvious attraction for ducks and geese and, of course, the hunters who pursue them. The lake itself and its numerous sheltered bays and bordering wetlands serve as prime habitat for waterfowl. Native Americans hunted these birds for sustenance and, even with primitive techniques such as clubbing, took many. Whites brought firearms to Oneida and waterfowl suddenly became more vulnerable. Single shot rifles and scatter guns forced hunters to take careful aim and seldom accounted for large harvests - with one exception - the punt gun. This firearm, a weapon with a very wide barrel, was capable of holding several ounces of powder and metal shot. It was mounted on the bow of a sturdy, low-profile boat in which the hunter rested in a relatively prone position. The camouflaged craft was allowed to drift (or was slowly paddled) toward waterfowl flocks. When the hunter closed the firing range, the gun was aimed and fired. Shot would be spread over a wide area causing, at times, upwards of thirty birds to be killed. Gunners who used punts were, by in large, market hunters who preserved their kill and exported it to upstate cities.

In more recent times, waterfowling was still a productive and popular Oneida Lake pastime. Dr. Paul Cramer, of Liverpool, experienced the last years of Oneida's bountiful duck hunting and wrote of his sport for the Spring 1980 edition of the Oneida

Lake Association's *Oneida Lake Bulletin*:

> I remember going to Long Island in our boat. The wild rice was very plentiful and grew six feet tall. We cut a large bundle and took it ashore, where we proceeded to tie the stalks into smaller bundles about one inch through. These we then tied side by side to a 12-foot roll of chicken wire.
>
> This resulted in a light weight natural looking blind which could be rolled up and easily carried in a boat or car. Given reasonable care, it would last for years and I still have one that I built 50 years ago.
>
> I shall always remember that dawn of November 1, 1937, when the bluebills came down out of the western stratosphere by the thousands so that they darkened the sky over Brewerton. Skimming down onto the surface of the lake, they all settled into one huge raft a mile long. I remember flocks of 50 or even 100 swinging over our decoys.

The decoys Dr. Cramer and his father used were, for the most part, home-crafted. This was the decade of the Great Depression and commercially produced decoys cost one dollar, a princely sum then. Using whittling tools, the Cramers transformed cork into a duck's shape. They painted their birds and mounted eyes, which they had to purchase, into the head. These eyes were very important, for their absence would alarm incoming ducks. To the decoy's bottom was attached a cord and weight, the cord being long enough to allow the decoy to "swim" effectively.

Duck hunting was extremely popular in the '30s and '40s, so much so that opening day on Oneida sounded like a war's outbreak. Dr. Cramer relates how having a blind on one of the lake's points was a matter of prestige among waterfowlers. Some hunters were so rabidly enthused with their sport that they would row to one of the Duck Islands off Constantia and spend the night on that island, insuring that they would have a prime spot for the upcoming day's hunt. Most hunters used double-barreled shotguns then; Cramer's first weapon was an Ithaca gun that "kicked like nine mules." The abundance of birds made the use of calls unnecessary. Bluebills (scaup) and whistlers (goldeneyes) were the most common ducks, but blacks and canvasbacks added occasional variety to a day's bag.

Duck hunting success dropped considerably during the 1950's, possibly as a result of over-harvesting during the sport's glory years (there were no bag limits then). Other factors, such as alteration of the habitat - wild rice is now rare around Oneida -

undoubtedly took their toll. The sport survives today, however, and a few blinds protrude from the lake's autumn surface, supporting the sportsmen whose shots' muffled sounds give reminder to Oneida's waterfowling past.

MY PEOPLE

In writing this book, I was blessed to meet scores of informative, loquacious people who made my work possible and delightful besides. Some of these persons became good friends, others casual acquaintances, while many I observed from a distance, noting their roles in the contemporary lake scene. Let me introduce you to some of these fine folk.

Wally Keesler enjoys his golden retirement years by fishing the lake - sometimes five days per week. Spring, summer or fall - at the crack of dawn - Wally's on the water, where he belongs.

Father Leo Wimmet of Saint John's, North Bay, and Saint Mary's, Sylvan Beach, and Father Robert Jones of Saint Mary's, Cleveland, minister to the faithful in the tradition of J.G. Mertens, founding priest of the former two parishes.

Sails fill the air every Wednesday and Saturday evening as the Oneida Lake Sailing Club sponsors its version of America's Cup. These boats, at sunset, complement a marvelous scene.

"Skip" Aubeuf owns and manages "Yesterday's Royal," a Sylvan Beach restaurant restored to its early twentieth century magnificence. The lakeside hotel is a joy to experience.

Every month, the members of the Brewerton Historical Society gather, sometimes at their Oliver Stevens Blockhouse museum, other times at members' homes. Groups like this one preserve our past as an unforgotten treasure.

"Jigger" Smith counts out worms, crabs and minnows at South Bay Bait and Tackle. Gives a little fishin' advice, too.

Mike Mitchell of Canastota, an Environmental Conservation Officer (game warden, in the vernacular), pursues modern-day fish pirates. "Mitch" catches his share.

Every opening weekend of walleye season, the Cicero Lions' Club sponsors a pike tournament, earning thousands of dollars for charity. It's nice to think of fish concurrently providing fun and helping those in need.

Roy and Cherry Bridenbecker still live on their generations-old family farm, west of Lakeport. An older couple, they enjoy their garden, their memories and mementos, and they warmly share these with the occasional passing historian.

Norm Yeomans is the boss of the Oneida Hatchery, New York State's premier walleye-producing facility. Ably assisted by fish technicians like Wayne Masters, Norm coordinates this very significant conservation chore.

For over half a century, Eddie and Fifi Stewart have managed Eddie's Restaurant, Sylvan Beach, building the business from a tiny hot dog stand to a regionally famous family dining enterprise.

Oneida Limited Corporation maintains Lewis Point as a recreational facility for its employees. A benevolent organization, the company allows public access to the point during the winter season.

Leonard Cooper, adorned with straw hat, diligently works his large garden in Constantia. Leonard's the town historian and has made copious records of the lake's north shore history.

Courtney "Corky" Winn takes pride in his photo collection of the Constantia-Bernhard's Bay-Cleveland area. He should take pride - the images are grand.

Barge captains steer their ponderous craft through the lake. Once or twice a day, summer and fall, a Sears, Morania or Peckinpaugh vessel crosses Oneida, reminiscent of days when the lake was a major water transportation artery.

Don and Nancy Sheldon run their Toad Harbor marina in the peace and solitude provided by its location, three miles off the bustling thoroughfares that encircle the lake. Standing at the Sheldon marina, one is reminded of the "retreat" ideal that once characterized lake resorts.

Bob Igoe, his son Bob Jr. and daughter Sheila Orlin own and operate North Country Books, a local history-publishing company based in Sylvan Beach and Utica.

Judd and Dixie Glenney tend to the office and keep the outboards running and spinakers flying at South Bay's Oneida Lake Marina.

Michael and Lawrence Mazza, ages eleven and eight, take their first Oneida Lake fishing trip and catch seven big smallmouth bass in Messenger's Bay. Youth and fishing - what a superb time.

And in 1988 the congregation of the historic Trinity Church, Constantia, began restoration work on that structure, insuring that this gem of the lake's past would be there for generations to come.

May the future hold more Trinitys.

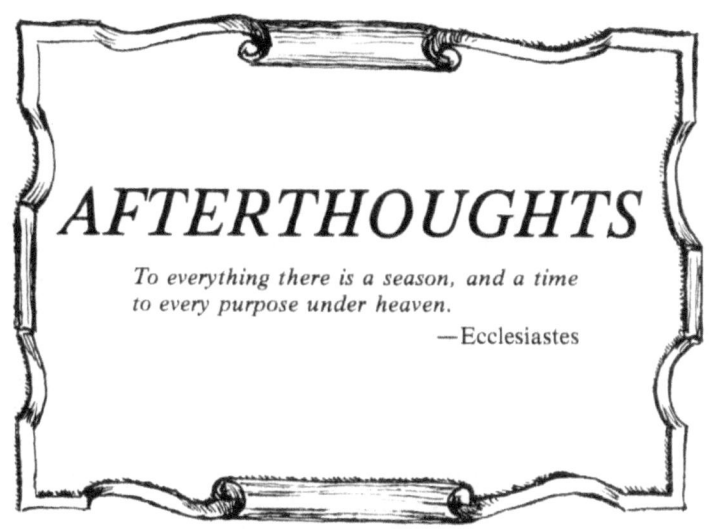

AFTERTHOUGHTS

To everything there is a season, and a time to every purpose under heaven.
—Ecclesiastes

The seasons and times of Oneida Lake history have manifested themselves in the story of the lake's place names. In titles like Chittenango Creek, Canaseraga Creek and Oneida Lake itself we note the period of Indian occupation. Brewerton and Wood Creek bear witness to the colonial era, while Scriba Creek and Frenchman's Island emanate from the time of pioneer settlement. The Yankee migration to New York State in the early 1800's, which resulted in the lake area's first significant growth, is evidenced in Spencer Creek, Billington Bay and Damon Point. From roughly 1850 until 1910, Oneida Lake tourism flourished and names like Larkin Point, Norcross Point, Messenger's Bay and Sylvan Beach sprouted from this boom. Concurrently, lake villages exhibited industrial traits, a phenomenon documented in the history of Cleveland, Colon Bay and Dickinson Isle. Early twentieth century fish pirates left their story in tales of Wood Point, Big Bay and Poddygut Shoals. The post-1920 spread of cottage development along the lakeshore finds example in the

Wilson, Godfrey and Hitchcock Points' sagas. Virtually every era of Oneida's past is depicted in its place names' analyses.

A distinguished visitor to Oneida Lake in the pioneer era was the French author Alexis de Tocqueville, who had read about the emigre of Frenchman's Island and wanted to further investigate that saga. In *Memoirs, Letters and Remains*, de Tocqueville mentioned his thoughts concerning the Frenchman's experience:

> ... the remembrance of the French couple on the Lake Onieda was never effaced from my memory. How often I had envied the peaceful joys of their solitude! Domestic bliss, the charms of conjugal union - even love - became mixed up in my mind with the image of the solitary island which my imagination had transformed into a new Eden. The story interested my companion. We often talked of it, and we every time ended by repeating, gayly or sadly, 'The only happiness in this world is on the Lakè Oneida.'"

De Tocqueville's last line has stayed with me since I first read it in Hamilton College's James Library in 1972. Although his words are romanticized, they reflect the fact that the lake has been and is a source of great happiness. When I muse about de Tocqueville's quote, I think of the lake's past inhabitants and of the importance that this water has played in their lives. I think of George Scriba, planning to build his empire along Oneida's shore. Of Anthony Landgraff and Crawford Getman, establishing industry at Cleveland. Of William Dunham, Abram Larkin, Louis Chesebrough and Clifford Beebe, developing resort hotels. And I think of Oneida Lake's current people. Of Earl Pearson, Paul Cramer and the devoted of the Oneida Lake Association, savoring every angling moment they can. Of John Forney, Ed Mills and their students, monitoring the lake's ecosystem. And of the masses, the boating zealots, vacationers, commuters, merchants and the average, ordinary person. For these people, past and present, Oneida Lake has brought a great degree of happiness, perhaps not that of de Tocqueville's imagination, but genuine joy nonetheless.

In writing about this happiness, I am compelled to think to the future Oneida Lake, and to hope that our descendants experience that same feeling. Thinking ahead raises concerns, however. Certain basic issues must be addressed in order to preserve, and improve, the Oneida Lake experience. Among the questions that we must answer are these. Will suburban development be allowed to replace productive lake-bordering wetlands? Will sewage treatment facilities be expanded to include the entire lakeshore area? Will restrictive zoning be adopted to remove eyesore structures and insure for proper expansion in lake communities? Will successful endeavors be made to preserve and restore historic sites such as Cleveland's Saint James' Church, the Sylvan Beach pier and the north shore's Marsden Cemetery? Will our country adequately tackle the acid rain problem or will this festering cancer be allowed to downgrade Oneida as it has the once pristine lakes of the Adirondacks? Will "sportsmen" continue to look aside when poaching violations occur? Will protest occur if the Federal Government again proposes to radically alter Oneida Lake's bed in a project that deepens the Barge Canal, making the waterway passable for ocean-going vessels? And, will people continue to love this wondrous lake, as many have in the past, and like those of us for whom de Tocqueville's happiness endures today?

Admittedly, I editorialize in writing these inquiries, but I am very concerned about Oneida Lake, for it has been a significant force in my life. A healthy lake and attractive lake area are invaluable assets to Central New York, but the reverse situation would prove a nightmare. My finest experiences on Oneida occurred during the innumerable fishing trips that I shared there with my grandfather, Stanley Alfred Osterhout. When I consider how I want to envision the future lake, my thoughts return to the last trip that Gramps and I shared. It was in November, 1984, a blustery, raw day, the type that heralds winter overtaking fall. Despite the conditions, the lake was navigable and the walleyes bit with gusto. Gramps landed the last pike in our limit that day, after which I turned to him and said, "The lake was good to us, Gramps." My grandfather smiled, his face slowed by the chill as he answered, "Yes, Jack. It always is."

MY DEBTS

The following persons and organizations have provided me with invaluable assistance in creating this book. To each, and to any I may have inadvertently omitted, I extend a sincere word of thanks.

William Barrett
Katherine App Bennett
Clarence Bitz
Mrs. Lloyd Blankman
Nat Boxer
John Boysen
Isabel Bracy
Brewerton Free Library
Brewerton Historical Society
Mr. and Mrs. Roy Bridenbecker
Richard Brown
Glenn Chesebrough
Leonard Cooper
Paul Cramer
Leon Damon
Fred David
Mr. and Mrs. George Davis
Ray Denman
Richard Devan
Mr. and Mrs. Marvin Dunham
David Ellis
Ray Ernenwein
Leona Flynn
John Forney
Lawrence Fournier
David Goff
Carol Greene
Charlie Griesmyer
Bob Grube
Marion Henke
Marshall Hope
Ann Hopkins
Clara Houck
Russell Hubbard
Bob Igoe
Irene
Father Robert Jones
Mr. and Mrs. Jack Kinney
Alice Kneeskern
Alfred Kolmer
Dora Krause
Cappy Kyser
Moe Labella
Marvin Ladd
Madison County Clerk's Office
Madison County Historical Society
Jill Maynard
Dave Millar
Ed Mills
Francis and Iva Money
Mabel Myer
Matie Nichols

My Debts 239

Ed Olmstead
Oneida County Historical
  Society
Oneida Lake Association
Oneida Limited, Inc.
Onondaga County Clerk's
  Office
Onondaga County Historical
  Association
Oswego County Clerk's Office
Oswego County Historical
  Society
Earl Lee Pindle
Hubert Prescott
Doug Preston
Barbara Revette
Millard Rogers
Jack Sauer

Isabelle Billington Saunders
Frederick Scriba
George Scriba
Don and Nancy Sheldon
Bruce and Erma Stallknecht
John, Teddy and Brian
  Stillman
Sullivan Free Library
Syracuse Public Library
Elden Taft
Utica Public Library
Ruth Weimer
Richard Will
Father Leo Wimmet
Harry Wing
Courtney Winn
Warren Wood

The Oneida Lake region, 1790's. This map, courtesy of the Oneida County Historical Society, shows several interesting points about the lake in the pre-Barge Canal era. Frenchman's Island was then called DeZeng's Island, after the Baron DeZeng, a colonial visitor to Oneida. Dunham's Island, just east of Frenchman's, has an illegible title. The other three islands shown are now submerged - the Barge Canal rose the lake level to accomplish this. Going from west to east (left to right) on the map, these isles are now Dakin's Shoal, Big Isle (Buoy 121) and Messenger's Shoal (Buoy 113).

BIBLIOGRAPHY

———, *Atlas of Madison County, New York*, D.G. Beers, Philadelphia, 1874.

———, *Atlas of Oneida County, New York*, D.G. Beers, Philadelphia, 1874.

———, *Brewerton, New York, U.S.A.*, Brewerton Library Association, Brewerton, 1973.

———, *Country Roads*, Madison County Board of Supervisors, Wampsville, 1981.

———, *Gazetteer and Business Directory of Madison County, New York*, Hamilton Child, Syracuse, 1868.

———, *Gazetteer and Business Directory of Oneida County, New York*, Hamilton Child, Syracuse, 1869.

———, *Gazetteer and Business Directory of Oswego County, New York*, Hamilton Child, Syracuse, 1866.

———, *Gazetteer and Directory of the County of Oneida*, Charles N. Gaffney, Utica, 1884.

———, *History of Oswego County*, L.H. Everts and Company, Philadelphia, 1877.

Bibliography

———, *New Century Atlas - Oneida County*, Century Map Company, Philadelphia, 1907.

———, *New Topographic Atlas of Oswego County, New York*, C. K. Stone, Philadelphia, 1867.

———, *Oswego City and County Directory and Gazetteer*, George Moss and Company, Oswego, 1869.

———, *Sweet's New Atlas of Onondaga County, New York*, Walker Bros., New York, 1874.

———, *Syracuse City Directory*, all volumes from 1890 to 1915.

———, *The Farm Journal Illustrated Directory of Onondaga County, New York*, Wilmer Atkinson Company, Philadelphia, 1917.

———, *The History of Oneida County*, C. L. Hutson Co., printers, published by Oneida County, 1977.

Adams, C. C., and Hankinson, T. L., "The Ecology and Economics of Oneida Lake Fish," *Roosevelt Wildlife Annals*, Syracuse University College of Forestry, Syracuse, 1928.

Beauchamp, William M., Rev., *Indian Names of New York*, H. C. Beauchamps, Fayetteville, 1893.

Beauchamp, William M., Rev., *Onondaga Revolutionary Soldiers*, The McDonnell Company, Syracuse, 1913.

Beauchamp, William M., Rev., *Past and Present of Syracuse and Onondaga County, New York*, S. J. Clarke Publishing Company, New York, 1908.

Blankman, Edgar, *Deacon Babbit*, John C. Winston Co., Philadelphia, 1907.

Boyd, Andrew, *Boyd's Directory of Principal Farmers and Businessmen in Onondaga County, New York*, Boyd Directory Printing Office, Syracuse, 1891.

Boyd, Andrew, *Boyd's Directory of Principal Farmers and Businessmen in Onondaga County, New York*, Central City Publishing House, Syracuse, 1887.

Bruce, Dwight (ed.), *Onondaga's Centennial*, The Boston History Company, Boston, 1896.

Churchill, John C., *Landmarks of Oswego County, New York*, D. Mann and Company, Syracuse, 1895.

Clark, Joshua, *Onondaga*, Stoddard and Babcock, Syracuse, 1849.

Clarke, T. Wood, *Emigres in the Wilderness*, MacMillan, New York, 1941.

De Tocqueville, Alexis, *Memoirs, Letters and Remains*, Ticknor and Fields, Boston, 1872.

Durant, Samuel, *History of Oneida County*, Everts and Fariss, Philadelphia, 1878.

Ellis, David, et. al., *A History of New York State*, Cornell University Press, Ithaca, 1967.

Gordon, William R. and Platukis, Joseph G., *Syracuse and South Bay Railroad to Oneida Lake*, Harold E. Cox, Forty Fort, Pennsylvania, 1985.

Hammond, L.M. *History of Madison County*, Truair, Smith and Company, Syracuse, 1872.

Harder, Kelsie B. (ed.), *Illustrated Dictionary of Place Names, United States and Canada*, Van Nostrand Reinhold Company, New York, 1976.

Jackson, Harry, *Scholar in the Wilderness*, Syracuse University Press, Syracuse, 1963.

Jones, Pomroy, *Annals and Recollections of Oneida County*, Pomroy Jones, Rome, 1851.

Landgraff, Harmon, *Oneida Lake - An Historical Sketch*, The Lakeside Press, Cleveland, 1926.

Nichols, Claude A., *Sullivan in History*, McHenry Press, Chittenango, 1939.

Parsons, Samuel H. (pub.), *Parsons Central New York Directory*, Syracuse Times Publishing Company, Syracuse, 1899.

Rochefaucault-Liancourt, Duke de la, *Travels Through the United States of North America, The Country of the Iroquois, and Upper Canada*, R. Phillips, London, 1799.

Seymour, John, *Centennial Address by John Seymour with Letters from Francis Adrian Van Der Kemp*, White and Floyd, Utica, 1877.

Simpson, Elizabeth, *Mexico - Mother of Towns*, J.W. Clement Co., Buffalo, 1949.

Smith, James H., *History of Chenango and Madison Counties*, D. Mason and Company, Syracuse, 1880.

Smith, John E. (ed.), *Our County and Its People, Madison County, New York*, The Boston History Company, Boston, 1899.

Snyder, Charles M., *Oswego: From Buckskins to Bustles*, Ira J. Friedman Inc., Port Washington, New York, 1968.

Stewart, George R., *American Place Names*, Oxford University Press, New York, 1970.

Thompson, Harold W., *Body, Boots and Britches*, J.B. Lippincott, New York, 1939, reprinted by Dover Publications, New York, 1967.

Wager, Daniel E., *Our County and Its People*, The Boston History Company, Boston, 1896.

Wheaton, Ellen, *The Diary of Ellen Birdseye Wheaton*, private printing, Boston, 1923.

PAPERS

_____, "History of the Bridgeport United Methodist Church," published by the church, 1969.

Bracy, Isabel, "Important Items in Madison County History," indexed, Madison County Historical Society files.

Brown, David, "History of Bridgeport," 1920's.

Burnham, Nan Marie, "Rotterdam to Constantia - the Vision to the Awakening," a paper for the State University College at Buffalo.

Bushnell, Charles, "Reminiscences of Charles R. Bushnell of the Town of Lenox," Madison County Historical Society, 1906.

Hubbard, Evalena, "Local History in Northern Sullivan," Sullivan Free Library files.

Johnson, Appalonia H. Douglas, "Colonel Zebulon Douglas," Sullivan Free Library files.

Mills, Edward and Gannon, John, "Oneida Lake Profile," New York State Department of Environmental Conservation and the Oneida Lake Association.

Myer, Mabel L. Bentley, "History of Verona Beach," Verona township historical files.

NEWSPAPERS

Articles from each of the following papers have been used in this book's preparation. The articles are far too numerous to list here.

Canastota Bee - Journal

Chittenango-Bridgeport Times
    Chittenango historian Clara Houck has been a regular contributor of lakeshore history columns to this paper. The Sullivan Free Library has most on file.

Madison County Times
    Predecessor of the Chittenango paper, the *Times* is preserved in bound volumes in the Sullivan Library. Many topics have been indexed by Clara Houck.

North Shore Citizens' Outlet
    This paper contained Fred Griesmyer's ultra-informative "Cleveland, Past and Present" series during the 1960's. The author dealt with many aspects of the lake's past, and many communities in addition to his native village.

Oneida Dispatch
    George W. Walter and Marshall Hope were two history writers for this paper. The Madison County Historical Society has many of their works on file.

Oneida Free Press
    Oneida Lake during the 1880's is depicted in these issues.

Oneida Lake Association *Bulletin*
    The official newsletter of the Association, this paper deals primarily with

environmental topics, though historical items show up occasionally. The Association maintains a file of all back issues.

Syracuse *Journal* and Syracuse *Standard*
    Articles relative to lake history in the 19th century are kept on file in the Onondaga Historical Association, Syracuse.

Syracuse *Post-Standard*
    The "Just Around the Corner" series by "Bertrande," in 1946, gives fascinating details of early 20th century life in Jewell.

Clippings relative to Oneida's history from several of the above papers and innumerable other sources are on file and categorized in the "Milton Papers," Brewerton Free Library, Brewerton.

CENSUSES

These are found in the county clerk's office of the four counties listed below.

Madison County - 1855 (indexed by county historian Isabel Bracy), 1865, 1875, 1892, 1905.

Oneida County - 1835, 1855, 1870

Onondaga County - 1880, 1892, 1905

Oswego County - 1855, 1892

MAPS

In addition to the atlases listed in the book section, the following maps were studied.

Madison County - 1853, plus maps of south shore lands, on file in the county's map room.

Oneida County - 1852, in the county's map room.

Oswego County - 1867, 1889, in the county clerk's office.

PROPERTY RECORDS

When required, property records (deeds) were examined to validate a particular place name's origin. Over the course of five years I read over five hundred deeds. Like individual news articles, there are too many to list.

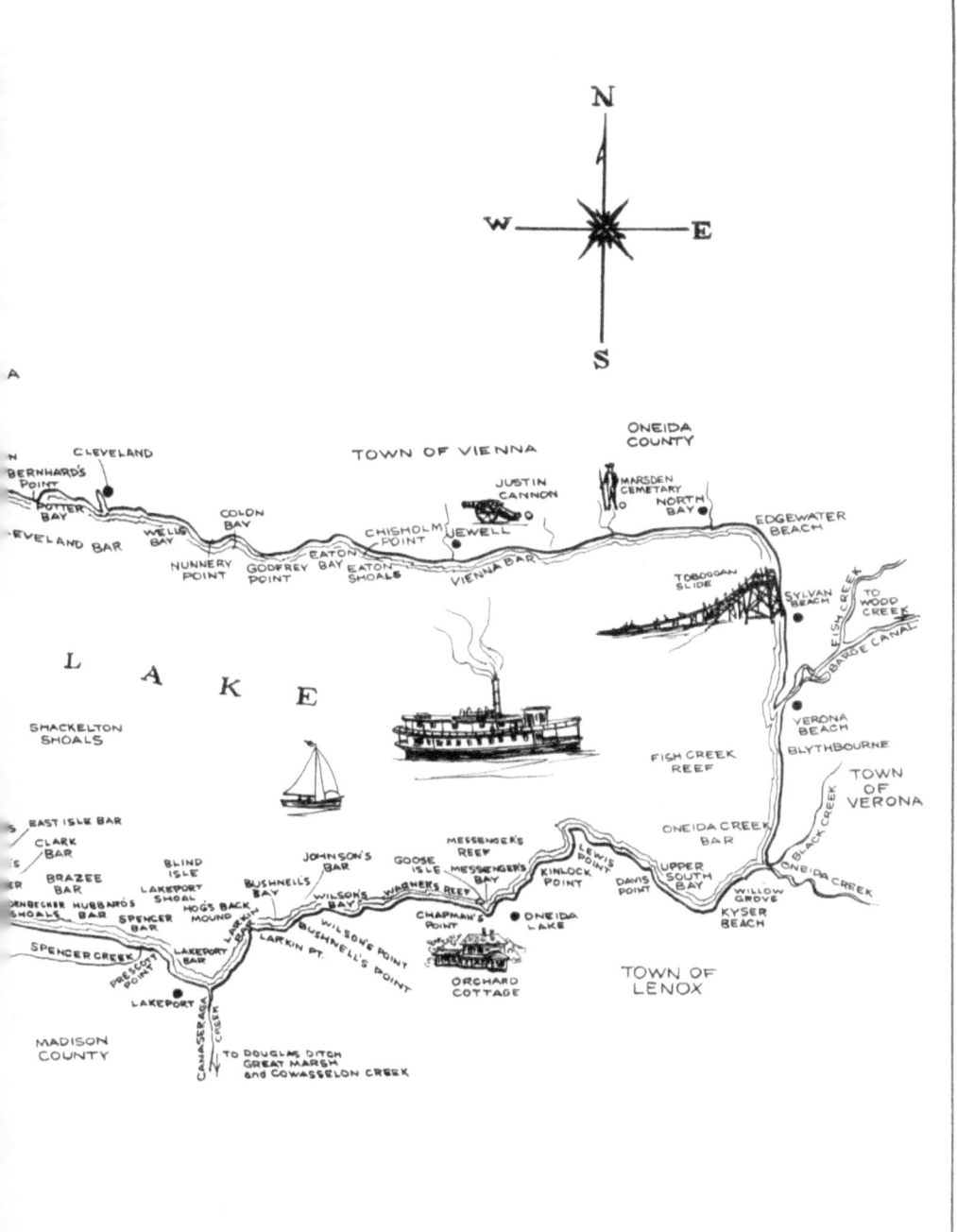